THE CATHOLIC UNIVERSITY OF AMERICA
CANON LAW STUDIES
No. 184

RELIGIOUS DISMISSED AFTER PERPETUAL PROFESSION

AN HISTORICAL CONSPECTUS AND COMMENTARY

BY THE

REV. CHARLES GERARD O'LEARY, C.SS.R., J.C.L.
Priest of the Baltimore Province

A DISSERTATION

Submitted to the Faculty of the School of Canon Law of the Catholic University of America in Partial Fulfillment of the Requirements for the Degree of Doctor of Canon Law

THE CATHOLIC UNIVERSITY OF AMERICA PRESS
WASHINGTON, D. C.
1943

Imprimi Potest:

MICHAEL A. GEARIN, C.SS.R., J.C.D.
Superior Provincialis.

Brooklynii, die 9 maii, 1943.

Nihil Obstat:

HIERONYMUS D. HANNAN, A.M., LL.B., S.T.D., J.C.D.,
Censor Deputatus.

Washingtonii, die 17 maii, 1943.

Imprimatur:

✠ MICHAEL J. CURLEY, D.D.,
Archiepiscopus Baltimoriensis-Washingtoniensis.

Baltimorae, die 17 maii, 1943.

Printed by
THE PAULIST PRESS
New York, N. Y.
51

TO

OUR MOTHER OF PERPETUAL HELP

TABLE OF CONTENTS

PART II
CANONICAL COMMENTARY

CHAPTER IV

CHAPTER V

CHAPTER VI

CHAPTER VII

CHAPTER VIII

CHAPTER IX

CHAPTER X

FOREWORD

EVERY society must have ways and means of expelling unfit members. Such a sanction is also necessary in the "societies" of the approved religious orders and religious congregations in the Church. Those who have entered the religious state must strive after evangelical perfection by observing the obligations of the vows of poverty, chastity and obedience, and the obligations of a particular approved rule. If they fail seriously and incorrigibly in their obligations, if they commit crimes which render them incompatible with the religious life, the sanctity of the religious state demands that they should be dismissed. Thus the Code of Canon Law determines the legal method of dismissing unfit members of the religious state.

The Code proceeds to state the canonical effects of this dismissal in reference to those who have professed perpetual vows. For them dismissal, in most cases, does not entail a complete separation from the organization as it does in the case of those who have made temporary profession. Hence in four canons the Code outlines the status of those who remain religious after dismissal. In the four canons, 669 to 672, no attempt is made to give a complete compendium of all the obligations which bind religious dismissed after perpetual profession, since this would prove too extensive for the limitations of a code of common law. An effort has been made to make such a compendium in this work. This has made it necessary to discuss not only the canons referred to, but also to treat certain obligations of religious arising from the common law and from the bond of religious profession.

The scope of this dissertation comprehends only those religious who have been dismissed after the profession of perpetual vows. It does not embrace any discussion on the action of dismissal itself, but is confined to the condition of such religious after dismissal has taken place. Moreover the complete canonical status of all these religious will not be found in this work, since no attempt has been made to treat the juridic effects of the various crimes that may cause dismissal. Occasionally some reference is given to the effects of particular crimes, but for the most part, the work is confined to the effects of dismissal itself. It is evident that any attempt to expound the complete status of all dismissed religious, including the effects of individual crimes, could not be confined to one volume.

The historical section of the dissertation treats the development of the effects of dismissal in pre-Code times. Little common law can be cited in direct reference to this matter. On that account, frequent reference is made to the opinions of pre-Code authors who wrote on this subject. The authors referred to have been greatly responsible for the complete discipline governing the effects of dismissal before the Code. Where common law was lacking in certain points, they took norms from the monastic rules and from the general principles of religious profession and religious life. Their reasoning on certain matters remains the basis of many of the opinions which have been expressed since the promulgation of the Code.

The writer realizes that a commentary on the status of religious dismissed after perpetual profession is subject to many difficulties. Authors of canonical commentaries disagree on important points concerning this matter. The writer is well aware that at times he has rejected the opinions of authors of international prominence. This was not done in a spirit of presumption or of intolerance toward their views, but only after a study of the individual difficulties and of the reasons proposed. Some of the conclusions advanced in this work have been deduced from common principles of law and from the obligations arising in perpetual profession and have not been found in any of the available commentaries written after the promulgation of the Code.

It may be stated here that in practice all the prescripts of law may not be observed exactly in actual cases of dismissed religious. It is evident that when serious delinquency and incorrigibility are concerned, cases may at times be best dealt with individually, especially when the delinquent is a cleric in major orders. However, this does not detract from the present commentary, for it is completely based on the prescripts of common law.

The writer takes this occasion to express his gratitude to the Congregation of the Most Holy Redeemer, to the former Provincial of the Baltimore Province, the Most Rev. William T. McCarty, C.SS.R., D.D., Titular Bishop of Anaea and Military Delegate, and to the present Provincial, the Very Rev. Michael A. Gearin, C.SS.R., for the opportunity offered for advanced study in canon law. He also expresses his indebtedness to all the members of the Faculty of the School of Canon Law of the Catholic University of America.

CHAPTER I

PRELIMINARY NOTIONS

It is important to understand the fundamental notions of dismissal and the purpose of dismissal, before approaching the question of the canonical status of dismissed religious. Confusion of thought about these basic ideas is bound to beget confusion in the determination of the status that follows dismissal. Much of the diversity of opinions, found in the writings of some of the pre-Code authors who treat of dismissed religious, is undoubtedly caused by the lack of a thorough understanding of these fundamental notions.

Moreover, it will be evident that what is said in this chapter is of special importance, since it will be used as a basis for certain interpretations that will be given in the following pages.

Article I. Dismissal From Religious Institutes

With reference to religious who have professed perpetual vows, dismissal is defined as an egress from the communal life of a religious organization, imposed by legitimate ecclesiastical authority upon a delinquent religious. A very clear presentation of this notion of dismissal has been given by Rotarius. By dismissal, he states, the religious is not made a free person or a member of the lay state without vows. On the contrary, he is merely separated from the community of all the confreres of his religious institute and is deprived of the special providence of his religious superiors. This separation is imposed as a punishment for his crimes and as a precaution lest his evil pestilential influence infect the other religious.[1]

It is unfortunate that the word *dismissal* is not well chosen and is responsible for serious misconceptions. It is ordinarily understood as a thorough and complete discharge or expulsion of a member from an organization. In this ordinary conception of *dismissal* there is no

[1] *Theologia Moralis Regularium* (3 tomes in 2, Venetiis, 1735), Tom. I, lib. III, c. II, punct. V, n. 1.

further bond between the organization and the dismissed member. The dismissed member ceases in every way to belong to the organization. It is evident that this conception of *dismissal* cannot be applied to the dismissal of religious after the profession of perpetual vows. The most that can be said, in this sense of the term, is that the religious is dismissed from the community of all the confreres of his religious institute. He is *de jure* and *de facto* separated from the community of his confreres by dismissal, but he is neither *de jure* nor *de facto* separated from the religious state nor from his religious institute.

For this reason the words *communal life* were inserted in the above definition of dismissal, instead of the words *religious institute,* usually found in the definition. From the above definition of dismissal two conclusions may well be drawn, first, that the dismissed person is still truly and substantially a religious, and secondly, that he is still a member of the religious organization which dismissed him.

It is true that in most cases of dismissal, the dismissed person is still a religious. The exceptions are cases in which, by virtue of the rules and constitutions of particular religious organizations, dismissal is accompanied by automatic dispensation from the religious vows. Only such a dispensation from the vows can completely sever a religious from the religious state. In most cases of dismissal there is no such dispensation and hence the religious remains bound by his vows.[2] He is therefore truly and substantially a religious. The authors have constantly testified to this fact.[3] This point may be

[2] Canon 669, § 1.

[3] Donatus, *Rerum Regularium Praxis Resolutoria* (2 tomes, Neapoli, 1652), Tom. I, pars II, tract. VIII, q. 50, n. 2; Leurenius, *Forum Ecclesiasticum, in quo Jus Canonicum Universum Explanatur* (5 vols. in 3, Venetiis, 1729), Lib. III, tit. XXXI, q. DCCCLVIII, n. 2 (hereafter to be cited as Leurenius); Passerinus, *De Hominum Statibus et Officiis Inspectiones Morales* (3 vols., Lucae, 1732), Q. CLXXXIX, art. VIII, nn. 600, 612, 624 (hereafter to be cited as *De Hominum Statibus*); Rotarius, *Theologia Moralis Regularium,* Tom. I, lib. III, c. II, punct. VI, n. 10; Schmalzgrueber, *Ius Ecclesiasticum Universum* (5 vols. in 12, Romae, 1843-1845), Lib. III, tit. XXXI, n. 249 (hereafter to be cited as Schmalzgrueber); Suarez, *Opera Omnia* (26 tomes, Parisiis, 1856-1861), Tract. VIII, lib. III, c. V, n. 1 (hereafter to be cited as Suarez); Coronata, *Institutiones Iuris Canonici* (5 vols., Taurini: Marietti, Vols. I and II, 2. ed., 1939, Vols. III, IV and V, 1. ed., 1933-1936), n. 658, 1° (hereafter to be cited as *Institutiones*).

brought out more convincingly by the manner of reception that a dismissed religious receives when he returns to his religious institute. No new profession of vows is made, but once he returns and the superiors accept him, he joins the other professed religious. Since it is only by the profession of religious vows that one is introduced into the religious state, there can be no doubt then, that a dismissed person is still a religious.

Even the quasi-permanent residence of a dismissed religious outside his monastery or convent, while he is separated from his confreres and superiors, can by no means be advanced as an argument that he is no longer essentially a religious. Religious bishops who because of their talents and piety have been elevated to ecclesiastical dignities are admittedly still religious. Yet, they maintain a permanent residence outside their convents or monasteries and are separated from their confreres and religious superiors. Therefore, how can the dismissed religious who is in this condition for a much less noble reason, namely for his serious delinquency, be said to be free from the religious state, and not a religious? Finally in the fourth chapter of the sixteenth title the Code does not treat of dismissed *persons*, but of dismissed *religious*. The title reads, "*De religiosis dimissis qui vota perpetua nuncuparunt.*"

Besides being a member of the religious state in general, the dismissed person is also a member of the particular religious institute in which he made the profession of his vows.[4] It is true that he is a separated member but he must still be reckoned among the members of his organization until he is dispensed from his vows, or until he transfers to another religious institute. Only by such means can a religious sever the juridical bond that binds him to a particular institute.

Another reason can also be advanced in proof of this contention. It has been shown that the dismissed religious is still bound by his

[4] Rotarius, *Theologia Moralis Regularium*, Tom. I, lib. III, c. II, punct. V, n. 1, punct. VI, n. 1; Leurenius, Lib. III, tit. XXXI, q. DCCCLVIII, n. 2; Passerinus, *De Hominum Statibus*, Q. CLXXXIX, art. VIII, nn. 612, 624; Wernz-Vidal, *Ius Canonicum ad Codicis Normam Exactum* (7 tomes in 8 vols., Romae: Apud Aedes Universitatis Gregorianae), Tom. III, *De Religiosis* (1933), n. 451 (hereafter to be cited as *De Religiosis*).

religious vows, but these vows, particularly the vows of poverty and obedience cannot be adequately understood without reference to the rules and constitutions of a particular religious institute. A religious does not profess the vows of poverty, chastity and obedience in general, but he professes them as they are determined by the rules and constitutions of the religious institute which he enters. Therefore, since the dismissed religious is admittedly bound by the vows, he is still bound to the religious institute which dismissed him, because the obligations of those vows are determined by that institute.

For these reasons St. Thomas [5] presents an analogy between excommunication and dismissal from a religious institute. One who has been excommunicated is separated and excluded from the communion of the faithful of the Catholic Church. Yet he, by no means, ceases to remain a Catholic, because the bond arising in valid baptism still persists and even though he is separated from the communion of the faithful, he still remains a member of the Church *jure et debito,* because of that bond.[6] Likewise the dismissed is excluded and separated from the community of all of his confreres without losing either the religious state or membership in the religious organization, because of the bond arising from his profession in that religious institute.

Suarez makes an analogy between dismissal and separation because of adultery after a valid marriage.[7] In this case, although there is in fact a real separation since the use of matrimony and cohabitation ceases, still the bond of valid marriage persists and the persons are still recognized as husband and wife. So, after the separation from the communal life, caused by dismissal from a religious institute, the professed person should be recognized as a religious and as a member of the religious institute.

Finally, concerning dismissal it should be noted that the term "dismissal" has sometimes been inaccurately applied. It should not be used in reference to those religious who follow the suggestion of their superiors, when for the purpose of preserving their good name,

[5] St. Thomas Aquinas, *Opera Omnia* (24 tomes in 15, Parmae, 1852-1869), *Quodlibet* XII, art. 36.

[6] Connell, *De Sacramentis Ecclesiae* (Brugis: Beyaert, 1933), n. 130.

[7] Suarez, Tract. VIII, lib. III, c. V, n. 1.

the superiors urge them to petition for a dispensation of their own accord, when their conduct actually merits dismissal. These religious cannot be called canonically dismissed and hence such cases are not treated in this work. Also from the definition of dismissal which has been given, it is evident that dismissal does not comprehend simple voluntary egress from a religious institute by an indult of exclaustration or an indult of secularization, or by apostasy from a religious institute, or by exclusion from the renewal of vows or by transfer to another religious institute.

Article II. The Term "Dismissed Religious"

In the present Code of Canon Law the term "dismissed religious" is applied to all religious who, for guilty conduct, have been discharged from the communal life of a religious institute or have been entirely separated from the religious institute by competent ecclesiastical authority. It matters not whether the religious are professed with solemn or with simple vows, whether their vows are perpetual or temporary, whether they belong to an institute of pontifical or an institute of diocesan approval. The same term "dismissed" is applied to all of these classes by the Code.[8]

In pre-Code legislation other terms as *"ejecti"* and *"expulsi"* were used besides *"dimissi"* and usually each of these terms had its own restricted meaning. As a rule *"ejecti"* and *"expulsi"* referred only to those discharged from a religious order after solemn profession.[9] It must be noted that the term *"ejecti"* as used by the old monastic rules and by the monastic writers did not always have the exact meaning of "dismissed" in our present legislation. The old monastic writers once divided the dismissed *(ejecti)* into two classes, namely, those who were dismissed from their religious institute permanently and those who were dismissed until they amended and asked for

[8] Only in two canons, 653 and 668, does the Code use the expression *"ad saeculum remitti"* when the term *"dimitti"* might be expected. These canons refer to the action that can be taken against a guilty religious in cases of great scandal and when there would be danger to the good name of the community in delay. The variant expression is used advisedly. Cf. *infra,* pp. 50-51.

[9] Cf. Palombo, *De Dimissione Religiosorum* (Taurini, Romae: Marietti, 1931), n. 2.

readmittance. This distinction ceased after the first universal legislation on dismissal was enacted in the seventeenth century. From that time on, it was clear that no one could be permanently dismissed from the religious life by religious superiors and the term *"ejecti"* was applied only to the latter class, namely to those who were expelled from the monastery until they repented of their crimes, amended their lives and asked to be received again into the community. The period of time spent outside the monastery remained indefinite, depending on the dispositions of the delinquent religious.

Sometimes the term *"ejecti"* was used for those religious who were put outside the monastery for a stated time determined by the superiors, in expiation of their faults. However the more usual term applied to these religious was the term *"expulsi."* [10] But again, this class of punished religious was found only before the first universal legislation on dismissal.

After the introduction of institutes with simple vows only, the term *"dismissi"* was reserved for such religious.[11] The use of *"ejecti"* or *"expulsi"* and *"dismissi,"* distinguishing between religious who had made profession of solemn vows and religious who had made profession of simple vows was from that time on treated fairly consistently by the authors.

Enactments of the Holy See can be cited as proof that the Church also recognized the specific and restricted meaning of these terms as used by the authors. In the declaration *Sanctissimus* [12] in which only simple vows are spoken of in regard to dismissal, the word *"dimissi"* is used exclusively. In the decree *Auctis admodum* [13] *"expulsi"* is used concerning religious of solemn vows and the word

[10] S. Benedicti Abbatis Anianensis, "Concordia Regularum"—Migne, *Patrologiae Cursus Completus, Series Latina* (221 vols., Parisiis, 1844-1864), CIII, 988, note f (hereafter to be cited as *MPL*); cf. *(Regula S. Pachomii)*, c. 84—*MPL*, L, 293.

[11] Palombo, *loc. cit.*

[12] S. C. super Statu Regularium, 12 iun. 1858—*Codex Iuris Canonici Fontes cura Emi. Petri Card. Gasparri editi* (9 vols., Vols. VII, VIII, IX ed. *cura et studio Emi. Justiniani Card. Serédi,* Romae [postea Civitate Vaticana]: Typis Polyglottis Vaticanis, 1923-1939), n. 4383 (hereafter to be cited as *Fontes*).

[13] S. C. Ep. et Reg., 4 nov. 1892, ad 4—*Fontes*, n. 2020.

"dimissi" concerning those who had taken simple vows. In 1896 the Sacred Congregation explicitly stated, *"Improprium est dicere sorores expelli, sed dicitur dimitti."* [14]

However it must be noted as Wernz [15] points out that the use of these terms according to the above distinctions was not always consistent. At any rate, there is no longer place for consideration of these distinctions since the Code applies the term *"dimissi"* to all classes of dismissed religious.

Since this work is concerned with religious who are dismissed after the profession of perpetual vows, they will be referred to always, even if the term "dismissed religious" is not further modified. Where there is question of other classes of religious care will be taken to make the necessary distinction.

Moreover, the dismissed religious under consideration are those who have been expelled from their religious organizations according to the principles of the Code of Canon Law, or according to the approved constitutions of religious institutes or by virtue of privileges concerning dismissal which have been granted to certain institutes by the Holy See. Nothing will be said therefore, of those who have been unjustly or illegally dismissed, or of those who have been "dismissed" because their profession was null and void. Also no reference will be made to those who have been "dismissed" from their monasteries or convents because of civil force or violence. Finally nothing will be said about those societies whose members live in common without vows, although the Code applies the canons treated here to the dismissed members of such organizations.[16]

[14] Filles de l'Immaculée Conception, 22 maii 1896, ad 34—apud Battandier, *Guide canonique pour les constitutions des instituts a voeux simples* (5. ed., Paris, 1911), p. 262 (hereafter to be cited as *Guide canonique*); cf Tabera, "De Dimissione Religiosorum,"—*Commentarium pro Religiosis* (later [1935], *Commentarium pro Religiosis et Missionariis*), XI (1930), 279, note 16 (hereafter to be cited as *CpR* up to 1934 inclusive and as *CpRM* from 1935 onward).

[15] *Ius Decretalium ad usum Praelectionum in Scholis Textus Iuris Canonici, sive Iuris Decretalium* (2. ed., 6 vols., Romae: Typographia Polyglotta S. C. de Prop. Fide, 1908), Tom. III, pars II, n. 676 (hereafter to be cited as *Ius Decretalium*); cf. Tabera, "De Dimissione Religiosorum,"—*CpR*, XI (1930), 279.

[16] Canon 681.

Article III. The Purpose of Dismissal

There is a twofold purpose to the institute of dismissal, one, on the part of the religious institute and the other, on the part of the dismissed religious.[17] This was expressly stated in a decree of the Sacred Congregation of the Council of 1694.[18]

On the part of the religious institute, dismissal is used lest the delinquent religious by his bad example ruin the spiritual and religious life of his confreres and lest, by his scandal, he harm the good name of religion in general.[19] This is the primary purpose of dismissal and must receive the first consideration. Therefore the common good of the religious institute is the prime end of dismissal rather than the private good of the guilty religious.[20]

On the part of the dismissed religious, the further end of dismissal is the hope that by such action the delinquent may, the more readily, ackowledge his faults and amend his ways. By placing the guilty religious outside the convent or monastery, away from the charity of his confreres, by the shame that will come to him before his relatives and friends, the last extreme measure is taken to correct the religious.[21]

It is evident that these two ends of dismissal, namely the restoration of the social order and the emendation of the guilty party, are notions corresponding to the purposes of ecclesiastical penalties.[22] Can dismissal then, be called a canonical penalty? It must be answered that it is at most merely a quasi-penalty, or as the authors state, it has a *ratio poenae.*[23] It should be noted that in purpose

[17] Donatus, *Rerum Regularium Praxis Resolutoria,* Tom. I, pars II, tract. VIII, q. II; Piatus Montensis, *Praelectiones Juris Regularis* (3. ed., 2 vols., Tornaci, 1906), I, q. 240.

[18] ". . . ne consortio morbidarum pecundum caeterae corrumpantur, et remedia . . . ad sanitatem oblata male affectis . . . prosint"—S. C. C., decr. *Instantibus,* 24 iul. 1694—*Fontes,* n. 2942.

[19] Rotarius, *Theologia Moralis Regularium,* Tom. I, lib. III, c. II, punct. V, n. 1, punct. VI, n. 1; Coronata, *Institutiones,* n. 645.

[20] Rotarius, *op. cit.,* Tom. I, lib. III, c. II, punct. I, nn. 1, 6.

[21] Donatus, *Rerum Regularium Praxis Resolutoria,* Tom. I, pars II, tract VIII, q. II; Piatus Montensis, *Praelectiones Juris Regularis,* I, q. 240.

[22] Canon 2215.

[23] Palombo, *De Dimissione Religiosorum,* n. 5.

the similarity between dismissal and a canonical penalty extends more toward the purpose of a vindicative penalty [24] than to the purpose of a medicinal penalty or censure.[25] However in vindicative penalties, although the Church primarily and directly intends the restoration of the social order, still as a kind mother, she also intends indirectly the emendation of the guilty party. To the amendment of the guilty party all ecclesiastical penalties are of their nature necessarily, although in some cases only secondarily, directed.[26] So in dismissal the religious superiors should not act without any consideration for the delinquent's amendment, even though they act primarily for the common good of the institute.

Moreover, in accordance with the mildness of canon 2214, § 2, in reference to canonical penalties, religious superiors should leave nothing untried to avert the calamity of dismissal. It should be remembered that the institute of dismissal has always been recognized as a very drastic measure. For this reason it must be used sparingly. The words of the decree of the Sacred Congregation of the Council will be a stirring reminder: "The religious superiors are earnestly admonished to remember the paternal charity and meekness which they profess and to leave nothing untried that they may gain the souls of their brethren who have fallen almost into the pit of the wicked, before they try the most serious and extreme remedy of expulsion. And all the more because Our Lord Jesus Christ in the last judgment will require from the hands of superiors the blood of those subjects who perished under the rule of superiors who were maliciously negligent and forgetful of their office." [27]

Finally, lest the objection be raised, it certainly is not too harsh to state that in dismissal the superiors intend primarily and directly the common good of the religious institute and not the private good of the individual religious.[28] Dismissal is in most cases, the final

[24] Canon 2286.

[25] Canon 2241.

[26] Cf. Palombo, *De Dimissione Religiosorum*, n. 4.

[27] S. C. C., decr. *Sacra Congregatio*, 21 sept. 1624—*Fontes*, n. 2454, the writer's translation.

[28] Cf. Suarez, Tract. VIII, lib. III, c. IV, n. 5; Palombo, *De Dimissione Religiosorum*, nn. 5, 6.

and extreme measure employed by the superiors to correct the subject, after all other efforts have failed. The long list of less extreme efforts to urge the religious to amend are exhortations, admonitions, privations, punishments, prescription of penances, removal from the occasion of sin and transfer to another house of the religious institute. When all these have failed to bring about amendment, it is high time for the superiors to look directly to the good of the institute and to protect it against the evils of seriously bad example by means of dismissal.

PART I

HISTORICAL CONSPECTUS

CHAPTER II

STATUS OF DISMISSED RELIGIOUS BEFORE URBAN VIII

ARTICLE I. STATUS BEFORE THE DECRETALS OF GREGORY IX

SEVERAL factors can be stated as reasons why there was no general legislation on the status of dismissed religious until the beginning of the seventeenth century. In the early ages the Church was occupied with more serious problems and hence was slow to consider even some of the more important phases of monastic life. Thus it was only at the Council of Chalcedon (451) that the Church took a hand in the approbation of religious institutes by committing them to the care of the bishop of the city.[1] Moreover it was common for the early monastic founders to include general norms on dismissal in their primitive rules and with these rules as their basis, the monastic authors formed a thorough and practical discipline on the institute of dismissal.

There are a few references to dismissal of monks in Roman law,[2] but in these enactments nothing is stated on the status of the dismissed monks. In the Novels of Justinian mention is made of monks

[1] C. 4—Mansi, *Sacrorum Conciliorum Nova et Amplissima Collectio* (53 vols. in 59, Florentiae, Parisiis, Arnhem et Leipzig, 1901-1927), VII, 359, c. 8, 362 (hereafter to be cited as Mansi); cf. Orth, *The Approbation of Religious Institutes,* The Catholic University of America Canon Law Studies, n. 71 (Washington, D. C.: The Catholic University of America, 1931), pp. 13-20.

[2] C. (1.7) 6; N. (133.5) 1; N. (133.6). *Corpus Iuris Civilis,* 3 vols., Berolini, 1928-1929. *Institutiones,* quas recognovit P. Krueger; *Digesta,* quae recognovit T. Mommsen, et retractavit P. Krueger; *Codex Iustinianus,* quem recognovit et retractavit P. Krueger; *Novellae,* quas recognovit R. Schoell, et absolvit G. Kroll.

who, after the reception of orders, attempted marriage, or who lived with concubines, or who otherwise led a wicked life. Such monks were to be dismissed from the clerical state and from the monastic life. As a result they were to live thereafter as private persons and they could not seek to enter military service or any public office without incurring the enacted penalties of law. Left to their own resources, it was hoped that such monks would repent and become aware of the satisfaction which they owed to God.[3] This last section seems to imply that a monk who married, or who lived a wicked life and was dismissed, was not subject to further sanctions or to prosecution on the part of civil authorities, on the ground that he was accountable to God alone for his crime and for his infidelity to his profession.[4]

Provision was made for the dismissal of monks even in the earliest rules of monastic life as may be noted in the rule of St. Macarius (+395), the disciple of St. Anthony (+356).[5] Mention of dismissal was also made in the rules of St. Basil (+379),[6] of Cassian (+435),[7] of St. Isidore of Seville (+636),[8] of St. Columbanus (+615),[9] of St. Fructuosus (+665),[10] in the so called rule of St. Augustine (+430),[11] and in the Oriental Rule.[12] The norm found in the rule of St. Benedict (480-543) is illustrative of all these rules. His rule

[3] N. (5. 8).

[4] "Poena igitur civili non adficitur monachus qui uxorem duxerit."—Gothofredi, *Corpus Juris Civilis* (Lugduni, 1781), N. (5. 8), note.

[5] C. 17, "Regula S. Macarii,"—*MPL,* CIII, 449.

[6] Interr. 28, "S. Basilii Magni Regulae Fusius Tractatae,"—Migne, *Patrologiae Cursus Completus, Series Graeca* (161 vols., Parisiis, 1856-1866), XXXI, 987-990, interr. 47, 1035, interr. 44, "S. Basilii Magni Regulae Brevius Tractatae," 1110-1111, interr. 57, 1122, interr. 102, 1154.

[7] C. 6, "Joannis Cassiani De Institutis Renuntiantium,"—*MPL,* XLIX, 159.

[8] C. 14, "S. Benedicti Abbatis Anianensis Concordia Regularum, Ex Regula Sancti Isidori Episcopi,"—*MPL,* CIII, 1033.

[9] C. 10, "S. Columbani Abbatis Regula Coenolialis,"—*MPL,* LXXX, 223.

[10] Cc. 14, 15, 20, "S. Fructuosi Bracarensis Episcopi Regula Monastica Communis,"—*MPL,* LXXXVII, 1122, 1123, 1127.

[11] N. 7, "S. Augustini Regula Ad Servos Dei,"—*MPL,* XXXII, 1381-1382.

[12] "S. Benedicti Abbatis Anianensis Concordia Regularum, Ex Regula Orientali,"—*MPL,* CIII, 1034; N. 35, "Vigilii Diaconi Regula Monachorum,"—*MPL,* L, 379-380.

is of greater importance because within two hundred years after his death it was observed throughout the whole West. It had gradually supplanted all other rules.[13] His rule states, "*Quod si nec . . . sanatus fuerit, tunc iam utatur Abbas ferro abscissionis, ut ait Apostolus: 'Auferte malum ex vobis,'* [14] *et iterum: 'Infidelis si discedit, discedat,'* [15] *ne una ovis morbida omnem gregem contaminet.*" [16] A special norm was also given by St. Benedict for the dismissal of monks who were priests. This rule demanded the intervention of the bishop before the dismissal of such monks.[17]

This is not a complete enumeration of the monastic rules mentioning dismissal and besides there were other rules for monks which were never put down in writing,[18] but the above cited rules represent the practice of monastic life in this period. Only general norms for dismissal were given and there was little mentioned about the status of the dismissed monks. Certain rules treated about the readmittance of the dismissed monks and indicated under what conditions they could be received. Above all they had to show a thorough amendment of the vice for which they were expelled and they, on being received, should take the last place.[19]

[13] Cf. Wernz, *Ius Decretalium*, Tom. III, pars II, n. 603.

[14] I Cor. V, 13.

[15] I Cor. VII, 15.

[16] C. 28, "S. P. Benedicti Regula Commentata,"—*MPL,* LXVI, 519-520; Butler, *Sancti Benedicti Regula Monasteriorum* (3. ed., Friburgi Brisgoviae: Herder, 1935), p. 63.

[17] C. 62, ". . . et saepe admonitus si non correxit, etiam episcopus adhibeatur in testimonium. Quod si nec sic emendaverit, clarescentibus culpis projiciatur de monasterio, si tamen talis fuerit ejus contumacia, ut subdi aut obedire Regula nolit."—"S. P. Benedicti Regula Commentata,"—*MPL,* LXVI, 864.

[18] As late as the eleventh century, St. Romuald (+1027) left no written rule for his monks, but transmitted his mode of life by oral tradition. Cf. Schroeder, *Disciplinary Decrees of the General Councils* (St. Louis: Herder, 1937), p. 255.

[19] C. 20, "S. Fructuosi Bracarensis Episcopi Regula Monastica Communis," —*MPL,* LXXXVII, 1127. It should be noted that where St. Benedict speaks of receiving back one who had been dismissed ("*projicitur*"), he was not speaking of one dismissed in the strict sense, but of one who was put outside the monastery for a time as a penance. The words "*aut projicitur*" are found in the text of *MPL,* LXVI, 523-524, but in Butler, *Sancti Benedicti Regula Monasteriorum,* p. 64, they are omitted. The authors taught that St. Benedict was silent

Some particular legislation on dismissal, outside the monastic rules, was enacted at the particular Council of Meaux (845), where it was stated that a monk should not be dismissed from the monastery without the council and the presence of the bishop, or of his vicar, by whose disposition and authority the future life and abode of the dismissed monk should be discerned, lest the dismissed monk be forever lost, when he could be in some way saved.[20] The bishop then, had the duty of vigilance over all the dismissed monks in his diocese. He determined how they could best be corrected outside the monastery and he reported to the regular superiors on their improvement.

Gratian in his *Decretum,* mentioned dismissal twice [21] but he did not discuss it from the standpoint of a legal institute. Neither did he discuss any of the effects which follow upon dismissal.

Before the time of the Decretals it became evident that some regular superiors were prone to dismiss their monks and hence the latter had the occasion to wander about with evident detriment to their eternal salvation and with public scandal to the faithful. Therefore sqmething had to be done to enforce the return of such monks to their monsteries.[22] This condition brought about the first general law referring to dismissed monks in the *Decretals of Gregory IX.*

Article II. Development From Gregory IX to Urban VIII

There are some instances of the mention of dismissal in the *Decretals of Gregory IX.* Three of these enactments merely apply to the general monastic norms. They involve as the only cause of dismissal incorrigibility in certain offenses.[23] One reference is a new canon and had the force of universal law, as did all the decretals of

about the obligation of receiving back those who were dismissed in the strict sense. Cf. C. 29, "S. P. Benedicti Regula Commentata,"—*MPL,* LXVI, 525.

[20] C. 59—*Monumenta Germaniae Historica, Legum Sectio II, Capitularia Regum Francorum,* Tom. II (ed. V. Krause, Hannoverae, 1897), p. 412 (hereafter the *Monumenta* will be cited as *MGH*).

[21] C. 11, C. XXVII, q. 1; c. 17, C. XXVII, q. 1.

[22] Van Espen, *Jus Ecclesiasticum Universum* (ed. noviss., 10 tomes in 5 vols., Venetiis, 1769), Tom. I, pars I, tit. XXVII, c. VII, n. V.

[23] Cc. 6, 8, X, *de statu monachorum et canonicorum regularium,* III, 35; c. 7, X, *ne clerici vel monachi,* III, 50.

Gregory IX,[24] from the constitution, *Rex pacificus* of September 5, 1234.[25] This canon was a decree enacted by Gregory IX (1227-1241) himself. It ordered all religious superiors to search for their dismissed subjects *annually*. It stated, "If these monks (dismissed) can be received back into the monastery according to the rules of their order their abbots or priors can, after a previous warning, be compelled to receive them under ecclesiastical censure, saving always the discipline of the order. But if the order does not allow this, the dismissed monks shall be provided for by Our Authority, so that they may be given the necessities of life to fulfill their penance in befitting places near the monasteries from which they have been expelled, if this can be done without grave scandal. If not, they shall be placed in other religious houses of the same order. However if the regular superiors find the dismissed subjects disobedient they shall excommunicate them and shall see that the excommunication is publicly announced by the prelates of the churches until such monks return to obedience."[26]

The interpretations of this canon were by no means uniform. Many famous theologians decided that after the promulgation of this enactment dismissal could no longer be employed in monastic life.[27] They held that from then on incorrigible monks should be punished and imprisoned in the monastery, or should be sent to other monasteries to do penance. Their opinions favored the imprisonment of incorrigible monks within the monastery in contradistinction to dismissal. Some testimony can be found for this statement in the

[24] Van Hove, *Commentarium Lovaniense in Codicem Iuris Canonici,* Vol. I, Tom. I (*Prolegomena*) (Mechliniae, Romae: Dessain, 1928), n. 206 (hereafter to be cited as *Prolegomena*).

[25] Gregorius IX, const. *Rex pacificus,* 5 sept. 1234—*Bullarum, Diplomatum et Privilegiorum Sanctorum Romanorum Pontificum Tauriensis Editio* (24 tomes in 25 vols., Augustae Taurinorum, 1857-1872), III, 485 (hereafter to be cited as *Bull. Rom. Taur.*).

[26] C. 24, X, *de regularibus et transeuntibus ad religionem,* III, 31, the writer's translation.

[27] Cf. Fagnanus, *Commentaria in Quinque Libros Decretalium* (5 vols., Romae, 1661), Lib. III, tit. XXXI, c. 24, nn. 37-38; Van Espen, *Jus Ecclesiasticum Universum,* Tom. I, pars I, tit. XXVII, c. VII, n. VI; Suarez, Tract. VIII, lib. III, c. IV, nn. 1-8; Sebastianelli, *Praelectiones Iuris Canonici, De Personis* (Romae, 1896), n. 363 (hereafter to be cited as *De Personis*).

statutes of certain religious orders, e. g., in the statutes of the Carthusians in 1368, *"Nullus pro quocumque crimine de Ordine expellatur, sed pro modo criminis et delicti carceri perpetuo vel ad tempus intrudatur,"* [28] whereas the older rules and constitutions of the Carthusians in 1259 had norms for dismissal similar to those found in the monastic rules.[29] Also in the time of Pius IV (1559-1565) the Sacred Congregation of the Council issued several decrees to the Generals of religious orders stating that they should imprison delinquent monks within the monastery and not expel them, even when their emendation was dispaired of.[30] Indeed in the thirteenth century and for some time following it seems that such was the practice within the Church.[31]

However the difficulties of such a system urged the religious superiors to petition the Holy See for certain privileges regarding the dismissal of monks. Such privileges were granted for example to the order of Somascha under Pope Pius V (1566-1572), and to the order of Friars Minor under Popes Innocent IV (1243-1254), Alexander IV (1254-1261), Sixtus IV (1471-1484) and Alexander VI (1492-1503). In the Apostolic Letter of June 15, 1501, *Cum sicut nobis*, Pope Alexander VI granted the power of expelling incorrigible subjects to the General and Provincials of the Order of Friars Minor.[32] Other orders participated in such favors granted by the Holy See and mention of dismissal again began to appear in the approved constitutions of certain orders. Gradually then, by privilege and by approved constitutions the discipline of dismissal was integrally constructed, even though there was little reference to it in universal law.[33]

Thus the Holy See in 1596 expressed its mind on the matter in

[28] Apud Bastien, "De Evolutione Historico-Iuridica Processus Dimissionis," —*Jus Pontificium*, XI (1931), 24.

[29] Cf. Bastien, *op. cit.*, pp. 21-22.

[30] Cf. Fagnanus, *Commentaria in Quinque Libros Decretalium*, Lib. III, tit. XXI, c. 24, n. 36; Benedict XIV, *De Synodo Dioecesana* (ed. noviss., Prati, 1844), Lib. XIII, c. XI, n. XV.

[31] Cf. Bastien, "De Evolutione Historico-Iuridica Processus Dimissionis,"—*Jus Pontificium*, XI (1931), 23.

[32] Apud Tabera, "De Dimissione Religiosorum,"—*CpR*, XI (1930), 280, note 29.

[33] Cf. Tabera, *op. cit.*, p. 280.

stating that the right of dismissal should not be denied to religious superiors when they acted according to the norms of their rules which had been approved by the Apostolic See.[34] From the privileges granted by the Holy See, from interpretations of the older monastic norms on dismissal and from the fundamental notions of monastic life, the authors then formed an integral discipline on dismissal, not however, without disputing many relative questions.

Concerning the disputed canon of Gregory IX, the Council of Salzburg (1281) stated that if a regular superior did not readmit a dismissed subject on the recommendation of the bishop, the superior was thenceforth suspended from the administration of temporal goods, until he received the dismissed monk into the monastery.[35]

The discipline on dismissal which the authors formed in this period may be summarily explained as follows. As for the observance of the religious vows, they generally agreed that the dismissed subject was not freed from the bonds of the three substantial vows, but they gave norms concerning these obligations after dismissal.[36] Soto however disagrees with the common opinion in certain circumstances. He states, "*. . . si autem correcta vita ad claustra rediens non admittatus, tutus manet in saeculo. Quod si scisciteris, an teneatur in saeculo religionis vota servare, respondetur: A voto quidem obedientiae absolutus manet; postquam praelata eum reiecit, ac subinde a voto paupertatis, quando-quidem conventus eum non alit.*" [37] Concerning the vow of chastity, the dismissed monk was absolutely bound to its obligations. Concerning the vow of obedience, there were two opin-

[34] S. C. Ep. et Reg., *Lisbonen.*, 22 ian. 1596—*Fontes*, n. 1547.

[35] C. 6—Mansi, XXIV, 399.

[36] Navarrus (Martin de Azpelcueta), *Opera Omnia* (6 vols., Venetiis, 1618, 1621), Tom. II, comment. II *de regularibus*, nn. 33-35 (hereafter to be cited as Navarrus); Molina, *De Iustitia et Iure Tractatus* (2 tomes, Venetiis, 1611), Tom. I, disp. 140, tom. II, disp. 276 (hereafter to be cited as *De Iustitia*); Azor, *Institutum Moralium in Quibus Universae Quaestiones* (3 vols., Brixiae, 1617), Pars I, lib. XII, c. XVI, q. 9 (hereafter to be cited as *Institutum Moralium*); Vasquez, *Commentarii in Summam S. Thomae* (2 tomes in 6 vols., Lugduni, 1631), Iam IIae, q. 96, art. 4, disp. 165, n. 87; Sanchez, *Opus Morale in Praecepta Decalogi* (2 vols., Parmae, 1723), Lib. VI, c. IX, nn. 24-29 (hereafter to be cited as *Opus Morale*); Suarez, Tract. VIII, lib. III, c. V, n. 1; Lessius, *De Iustitia et Iure* (3. ed., Mediolani, 1613), Lib. II, c. 41, dub. XIV, n. 115.

[37] *De Iustitia et Iure* (Venetiis, 1568), Q. VII, art. I, n. 3.

ions expressed. The first stated that the dismissed monk was obliged to obey the bishop by reason of his vow.[38] The second opinion stated that he was bound to obey the bishop as the other clerical members of the diocese, merely by reason of the bishop's jurisdiction over him as a cleric.[39] It should be noted that Molina stated that the first opinion was contrary to the practice of the Church and was improbable.[40] The authors who asserted that the dismissed monk was obliged by obedience to obey the bishop, disputed among themselves as to which bishop should receive this obedience. Navarrus claimed that the proper bishop was the bishop of origin,[41] but Suarez claimed that the monk was free to present himself either to the bishop of origin or to the bishop of the place where the monastery which dismissed him was located.[42]

Concerning the vow of poverty, the authors were careful to point out that the dismissed monk could not acquire property for himself because of his vow.[43] There was little agreement as to who should acquire the goods of the dismissed monk. Some authors claimed acquisition by the monastery; [44] others, by the church or by the prelate to whom the dismissed was subjected, or when the dismissed monk was not subjected to anyone, by the monastery.[45] A third group claimed acquisition by either the Roman Pontiff or the bishop.[46] One opinion stated that the goods were acquired by God alone, but

[38] Navarrus, Tom. II, comment. II *de regularibus,* n. 35, comment. III *de regularibus,* n. 46; Suarez, Tract. VIII, lib. III, c. VI, n. 4.

[39] Molina, *De Iustitia,* Tom. I, disp. 140; Azor, *Institutum Moralium,* Pars I, lib. XII, c. XVI, q. 11; Sanchez, *Opus Morale,* Lib. VI, c. IX, n. 29; Lessius, *De Iustitia et Iure;* Lib. II, c. 41, dub. XIV, n. 114.

[40] *Loc. cit.*

[41] Tom. II, comment. II *de regularibus,* n. 34.

[42] Tract. VIII, lib. III, c. VI, n. 9.

[43] Molina, *De Iustitia,* Tom. I, disp. 140; Azor, *Institutum Moralium,* Pars I, lib. XII, c. XVI, q. 9; Sanchez, *Opus Morale,* Lib. VI, c. IX, n. 45; Suarez, Tract. VIII, lib. III, c. VI, n. 20; Lessius, *De Iustitia et Iure,* Lib. II, c. 41, dub. XIV, n. 112.

[44] Molina, *loc. cit.*; Lessius, *loc. cit.*

[45] Cf. Suarez, Tract. VIII, lib. III, c. VI, nn. 20-22.

[46] Azor, *Institutum Moralium,* Pars I, lib. XII, c. XVI, q. 9; Sanchez, *Opus Morale,* Lib. VII, c. XXXIII, n. 27.

that their administration pertained to the bishop.[47] Certainly after the declaration, *Officii nostri,* on January 21, 1577, all things however acquired by such monks pertained to the Apostolic Camera if the monk died outside the monastery.[48]

Anything that was of the proprietary spirit was denied to the dismissed monk. Thus he could not make illicit and superfluous expenses, nor could he accumulate riches or make a will.[49] However he was allowed the use of those things which he needed for food, clothing and habitation, which use was expressed as the mere *usus facti.*[50] Navarrus alone demanded the permission of the bishop for the use of necessities.[51]

Some authors as Antoninus, Sylvester and Armilla obliged the dismissed monks to the observance of the rule,[52] but the authors commonly freed them from such observance or at least from the observance of the accidentals of the monastic rules.[53]

Since the authors taught that the dismissed monk was still bound by the religious vows, they also treated his obligation of returning to religious life and the obligation of the religious institute to accept him. Concerning the obligation of returning to religious life, there were three opinions advanced. Certain authors taught that there was no obligation to return to the monastery.[54] Others stated that the

[47] Navarrus, Tom. II, comment. II *de regularibus,* n. 33.

[48] Gregorius XIII, declar.—*Bull. Rom. Taur.,* VIII, 162; cf. Ferraris, *Prompta Bibliotheca Canonica, Juridica, Moralis, Theologica, necnon Ascetica, Polemica, Rubristica, Historica* (8 vols., Parisiis, 1860-1863), s. v. "Ejecti a Religione," n. 72 (hereafter to be cited as *Prompta Bibliotheca*).

[49] Molina, *De Iustitia,* Tom. II, disp. 276; Sanchez, *Opus Morale,* Lib. VI, c. IX, nn. 46-47; Lessius, *De Iustitia et Iure,* Lib. II, c. 41, dub. XIV, n. 113.

[50] Molina, *op. cit.,* Tom. I, disp. 140; Sanchez, *op. cit.,* Lib. VI, c. IX, n. 45; Lessius, *op. cit.,* Lib. II, c. 41, dub. XIV, n. 112; Azor, *Institutum Moralium,* Pars I, lib. XII, c. XVI, q. 4.

[51] Tom. II, comment. II *de regularibus,* n. 35.

[52] Cf. Sanchez, *op. cit.,* Lib. VI, c. IX, n. 51.

[53] Cf. Navarrus, Tom. II, comment. II *de regularibus,* n. 46; Molina, *De Iustitia,* Tom. I, disp. 140; Sanchez, *Opus Morale,* Lib. VI, c. IX, n. 52; Suarez, Tract. VIII, lib. III, c. VI, n. 10; Lessius, *De Iustitia et Iure,* Lib. II, c. 41, dub. XIV, n. 115.

[54] Cf. Navarrus, Tom. II, comment. II *de regularibus,* n. 36, comment. III *de regularibus,* n. 52. Authors who held this view stated that the disputed canon of Gregory IX did not refer to those justly and absolutely dismissed.

first obligation of the dismissed was to amend his life so that he could return and that this obligation to return ceased after the monk had amended, asked for readmittance and was refused.[55] The third opinion imposed the obligation to return and stated that it was always binding even though the superiors rejected the dismissed subject after he had amended.[56]

Concerning the obligation of religious superiors of seeking dismissed subjects annually, Navarrus and others interpreted the canon of Gregory IX as referring only to those who had been unjustly dismissed or to those who had been dismissed without the observance of the juridic order.[57] Gonzalez states that the canon refers not to those who were absolutely dismissed, but to those dismissed only for a time.[58] Sanchez [59] and Azor [60] were of the opinion that this canon had been abrogated by custom. However if there was no obligation of seeking dismissed subjects there certainly was present the obligation of receiving them if they amended and returned, unless the religious institute had just causes for not receiving them.[61] When such subjects were received most authors stated that no new profession was necessary,[62] but Navarrus demanded a new profession.[63]

If a dismissed monk were not received into his own order, some taught that he should enter another institute,[64] but this opinion was commonly rejected.[65] Whether such a monk could go to another

[55] Soto, *De Iustitia et Iure,* Q. II, art. I, n. 3.

[56] Suarez, Tract. VIII, lib. III, c. V, n. 4; Sanchez, *Opus Morale,* Lib. VI, c. IX, n. 27.

[57] Navarrus, Tom. II, comment. II *de regularibus,* n. 36; Azor, *Institutum Moralium,* Pars I, lib. XII, c. XVII, q. 2, c. XVI, q. 2.

[58] *Commentaria Perpetua in Singulos Textus Quinque Librorum Decretalium* (5 tomes in 4 vols., Venetiis, 1699), Lib. III, tit. XXXI, c. XXIV.

[59] *Opus Morale,* Lib. VI, c. IX, n. 27.

[60] *Institutum Moralium,* Pars I, lib. XII, c. XVII, q. 2.

[61] Navarrus, Tom. V, lib. III, cons. LXXVIII; Molina, *De Iustitia,* Tom. I, disp. 140; Sanchez, *Opus Morale,* Lib. VI, c. IX, n. 32.

[62] Suarez, Tract. VIII, lib. III, c. V, n. 16; Sanchez, *op. cit.,* Lib. VI, c. IX, n. 33.

[63] Tom. V, lib. III, cons. LXIV, LXXX.

[64] D. Bonaventura, D. Antoninus et Sylvester, apud Sanchez, *Opus Morale,* Lib. VI, c. IX, n. 34.

[65] Navarrus, Tom. II, comment. II *de regularibus,* n. 36; Azor, *Institutum*

religious institute on his own authority was also disputed. Some authors affirmed that the religious prelate had the power of compelling a dismissed subject to enter another religious institute,[66] but many authors rejected this contention.[67]

Although no general legislation was advanced during this period concerning the status of monks who were priests, there is some evidence toward the end of the sixteenth century that they were forbidden to exercise their Orders and to minister to the care of souls. In the Provincial Synod of Lima in 1583 it was enacted that dismissed monks who were priests were to be prohibited all exercise of the ecclesiastical ministry by the bishops and also that they should be excluded from any ecclesiastical benefice.[68] The Holy See later expressed its attitude on at least two different occasions, when it forbade certain bishops to allow these dismissed religious to exercise their Orders. The bishops were reminded that they should urge the dismissed religious to go back to their monasteries and to accept the punishment for their faults. The approval of the Holy See was required for any case in which these religious were to be allowed to exercise their Orders.[69]

So far the case of only dismissed monks, religious who had professed solemn vows, has been treated here. The first explicit use of the term *simple vow* is found in Gratian.[70] Simple vows as distinct from solemn vows surely existed in fact but not in name in some localities before his time. The first foundation of the Institute of

Moralium, Pars I, lib. XII, c. XVI, qq. 6, 13, c. XVII, q. 2; Lessius, *De Iustitia et Iure,* Lib. II, c. 41, dub. XIV, n. 111; Molina, *De Iustitia,* Tom. I, disp. 140; Sanchez, *loc. cit.*; Suarez, Tract. VIII, lib. III, c. VI, n. 20.

66 Cf. Sanchez, *Opus Morale,* Lib. VI, c. IX, n. 41; "Ordo noster auctoritatem habet concessam a SS. PP., licentiandi supradictos, quo non recipiuntur ad Ordinem propter aliquam causam, ut transferantur ad alios Ordines, et puniendi eos si non fecerint." Miranda, apud Tabera, "Excursus Historicus de Regularium Eiectione a Religione,"—*CpR,* XIII (1932), 285.

67 Azor, *Institutum Moralium,* Pars I, lib. XII, c. XVIII, q. 43; Sanchez, *Opus Morale,* Lib. VI, c. IX, n. 41; Lessius, *De Iustitia et Iure,* Lib. II, c. 41, dub. XIV, n. 112; Suarez, Tract. VIII, lib. III, c. VI, n. 20.

68 Cf. Benedict XIV, *De Synodo Dioecesana,* Lib. XIII, c. XI, n. XXI.

69 S. C. Ep. et Reg., *Mazarien.,* 10 mart. 1592—*Fontes,* n. 1453; *Lisbonen.,* 22 ian. 1596—*Fontes,* n. 1547.

70 C. 8, D. XXVII.

the Society of Jesus was approved by Paul III, on September 27, 1540,[71] and Paul III on June 5, 1546 approved the plan for the Jesuit vows. The members of the Society who professed simple vows and who were later dismissed were automatically freed from the vows and there was no need of a dispensation. However the superiors were rquired to get a dispensation, rather than use the dispensing power of dismissal if there were time.[72] Members of the Society who had professed solemn vows were not dispensed from them by dismissal. Those members who had professed simple vows were true and formal religious. The simple vows which they took were quasi-temporary on the part of the Institute and perpetual on the part of the religious. This was officially decided in the constitution *Quanto fructuosius*.[73]

The sixteenth century was for the Church an age of much needed reform. After more weighty and fundamental questions had been settled by his predecessors Pope Clement VIII considered the condition of the religious state and enacted thorough legislation concerning most of its phases. He legislated for the promotion of sanctity and fervor in the religious life, propounding in detail prescriptions on the internal government, the reception of members, the novitiate, the profession of vows, the religious observance, the Divine Office, poverty, dress, common life, meals, etc.[74] The next step was to provide a general legislation on the institute of dismissal and its effects.

[71] Const. *Regimini militantis—Bull. Rom. Taur.*, VI, 303-306.

[72] *Institutum Societatis Iesu* (3 vols., Florentiae, 1892-1893), I, 560, II, 41-42; Gregorius XIII, const. *Ascendente Domino*, 25 maii 1584, n. 20—*Fontes*, n. 153.

[73] Gregorius XIII, const. *Quanto fructuosius*, 1 febr. 1582—*Fontes*, n. 150; repeated in const. *Ascendente Domino*, 25 maii 1584—*Fontes*, n. 153, cf. *Institutum Societatis Iesu*, II, 92, B.

[74] Clemens VIII, const. *Regularis disciplinae*, 12 mart. 1596—*Fontes*, n. 183; decr. *Sanctissimus*, 20 iun. 1599—*Fontes*, n. 186; decr. *Nullus omnino*, 25 iul 1599—*Fontes*, n. 187; const. *Cum ad regularem*, 19 mart. 1603—*Fontes*, n. 189

CHAPTER III

FROM URBAN VIII TO THE CODE

Article I. The Decree *Sacra Congregatio*

Pope Urban VIII (1623-1644), who came to the throne of Peter toward the beginning of the seventeenth century, approved the first universal legislation on religious dismissal and on its canonical effects. On September 21, 1624, the Sacred Congregation of the Council issued a decree under his approbation which reorganized in an authentic manner the norms that had been used thus far.[1]

The decree stated that as long as the dismissed subject remained outside the monastery, he should go about in the clerical habit and should be under the jurisdiction of the local ordinary and under obedience to him. Because of this enactment the religious Superior General was bound to notify the ordinary immediately when the sentence of dismissal was given. In such dismissal the religious superiors could not grant to the dismissed religious testimonial letters, dismissing them to the Holy See or commanding them to enter another religious institute. It was also stated that as long as a clerical dismissed religious lived outside the religious institute he was perpetually suspended from the exercise of Orders and that ordinaries had no faculty of interfering with this suspension.

The decree renewed again the constitution of Gregory IX, which demanded that the superiors search for their dismissed subjects at least annually.[2] This was of obligation, it stated, even for those who had been justly and finally dismissed according to the juridic norms, but only when there was evident hope of emendation based at least on the testimonial letters of the ordinary. The Sacred Congregation also imposed a serious obligation on the consciences of the

[1] S. C. C., decr. *Sacra Congregatio,* 21 sept. 1624—*Fontes,* n. 2454.

[2] C. 24, X, *de regularibus et transeuntibus ad religionem,* III, 31.

ordinaries as to truthfulness in granting these testimonial letters to the religious superiors.

The decree concluded by stating that no matter what was said in the constitutions of the various religious orders, whether mendicant or non-mendicant, no matter what was said in the constitutions of congregations, of convents, of houses, and of places of regulars, all were bound to follow this decree, notwithstanding all customs, exemptions, indults and privileges, however they were approved. As an added precaution it enacted that if anyone presumed to infringe the above norms he automatically incurred the penalty of privation of all the offices which he held at the time, and of the right to vote and to be voted for and furthermore he became perpetually incapable of enjoying these rights in the future. These penalties were reserved to the Holy See and no religious superior had any power to interfere with them.

The injunctions of the decree *Sacra Congregatio* were for the most part renewed in the decree *Instantibus,* under Innocent XII (1691-1700).[3] Nothing new was added to the existing legislation concerning the status of dismissed religious by this decree. The discipline of these two decrees remained unchanged and was observed in the Church until the decree *Quum singulae* [4] of May 16, 1911.[5]

It should be noted that this decree referred only to those who had taken solemn vows in religious orders. Thus the superiors of the Society of Jesus could dismiss without the required form subjects who had professed only simple vows.[6] The Sacred Congregation of the Council on February 11, 1662 decided that the religious of the Society of Jesus who had professed simple vows were not comprehended in the decree *Sacra Congratio.*[7]

[3] S. C. C., decr. *Instantibus,* 24 iul. 1694—*Fontes,* n. 2492.

[4] S. C. de Rel., decr. *Quum singulae,* 16 maii 1911—*Acta Apostolicae Sedis,* III, 235-238 (hereafter to be cited as *AAS*); *Fontes,* n. 4409.

[5] Cf. Tabera, "Excursus Historicus de Regularium Eiectione a Religione," —*CpR,* 13 (1932), 282.

[6] *Institutum Societatis Iesu,* I, 561.

[7] Cf. Benedict XIV, *De Synodo Dioecesana,* Lib. XIII, c. XI, nn. XXI, XXII, Piatus Montensis, *Praelectiones Juris Regularis,* I, q. 223.

Article II. The Vows

It was unanimously taught in this period that the dismissed regular was bound *per se* to the essential vows of the religious state.[8] Most of the authors proceeded to state that the vows, with the exception of the vow of chastity, were suspended as to their obligation after dismissal, but some of the authors insisted that dismissed regulars were strictly bound by their vows as far as was possible in their new status.[9]

Whatever their explanation of the question, the authors agreed that certain things were allowed to the dismissed regular which he could not do in the cloister. Thus he could without the permission of the superiors change his domicile and go about freely.[10] Because of the vow it was taught that such religious remained under the obedience of the regular superior.[11] The dispute about what type of obedience should be given to the bishop still continued. Some obliged the dismissed religious to obey by reason of the vow the bishop under

[8] Donatus, *Rerum Regularium Praxis Resolutoria,* Tom. I, pars II, tract. VIII, q. 50; Passerinus, *De Hominum Statibus,* Q. CLXXXIX, art. VIII, n. 600; De Ameno, *Opera Omnia* (3 tomes, Romae, 1753-1754), Tom. II, *De Incorrigibilium Expulsione,* Pars III, q. VI, n. 37 (hereafter to be cited as *De Incorrigibilium Expulsione*); Rotarius, *Theologia Moralis Regularium,* Tom. I, lib. III, c. II, punct. VI, n. 1; Bonacina, *Opera Omnia* (3 tomes, Lugduni, 1639), Tract. V, *De Clausura et poenis violatoribus eius impositis,* q. II, punct. XII, § III (hereafter this tract will be cited as *De Clausura*); Tamburini, *De Iure Abbatum* (4 tomes, Coloniae Agrippinae et Augustae Vindelicorum, 1691-1698), Tom. III, disp. VIII, q. VIII, nn. 5-8; Benedict XIV, *De Synodo Dioecesana,* Lib. XIII, c. XI, n. XX; Schmalzgrueber, Lib. III, tit. XXXI, n. 249; Ferraris, *Prompta Bibliotheca,* s. v. "Ejecti a Religione," n. 49; Bouix, *Tractatus de Iure Regularium* (2. ed., 2 tomes, Bruxellis, 1867), Tom. II, pars VI, sec. IV, c. III, q. IV; Wernz, *Ius Decretalium,* Tom. III, pars II, n. 676; Piatus Montensis, *Praelectiones Juris Regularis,* I, q. 244; cf. "Disceptatio Synoptica," S. C. Ep. et Reg., resp. *Montis Pessulani,* 1 iul. 1898—*Acta Sanctae Sedis,* XXXI (1898-1899), 397 (hereafter to be cited as *ASS*).

[9] De Ameno, *loc. cit.*; Passerinus, *op. cit.*, Q. CLXXXIX, art. VIII, n. 623; Rotarius, *loc. cit.*; Ferraris, *loc. cit.*; Wernz, *loc. cit.*; Piatus Montensis, *loc. cit.*

[10] Ferraris, *Prompta Bibliotheca,* s. v., "Ejecti a Religione," nn. 49-50; Benedict XIV, *De Synodo Dioecesana,* Lib. XIII, c. XI, n. XX.

[11] Schmalzgrueber, Lib. III, tit. XXXI, n. 250, 3; Passerinus, *De Hominum Statibus,* Q. CLXXXIX, art. VIII, n. 619; De Ameno, *De Incorrigibilium Expulsione,* Pars III, q. VII, nn. 50-52; Ferraris, *Prompta Bibliotheca,* s. v. "Ejecti a Religione," n. 49.

whose jurisdiction he lived while outside the monastery.[12] Others however holding to the more common view stated that he was not bound by vow to obey this bishop.[13]

Concerning the vow of poverty, generally the same questions were treated as in the former period. The dismissed regular was allowed the use and administration of goods for food, clothing, habitation and the other necessities of life. With regard to the goods in his possession he acted as "*administrator nomine religionis in ordine ad supradictos usus necessarios.*"[14] This was the common teaching that the dismissed monk had the mere use and the administration of the goods which he had in his possession and that he did not acquire them as his own.[15] In 1635 the Sacred Congregation of Bishops and Regulars stated, ". . . *qui eiecti fuerint adhuc teneri votis, ad quae se per professionem obligaverint, ita ut castitatem absolute servare debeant, paupertatem quatenus rerum dominium acquirere non possunt, nec eas ut proprias sed usum tantum retinere. . . .*"[16] Again in 1821 the same Congregation repeated, ". . . *eiectos bonorum habere tantum usum et administrationem. . . .*"[17] Rotarius pointed out that if the religious institute had not explicitly granted the permission for this use and administration of goods, it was conceded automatically

[12] Leurenius, Lib. III, tit. XXXI, q. DCCCLXIV; Schmalzgrueber, Lib. III, tit. XXXI, n. 250, 3; Bouix, *Tractatus de Iure Regularium,* Tom. II, pars VI, sec. IV, c. II, q. IV.

[13] Passerinus, *De Hominum Statibus,* Q. CLXXXIX, art. VIII, n. 629; De Ameno, *De Incorrigibilium Expulsione,* Pars III, q. VIII; Rotarius, *Theologia Moralis Regularium,* Tom. I, lib. III, c. I, punct. V, nn. 4-5; Tamburini, *De Iure Abbatum,* Tom. III, disp. VIII, q. VIII, n. 9; Bonacina, *De Clausura,* Q. II, punct. XII, § 5; Reiffenstuel, *Jus Canonicum Universum* (5 vols., Antverpiae, 1743), Lib. III, tit. XXXI, n. 241 (hereafter to be cited as Reiffenstuel).

[14] Passerinus, *De Hominum Statibus,* Q. CLXXXIX, art. VIII, nn. 529, 605, 2.

[15] Bonacina, *De Clausura,* Q. II, punct. XII, § III, § VII; Tamburini, *De Iure Abbatum,* Tom. II, disp. VIII, q. VIII, nn. 6-7; Engel, *Collegium Universi Juris Canonici* (Venetiis, 1760), Lib. III, tit. XXXI, § IV, q. IV, n. 57; Ferraris, *Prompta Bibliotheca,* s. v. "Ejecti a Religione," nn. 67-74; Schmalzgrueber, Lib. III, tit. XXXI, n. 250; Donatus, *Rerum Regularium Praxis Resolutoria,* Tom. I, pars II, tract. VIII, qq. XLVI, XLIX.

[16] S. C. Ep. et Reg., *Cisterciensium,* 1 iun. 1635—*Fontes,* n. 1748.

[17] Cf. *Analecta Iuris Pontificii,* XVI, 868, n. 1491.

in dismissal.[18] Some authors allowed the dismissed to carry on business and to contract obligations under civil law, but others disagreed, stating that business should not be allowed, particularly for those monks who had been ordained, but exception was made for true necessity.[19]

Some religious institutes took vows in addition to the three essential vows. The question of the obligation of these vows after dismissal was also disputed. According to some authors dismissed religious were still bound by the obligation of these additional vows,[20] but according to others these vows were suspended after dismissal.[21] The question was officially settled for the Society of Jesus. According to explicit papal statements the vows that its members professed of not accepting dignities or prelacies outside the Society and the vow of preserving the spirit and customs relative to the poverty of their Institute still bound the dismissed religious. The Pope alone could dispense from these vows.[22]

Concerning the simple vows which were professed in anticipation of solemn vows, the Holy See stated in the decree *Sanctissimus* that religious who had made profession of these vows were automatically dispensed from them in dismissal.[23] Such dissolution it was stated arose from a tacit condition in the profession, namely the professed condition, *"while I live in the religious institute."* It should be noted

[18] *Theologia Moralis Regularium,* Tom. I, lib. III, c. II, punct. VI, n. 2.

[19] Cf. Ferraris, *Prompta Bibliotheca,* s. v. "Ejecti a Religione," n. 50, note 2.

[20] Donatus, *Rerum Regularium Praxis Resolutoria,* Tom. I, pars II, tract. VIII, q. LI; Rotarius, *Theologia Moralis Regularium,* Tom. I, lib. III, c. II, punct. VI, n. 11; Ferraris, *op. cit.*, s. v. "Ejecti a Religione," nn. 51-52.

[21] Barbosa, *Collectanea Doctorum in Jus Pontificium Universum* (6 tomes in 3 vols., Lugduni, 1716), Lib. III, tit. XXXI, c. XXIV, n. 12; Leurenius, Lib. III, tit. XXXI, q. DCCCLXV; Schmalzgrueber, Lib. III, tit. XXXI, n. 251; Appeltern, *Compendium Praelectionum Juris Regularis* (2. ed., Parisiis, 1913), Q. 143, 2°.

[22] Paulus V, litt. apost. *Ex incumbente Nobis,* 31 ian. 1618—*Institutum Societatis Iesu,* I, 138; Urbanus VIII, const. *Vota quae Deo,* 25 ian. 1632—*Institutum Societatis Iesu,* I, 170, litt. apost. *Honorum dignitatumque,* 26 febr. 1643—*Institutum Societatis Iesu,* I, 174.

[23] S. C. super Statu Regularium, declar. *Sanctissimus,* 12 iun. 1858—*Fontes,* n. 4383; cf. S. C. super Statu Regularium, resp., 20 ian. 1860, ad 4—*Fontes,* n. 4385.

that in pre-Code law the Church recognized the simple vows that should be taken before solemn profession as perpetual on the part of the religious [24] and not as temporary vows as are now professed according to the Code.[25] It is true that the decree *Sanctissimus* was originally given to the Superior General of the Dominicans, but the same grant was extended to other orders which petitioned for it,[26] so that it became a common practice for religious orders.

Concerning the dismissal of men who had professed simple vows in congregations, there was no disposition of common law concerning their dismissal until recent times. By the decree *Auctis admodum* of 1892,[27] the solemnities of expulsion as prescribed by the decrees *Sacra Congregatio* and *Instantibus* were to be observed in the dismissal of all those who had professed simple perpetual vows in Congregations.[28] Unless the constitutions stated otherwise, men who had professed simple vows in Congregations were not freed from them in dismissal. This it is true was the practice of the Church prior to the decree *Auctis admodum.* However there are early evidences of privileges granted to institutes of merely simple vows whereby dismissal brought about the dissolution of the vows, e.g., in the Congregation of the Mission,[29] and in the Congregation of Clerics of the Christian Doctrine in France.[30] Nevertheless the general norm existed that unless the Holy See had made a particular grant in the matter, those who had professed vows in institutes of merely simple vows were not dispensed from them in dismissal. Members of such institutes were the only persons comprehended in the decree *Auctis admodum* and therefore the norm of the decree *Sanctissimus* in reference

[24] S. C. super Statu Regularium, ep. encycl. *Neminem latet,* 19 mart. 1857—*Fontes,* n. 4381; declar. 12 iun. 1858—*Fontes,* n. 4383.

[25] Canon 574, § 1.

[26] *Collectanea in Usum Secretariae Sacrae Congregationis Episcoporum et Regularium* (ed. noviss. Bizzarri, Romae, 1885), p. 857, N. B. (hereafter this work will be cited as Bizzarri).

[27] S. C. Ep. et Reg., decr. *Auctis admodum,* 4 nov. 1892—*Fontes,* n. 2020.

[28] Cf. Tabera, *"De Dimissione Religiosorum"—CpR,* XI (1930), 279.

[29] Alexander VII, const. *Ex commissa,* 22 sept. 1655—*Bull. Rom. Taur.,* XVI, 67-69.

[30] Alexander VII, const. *Sacrosancti apostalatus,* 15 mart. 1659—*Bull. Rom. Taur.,* XVI, 445-447.

to those who had taken simple vows in religious orders was left unchanged.[31]

The constitution *Conditae a Christo* in 1900 [32] contemplated the discipline of dismissal in reference to the rights of bishops in this matter. It stated that in regard to diocesan institutes, the bishop had the right to dismiss delinquent members and that in so dismissing them he could dispense with the vows with the exception of the perpetual vow of chastity. This obtained even though the vows were perpetually professed. The same power was enjoyed by the bishops in regard to additional vows which were professed according to the rules and constitutions. Lanslots pointed out that the proper bishop to use these powers was the bishop in whose diocese the person was dismissed and not the bishop of the place where the Motherhouse was located. He observed too that the bishops had generally received from Rome indults to dispense in dismissal from the vow of perpetual chastity.[33]

Concerning women religious with solemn vows, their expulsion was seldom employed in pre-Code practice, although speaking strictly the same reasons for dismissal could exist for them as for men in religious orders. The decisions of the Sacred Congregation of Bishops and Regulars in 1603 and in 1726 testify to the practice of punishing such religious within the cloister and of not dismissing them.[34] However at times, particularly in recent centuries, the Holy See has permitted the dismissal of such religious and it has stated in these cases that at least the substantials of the religious vows must be observed by the dismissed.[35] In pre-Code practice the dismissal of such religious

[31] Cf. Wernz, *Ius Decretalium*, Tom. III, pars II, n. 676.

[32] Leo XIII, const. *Conditae a Christo*, 8 dec. 1900—*Fontes*, n. 644; cf. S. C. Ep. et Reg., *Canarien.*, 16 maii 1902—*ASS*, XXXV (1902-1903), 245.

[33] Lanslots, *Handbook of Canon Law for Congregations of Women Under Simple Vows* (6. ed., New York, 1911), n. 177.

[34] S. C. Ep. et Reg., *in Volaterran.*, 15 iul. 1603—Bizzarri, p. 459; S. C. Ep. et Reg., *Vilnen.*, iun. 1726—Bizzarri, p. 320.

[35] S. C. Ep. et Reg., *Catanien.*, 9 nov. 1744—Bizzarri, pp. 365-366; ". . . Sua Beatitudine ha commandato scriversi a voi, che espellendo dal Monastero delle Orsoline la detta NN. la rimandiate in Casa de' suoi Parenti nella Bastia, spogliata dell Abito Religioso, ma soggetta ai voti di sua professione, sull' osservanza dei quali doverte seriamente ammonirla in quanto al vota di Castità assoluta-

was always referred to the Holy See. Likewise in 1902 the decree *Perpensis,* which referred to women religious in institutes which took solemn vows, stated that those who took simple vows in anticipation of solemn profession in such institutes could be dismissed only by the Holy See. The decree stated that in the decree of dismissal a dispensation from the vows would be included for those who had professed simple vows.[36]

It should be noted that no legislation was enacted before the Code in reference to the dismissal of women in institutes of merely simple vows, if one excepts the few norms stated in the constitution *Conditae a Christo* in regard to the bishop's power over diocesan institutes. *The Normae of 1901* stated that a sister dismissed after simple profession, was not freed from her vows by the mere fact of dismissal, but that she should ask for a dispensation from the vows.[37] This also had been the practice in the Church prior to this time. No dispensation from the vows was admitted in dismissal unless the rules and constitutions or a particular indult stated otherwise.[38]

According to the discipline of pre-Code law, if there was a good reason why a religious with solemn vows should remain in the world, he was very rarely given an absolute dispensation from his vows. He received an indult of secularization. This indult however differed greatly from the indult of secularization which is granted according to the present Code.[39] When this indult was granted, the religious was not freed from his vows. He was not bound to the particular

mente, ed in quanto agli altri nel sostanziale compatibile col nuovo stato. . . ." —S. C. Ep. et Reg., *Fulginaten.*, mart. 1796—Bizzarri, pp. 401-402.

[36] S. C. Ep. et Reg., decr. *Perpensis,* 3 maii 1902 ad 13—*Fontes,* n. 2039; cf. S. C. Ep. et Reg., *Bononien.*, 28 iul. 1902—*Fontes,* n. 2040.

[37] *Normae secundum Quas S. Congr. Episcoporum et Regularium Procedere Solet in Approbandis Novis Institutis Votorum Simplicium* (Romae, 1901), nn. 197-198 (hereafter to be cited as *Normae of 1901*).

[38] "Quocumque tamen modo professa ab instituto, aut egressu aut dimissione egrediatur, dispensationem a votis sive temporaneis sive perpetuis ipsamet impetrare tenetur, coadiuvantibus sororibus quatenus opus sit."—Filles de l'Immaculée Conception, 22 maii 1896, ad 34—apud Battandier, *Guide canonique,* p. 269.

[39] Piontek, *De Indulto Exclaustrationis Necnon Saecularizationis,* The Catholic University of America Canon Law Studies, n. 29 (Washington, D. C.: The Catholic University of America, 1925), p. 7.

rules of his religious institute, but he had to wear, at least under his outer garments, some sign of his religious habit, usually the scapular. Also by reason of the vow of obedience he was subject to the local ordinary. On the other hand, it was the practice even before the Code to dispense completely from simple vows and not to grant an indult merely of secularization to those who had professed such vows.

Article III. The Suspension of Orders

In regard to the suspension which was inflicted on the dismissed clerical religious, the decree *Sacra Congregatio* [40] and many later enactments reserved the power of dispensing from it to the Holy See alone while the religious remained outside the institute. The bishop therefore had no power over this suspension. His duty was to exercise vigilance over the dismissed religious and to report on his amendment to the regular superiors. Moreover he had no authority to judge the action of dismissal, in order to determine if it were just or unjust.[41] If in any case there was cause for appeal, the matter was to be referred to Rome.[42]

In 1672 the Sacred Congregation of the Council was asked whether this suspension could be remitted in any way by the ordinary, at least for the internal forum of conscience. It was asked if such power could be granted by force of an apostolic constitution even in the future, if in that constitution the decree *Sacra Congregatio* were not expressly abrogated. It was answered that without express abrogation no such power could be given.[43] Even though a dismissed cleric had been freed from the infamy of fact of dismissal by his emendation, and even though he was offered a patrimony, these were not sufficient reasons to dispense with this suspension. In 1751 a priest

[40] S. C. C., 21 sept. 1624—*Fontes,* n. 2454.

[41] Sebastianelli, *De Personis,* n. 363; Mocchegiani, *Jurisprudentia Ecclesiastica ad Usum et Commoditatem Utriusque Cleri* (3 vols., Ad Claras Aquas, 1904-1905), III, n. 895.

[42] Donatus, *Rerum Regularium Praxis Resolutoria,* Tom. I, pars II, tract. VIII, q. LIII, n. 3; Ferraris, *Prompta Bibliotheca,* s. v. "Ejecti a Religione," n. 38.

[43] S. C. C., *Toletana,* 4 iun. 1672—*Fontes,* n. 2829.

in these circumstances was officially advised not to ask for a dispensation.[44]

This suspension impeded the exercise, not only of all the Orders which the clerical religious had received prior to dismissal, but also those which he might receive after dismissal.[45] By a violation of the suspension through the exercise of Orders, an irregularity was incurred. That the exercise of minor Orders effected an irregularity was by no means a universal opinion. Some authors stated that no irregularity was incurred by minorities in exercising the Orders which they had received.[46] The authors taught that by the common law, dismissed clerical religious were not suspended from the offices of preaching and teaching.[47] They based this opinion on the reason that the offices of preaching and teaching were not offices intrinsically connected with the exercise of holy orders. By the automatic suspension which was incurred at dismissal, the cleric was suspended solely from the exercise of holy orders. Therefore they stated that since there was question of a *lex odiosa,* the law should not be extended to offices which had not an absolute and intrinsic relation and dependence on the exercise of holy orders. However most of the religious orders enjoyed privileges whereby the superiors could excommunicate their dismissed subjects if they dared to preach or teach within the limits or the religious province or district.[48] Moreover many authors also

[44] S. C. C., *Lunen Sarzanen,* 31 iul. 1751—*Thesaurus Resolutionum Sacrae Congregationis Concilii* (167 vols., Romae, 1718-1908), XV, 116 (hereafter to be cited as *Thesaurus S. C. C.); Lunen Sarzanen,* 8 iul. 1752—*Thesaurus S. C. C.,* XVI, 93; cf. Pallottini, *Collectio Omnium Conclusionum et Resolutionum Quae in Causis Propositis apud Sacram Congregationem Cardinalium S. Concilii Tridentini Interpretum Prodierunt* . . . (18 vols., Romae, 1868-1893), s. v. "Regulares," § 1, n. 38 (hereafter to be cited as Pallottini).

[45] Bonacina, *Theologia Moralis* (3 tomes, Venetiis, 1687), Tom. III, disp. III, q. VIII, punct. XII, n. 4; Piatus Montensis, *Praelectiones Juris Regularis,* II, q. 752.

[46] St. Alphonsus de Liguori, *Theologia Moralis* (ed. Gaudé, 4 vols., Romae, 1905-1912), Lib. VII, n. 358, 1; Aertnys, *Theologia Moralis juxta Doctrinam S. Alphonsi Mariae de Ligorio, Doctoris Ecclesiae* (3. ed., 2 vols., Tornaci, 1893), Lib. VII, n. 172.

[47] Cf. Commentator, "De Suspensione lata in religiosos eiectos extra Religionem degentes"—*ASS,* XIX (1886), appendix XLVI, 397-398.

[48] For the Society of Jesus, *Institutum Societatis Iesu,* I,. 561, n. 161; for

forbade the exercise of these offices to all dismissed clerical religious because they stated that by reason of dismissal, such clerics were burdened with infamy of fact.[49] It was commonly admitted, that if a dismissed cleric exercised these functions, he did not become irregular.

The suspension incurred by regulars at dismissal ceased only when the religious had returned to the cloister or when the Holy See saw fit to dispense with it. The same suspension was mentioned among the *latae sententiae* penalties of the constitution *Apostolicae Sedis* of 1869.[50] That constitution stated that a *latae sententiae* perpetual suspension from the exercise of Orders was incurred by dismissed religious while they lived outside the religious institute. In agreement with former law, the constitution stated that the suspension was reserved to the Roman Pontiff. Likewise the suspension ceased after the dismissed cleric had returned to the religious institute or had entered another institute.[51] It therefore was not an absolutely perpetual suspension, but only one relatively so. Its purpose was to protect the Sacred Mysteries from profanation by guilty hands and to urge the religious to repent and to return to his monastery, by thus forbidding him, through the restriction of his Orders, the goods which would accrue to him from the exercise of the ministry.[52]

It must be noted that the suspension enacted by the constitution

the Conventuals of the Order of St. Francis, Clemens IV, ep. *Virtute conspicuos,* 21 iul. 1265—*Bull. Rom. Taur.,* III, 736, confirmed by Sixtus IV, const. *Regimini universalis,* 31 aug. 1474—*Bull. Rom. Taur.,* V, 217; for the Carmelites, Sixtus IV, ep. *Dum attenta,* 28 nov. 1476—*Bull. Rom. Taur.,* V, 245; for the Order of Minims, Julius II, const. *Virtute conspicuos,* 28 iul. 1506—*Bull. Rom. Taur.,* V, 435; for the Dominicans, Gregorius XI, const. *Virtute conspicuos,* 6 mart. 1374—*Bull. Rom. Taur.,* IV, 567, confirmed by Sixtus IV, const. *Regimini universalis,* 1474—*Bull. Rom. Taur.,* V, 224.

[49] Donatus, *Rerum Regularium Praxis Resolutoria,* Tom. I, pars II, tract. VIII, q. LX; Passerinus, *De Hominum Statibus,* Q. CLXXXIX, art. VIII, n. 640; Rotarius, *Theologia Moralis Regularium,* Tom. I, lib. III, c. II, punct. V, n. 10; Ferraris, *Prompta Bibliotheca,* s. v. "Ejecti a Religione," n. 44.

[50] Pius IX, const. *Apostolicae Sedis,* 12 oct. 1869—*Fontes,* n. 552.

[51] Laurentius, *Institutiones Iuris Ecclesiastici Quas in Usum Scholarum Scripsit* (3. ed., Friburgi Brisgoviae, 1914), n. 580, 5.

[52] Commentator, "De Suspensione lata in religiosos eiectos extra Religionem degentes"—*ASS,* XIX (1886), appendix XLVI, 393.

Apostolicae Sedis was incurred only by religious properly so called; that is, by religious who had professed solemn vows.[53] Also only the latter class of religious was affected by the suspension enacted in former law of the decree *Sacra Congregatio*. The new Code for the first time in universal ecclesiastical legislation considers as religious in the strict sense all those who take simple vows in religious institutes and applies to them generally the same legislation as it does to regulars. The members of the Society of Jesus who were dismissed after the profession of simple vows were not considered as dismissed according to the injunctions of *Sacra Congregatio*. Therefore they were not suspended at dismissal by common law, but were permitted to exercise their Orders and also to receive ecclesiastical benefices.[54]

The Church in time applied the same penalty to the dismissed cleric who had professed simple vows in institutes of pontifical approval. This application was made in the decree *Auctis admodum* of 1892.[55] Before this time such clerics returned after dismissal to the ordinary of their place of origin and they remained under his jurisdiction.[56] The decree *Auctis admodum* stated something new with regard to the cessation of this suspension. It enacted that such clerics should remain perpetually suspended while they lived outside the monastery, until they were informed in some manner by the Holy See and until they had found a bishop willing to accept them and had provided for themselves an ecclesiastical patrimony. This

[53] Avanzini, *De Constitutione Apostolicae Sedis* (2. ed., Romae, 1874), p. 87; Vecchiotti, *Institutiones Canonicae ex Operibus Joannis Card. Soglia* (16. ed., 3 vols., Augustini Taurinorum, 1875), II, 365, note 4; Elbel, *Theologia Moralis per Modum Conferentiarum* (2. ed., 3 vols., Paderbornae, 1894), Pars X, n. 737; D'Annibale, *In Constitutionem Apostolicae Sedis qua Censurae Latae Sententiae Limitantur Commentarii* (Prati, 1894), n. 203; Piatus Montensis, *Praelectiones Juris Regularis*, II, q. 751.

[54] ". . . Eiecti autem sive dimissi a Societate Iesu post tria vota dumtaxat, non comprehenduntur in Constitutione S. M. Urbani VIII de Apostatis et Eiectis in *Limana Eiectionis*, 11 febr. 1662"—Pallottini, s. v. "Regulares," § I, n. 37; cf. Benedict XIV, *De Synodo Dioecesana*, Lib. XIII, c. XI, nn. XXI, XXII.

[55] S. C. Ep. et Reg., decr. *Auctis admodum*, 4 nov. 1892—*Fontes*, n. 2020.

[56] S. C. Ep. et Reg., *Rhedonen.*, 27 feb. 1891—*ASS*, XXIV (1891-1892), 565.

same enactment applied to religious who had professed solemn vows in religious orders.

It was later asked, if the decree in stating the conditions for the cessation of the suspension, namely the finding of a bishop willing to accept the dismissed cleric and the provision of an ecclesiastical patrimony, meant that both conditions must be taken collectively. It was asked if the decree should be taken in the sense that for the suspension to be taken away, both conditions were necessary. It was answered officially that both conditions were necessary.[57] In the same response the Sacred Congregation granted permission to a particular bishop to allow certain dismissed religious to exercise their Orders for a time while they remained in his diocese. But those religious it stated were still bound by the obligations of finding a bishop willing to accept them and of seeking an ecclesiastical patrimony according to the injunctions of the decree *Auctis admodum.*[58]

Vermeersch observed in 1913 that the Sacred Congregation sometimes granted a dispensation from this suspension to a dismissed cleric for a period of a year, at the same time commanding the cleric to attempt to find a bishop willing to receive him. More rarely, he stated, the Sacred Congregation dispensed with the suspension *ad nutum S. Sedis*. In the cases in which it did, the dismissed cleric could with the permission of the ordinary of the place exercise ecclesiastical functions as long as the Holy See did not withdraw the faculty.[59]

[57] S. C. Ep. et Reg., *Abulen.*, 20 nov. 1895—*Fontes*, n. 2026.

[58] *Loc. cit.;* Piat mentions a custom which existed in some regions, to advance men to orders without a title and this custom favored those dismissed clerics who came to live in those regions. The bishop there would furnish them a source of income, just as he did for his secular clergy, whence they could sustain themselves in a becoming, clerical fashion. In these cases the Sacred Congregation sometimes dispensed from the suspension, even though the dismissed cleric had not provided for himself an ecclesiastical patrimony.—*Praelectiones Juris Regularis*, I, q. 227, 6°.

[59] "De Competentia et stilo S. C. Religiosorum"—*Periodica de Re Canonica et Morali utili praesertim Religiosis et Missionariis,* IV (1913), 332-333 (hereafter to be cited as *Periodica*).

Article IV. Sustenance

In this period, as well as in the period treated previously, those religious justly and legitimately dismissed could in no way demand sustenance and support from the religious institute. The religious was expelled through his own fault and he was left to himself and was deprived of the paternal aid of his order as a punishment proportionate to his malice, a punishment calculated to bring him more readily to his senses and to penance.[60] Donatus stated that the dismissed religious should present himself to the bishop of his place of origin and should inform that bishop that he was a dismissed religious and was ready to obey and to be provided for by him. If the bishop refused to provide for him, the dismissed religious should work at some becoming labor. If he could not do this, he should ask for alms.[61]

Before the time of Benedict XIII (1724-1730), several ex-religious of the Society of Jesus attempted to exact from the religious institute sustenance or support after dismissal. In these cases which concerned clerics who had professed merely simple vows, automatic dispensation from the vows took place at dismissal. In several law-suits these ex-religious made their claims on the basis of their ordination in the Society with no ecclesiastical benefice or patrimony, but merely with the title of poverty. Subsequently, Pope Benedict XIII enacted the constitution *Injuncti Nobis* wherein he stated that such dismissed clerics of the Society, even though they had been ordained to the priesthood on the title of poverty, could not allege any right to sustenance from the religious institute after dismissal. By no title or cause, he stated, could the Society be obliged to extend to them any support.[62]

The Holy See sometimes arranged in a limited way for the sustenance of women religious who were dismissed. In 1796 the Sacred

[60] Ferraris, *Prompta Bibliotheca*, s. v. "Ejecti a Religione," n. 45; Craisson, *Manuale Totius Juris Canonici* (6. ed., 4 vols., Pictavii, 1880), n. 3089.

[61] *Rerum Regularium Praxis Resolutoria*, Tom. I, pars II, tract. VIII, q. XXXI, nn. 1-2.

[62] Benedictus XIII, const. *Injuncti Nobis*, 12 iun. 1728—*Bull. Rom. Taur.*, XXII, 661; cf. Ferraris, *Prompta Bibliotheca*, s. v. "Ejecti a Religione," n. 46; Benedict XIV, *De Synodo Dioecesana*, Lib. XIII, c. XI, n. XXII.

Congregation of Bishops and Regulars stated that the dowry should be returned to a woman religious who had professed solemn vows and who had been dismissed from the monastery.[63] The same Congregation later arranged for those women who had taken simple vows in anticipation of solemn vows. In the decree *Perpensis* of 1902 it was stated that the institute was obliged at dismissal to restore also to them the whole dowry, without the income.[64]

The same practice was employed with regard to women who were members of institutes of merely simple vows. Moreover when such a member was dismissed, besides the dowry, whatever personal property she had brought with her to the community which had not been consumed, was to be restored to her.[65] These provisions gave rise to an obligation of justice. The authors also demanded that, if a dismissed woman's dowry was not sufficient to provide for her journey home, she was to be supplied with what she needed.[66] The *Normae of 1901* also stated that the dowry was to be restored to such women and also the belongings that they had brought to the convent with them. It was further enjoined that the institute should provide all that was required for the dismissed person to return home in a safe and becoming manner.[67]

Article V. Further Effects of Dismissal

In the decree *Sacra Congregatio* of the Sacred Congregation of the Council, it was stated that while a dismissed religious remained outside his religious institute, he should wear the clerical garb and not the habit of his order.[68] The wearing of the clerical garb was prescribed because of its propriety for the religious state and also to remove from the dismissed religious the occasion of wandering about.

[63] S. C. Ep. et Reg., *Fulginaten.*, mart. 1796—*Fontes*, n. 1889.

[64] S. C. Ep. et Reg., 3 maii 1902—*Fontes*, n. 2039.

[65] Soeurs de Notre-Dame du Bon Secours, Lyon, 24 sept. 1891, ad 8—apud Battandier, *Guide Canonique*, p. 270.

[66] Battandier, *Guide Canonique*, pp. 269-271; Piatus Montensis, *Praelectiones Juris Regularis*, I, q. 227, B.

[67] *Normae of 1901*, n. 200.

[68] S. C. C., decr. *Sacra Congregatio*, 21 sept. 1624—*Fontes*, n. 2454.

The decree did not distinguish between clerics and non-clerics. It merely stated that while dimissed religious remained outside their monasteries, they were obliged to wear the clerical garb. For this reason some authors claimed that the obligation extended also to non-clerics who had been dismissed.[69] The Sacred Congregation of the Council declared in 1628 that the injunction to wear the clerical garb was of obligation even to those who had minor orders, for they did not lose their Orders by dismissal, but still retained their status as clerics.[70] After this declaration, the interpretation seemed to be commonly accepted that those who had not been ordained, could go about in the garb of lay people.[71]

If those who were obliged to wear the clerical garb put it aside with the intention of resuming neither it nor the habit of their order, they were then excommunicated and became true apostates.[72] But if they put it aside with the intention of wearing it again, they were not excommunicated nor were they apostates from their religious institute.[73] Pius VI (1775-1799), in view of the grave conditions of his time, granted to the bishops of France the faculty of dispensing from the obligation of wearing the clerical garb.[74]

Relative to the religious obligations other than the vows, the authors generally excused the dismissed religious from the rules of the monastery, the monastic fasts, the vigils, the choice of foods

[69] Donatus, *Rerum Regularium Praxis Resolutoria,* Tom. I, pars II, tract. VIII, q. XLI, n. 2; Passerinus, *De Hominum Statibus,* Q. CLXXXIX, art. VIII, n. 597; Rotarius, *Theologia Moralis Regularium,* Tom. I, lib. III, c. II, punct. V, n. 67.

[70] S. C. C., declar., 1 apr. 1628—apud Ferraris, *Prompta Bibliotheca,* s. v. "Ejecti a Religione," n. 62.

[71] Cf. Ferraris, *Prompta Bibliotheca,* s. v. "Ejecti a Religione," nn. 62-63.

[72] Sebastianelli, *De Personis,* n. 363; Donatus, *Rerum Regularium Praxis Resolutoria,* Tom. I, pars II, tract. VIII, q. XLII, n. 1.

[73] Rotarius, *Theologia Moralis Regularium,* Tom. I, lib. III, c. II, punct. V, n. 8; Passerinus, *De Hominum Statibus, Q. CLXXXIX,* art. VIII, n. 637.

[74] Const. *In gravissimis,* 14 mart. 1792—*Bullarii Romani Continuatio Summorum Pontificum* (19 vols., Prati, 1756-1883), X, 2476 ad 14.

and the like.[75] However Passerinus[76] and Ferraris[77] stated that the dismissed religious was bound to regular observance. It was also taught that such religious were not bound to recite the Divine Office unless they were in holy orders.[78] Some authors however stated that even though they were not in holy orders, they were bound under grave sin to recite the Divine Office, if as religious, they had the obligation of reciting it outside the choir.[79]

The first obligation of the dismissed religious was to amend his life so that he could return to his religious institute.[80] He was always free to return and the religious superiors were obliged to receive him back, if he were truly repentant, unless by his readmittance scandal would ensue or the discipline of the religious institute would thereby suffer, or unless other grave reasons against his readmittance contravened.[81] If reasons against his admittance were not present and if he had testimonial letters from the bishop of the diocese where he had stayed, the religious institute could be forced to receive him.

The question continued to be raised whether after the dismissed religious had amended, he was permitted to go to another institute or whether he was required to petition for readmittance into his own order. Some authors stated that he needed the permission of the

[75] Tamburini, *De Iure Abbatum,* Tom. III, disp. VIII, q. VIII, n. 15; De Ameno, *De Incorrigibilium Expulsione,* Pars III, q. VI, n. 42; Barbosa, *Collectanea Doctorum in Jus Pontificium Universum,* Lib. III, tit. XXXI, c. XXIV, nn. 12, 14; Leurenius, Lib. III, tit. XXXI, q. DCCCLXV, n. 2; Schmalzgrueber, Lib. III, tit. XXXI, nn. 248-249; Rotarius, *Theologia Moralis Regularium,* Tom. I, lib. III, c. II, punct. VI, nn. 10, 12; Piatus Montensis, *Praelectiones Juris Regularis,* I, q. 224, 3°.

[76] *De Hominum Statibus,* Q. CLXXXIX, art. VIII, n. 624.

[77] *Prompta Bibliotheca,* s. v. "Ejecti a Religione," n. 61.

[78] St. Alphonsus, *Theologia Moralis,* Lib. IV, n. 81; cf. Piatus Montensis, *Praelectiones Juris Regularis,* I, q. 244.

[79] Donatus, *Rerum Regularium Praxis Resolutoria,* Tom. I, pars II, tract. VIII, q. LII; Passerinus, *De Hominum Statibus,* Q. CLXXXIX, art. VIII, n. 626.

[80] Huguenin, *Expositio Methodica Juris Canonici ad Usum Scholarum Clericalium* (4. ed., Parisiis, 1887), n. 580.

[81] Donatus, *Rerum Regularium Praxis Resolutoria,* Tom. I, pars II, tract. VIII, q. XXVI, nn. 1, 4; Passerinus, *De Hominum Statibus,* Q. CLXXXIX, art. VIII, nn. 615, 619, 651; Rotarius, *Theologia Moralis Regularium,* Tom. I, lib. III, c. II, punct. VII, n. 3; Schmalzgrueber, Lib. III, tit. XXXI, nn. 253-256.

Roman Pontiff to enter another religious institute. They argued to this opinion from the enactment of the decree *Sacra Congregatio* which commanded the dismissed religious to wear the clerical garb while he was outside his monastery.[82] However some allowed him the faculty of entering any other religious institute whether of equal, stricter, or even less strict observance, without any permission.[83] The Society of Jesus had the faculty to allow its dismissed members to enter another approved religious institute and at times even an institute of less strict observance.[84]

The authors pointed out that the dismissed religious was in no way obliged to enter a religious institute other than his own. If the petition for readmittance was once refused, some authors stated that the dismissed religious could remain in the world with a safe conscience and that he was not bound to enter another religious institute.[85] However other authors stressed the obligation to return and stated that he was obliged to ask, not once or twice, but repeatedly.[86]

Whether all such dismissed members incurred infamy by the fact of dismissal was also a disputed point but the better opinion was that they were not to be considered infamous unless they had committed some crime to which infamy was attached by law.[87]

The religious was not obliged to a new profession or novitiate after his return.[88] After return to the monastery it was held that the dismissed subject was to be given the same status which he previously

[82] Donatus, *Rerum Regularium Praxis Resolutoria,* Tom. I, pars II, tract. VIII, q. LVII, n. 2, who also required the permission of the religious superior; Passerinus, *De Hominum Statibus,* Q. CLXXXIX, art. VIII, n. 636; Rotarius, *Theologia Moralis Regularium,* Tom. I, lib. III, c. II, punct. VI, n. 6.

[83] Tamburini, *De Iure Abbatum,* Tom. II, disp. VIII, q. VIII, n. 14.

[84] Gregorius XIII, const. *Cum alias,* 22 sept. 1582—*Bull. Rom. Taur.,* VIII, 399.

[85] St. Alphonsus, *Theologia Moralis,* Lib. IV, n. 81; Ferraris, *Prompta Bibliotheca,* s. v. "Ejecti a Religione," n. 61.

[86] Donatus, *Rerum Regularium Praxis Resolutoria,* Tom. I, pars II, tract. VIII, q. XXVI; Passerinus, *De Hominum Statibus,* Q. CLXXXIX, art. VIII, n. 619.

[87] Commentator, "De Suspensione lata in religiosos eiectos extra Religionem degentes,"—*ASS,* XIX (1886), appendix XLVI, 399.

[88] Tamburini, *De Iure Abbatum,* Tom. III, disp. VIII, q. VIII, n. 5; De Ameno, *De Incorrigibilium Expulsione,* Pars III, q. XVI; Schmalzgrueber, Lib. III, tit. XXXI, n. 257.

enjoyed,[89] but many disagreed with this view, holding that he should not be given the same rank and honors which he possessed before his dismissal.[90]

In 1905 the Sacred Congregation of the Council decreed that no dismissed religious was to be admitted into a seminary unless the bishop first received by personal information from the religious moderators letters concerning the talents and character and the worthiness and fitness for the priesthood of the dismissed subject.[91]

In 1909 the Sacred Congregation of Religious in the decree *Ecclesia Christi* enacted that those professed men who were dismissed from one order or congregation could not without the permission of the Holy See be received into a novitiate or to the profession of vows and this under pain of nullity. The same prohibition also included those who were professed and were dismissed from one province of an order or congregation and who sought reception into the same province or into another province of the same order or congregation.[92] Later it was decided that those who had been dismissed from one institute and had been admitted to first profession in a second institute before the above decree was promulgated could be readily admitted to second profession, whether of solemn or of simple vows. However, the superiors were seriously obliged to seek secret and sworn information about the good morals of those subjects and also about their learning if they aspired to orders. The former superiors from whom this information was to be sought were bound in conscience to give secret information under oath.[93] In 1910 the prescripts of the decree *Ecclesia Christi* were extended to women who had professed either simple or solemn vows and were dismissed.[94]

If the dismissed person died in the world before returning to the

[89] Barbosa, *Collectanea Doctorum in Jus Pontificium Universum,* Lib. III, tit. XXXI, c. XXIV, n. 8; Passerinus, *De Hominum Statibus,* Q. CLXXXIX, art. VIII, nn. 600, 660; Schmalzgrueber, Lib. III, tit. XXXI, n. 257.

[90] Donatus, *Rerum Regularium Praxis Resolutoria,* Tom. I, pars II, tract. VIII, q. XXVII, n. 3; Leurenius, Lib. III, tit. XXXI, q. DCCCLXI, n. 2.

[91] S. C. C., decr. *Vetuit,* 22 dec. 1905, ad 4°—*ASS,* XXXVIII (1905-1906), 409; *Periodica,* II (1911), 65.

[92] S. C. de Rel., decr. *Ecclesia Christi,* 7 sept. 1909—*Fontes,* n. 4396.

[93] S. C. de Rel., declar,, 5 apr. 1910—*Fontes,* n. 4400.

[94] S. C. de Rel., declar., 4 ian. 1910—*Fontes,* n. 4399.

monastery, he was not to be buried in the cemetery of the religious institute. If he had not chosen a burying place, he was to be buried in the cemetery of the parish church.[95]

Those who were perpetually professed in any religious institute and had been dispensed from their vows at dismissal, in virtue of a privilege that some institutes possessed, were included in a decree of June 15, 1909. Also those who after dismissal received an indult of secularization or a dispensation from their vows were comprehended in the same legislation. The decree stated that all these were forbidden without a special indult of the Holy See to accept (a) any office, and in case of those who were capable of receiving a benefice, any benefice, in major or minor basilicas or in cathedral churches; (b) any professorship or office in clerical seminaries, major or minor, or in other institutions in which the clergy were educated, or in Universities or institutions which enjoyed the apostolic privilege of conferring academic degrees in philosophy, theology and canon law; (c) any office or position in the episcopal curia; (d) and the office of visitor or moderator of religious houses of communities of either sex, even in the case of merely diocesan congregations. They were forbidden further to establish an habitual domicile in any place where there was a convent or religious house of the province or mission to which such an ex-religious had been attached.[96]

Article VI. The Decree *Quum singulae*

The last enactment which treated of dismissal in pre-Code legislation was the decree *Quum singulae*.[97] Its purpose was to adapt the proceedings of dismissal to recent requirements and at the same time to reduce the laws existing in many sources to a convenient compendium. The statutes of this decree are contained substantially in the present Code.[98]

[95] Ferraris, *Prompta Bibliotheca*, s. v. "Ejecti a Religione," n. 74; Craisson, *Manuale Totius Juris Canonici*, n. 3091; Bachofen (Augustine), *Compendium Juris Regularium* (New York, 1903), p. 359.

[96] S. C. de Rel., decr. *Quum minoris*, 15 iun. 1909—*AAS*, I (1909), 523.

[97] S. C. de Rel., decr. *Quum singulae*, 16 maii 1911—*AAS*, III (1911), 235-238; *Fontes*, n. 4409.

[98] Cf. Tabera, "Excursus Historicus de Regularium Ejectione a Religione,"—*CpR*, XIII (1932), 290.

By this decree those in minor orders who were dismissed were forbidden to receive higher orders without the permission of the Holy See. Vermeersch stated that higher orders referred not only to major orders but also to minor orders when a dismissed cleric had not received all of the minor orders. Permission of the Holy See was also required for dismissed non-clerics in reference to first tonsure.[99] The same author was of the opinion that minor clerics were not to be considered irregular and that the permission required for their advancement to Orders was not to be confused with a dispensation from an irregularity.[100]

The decree also stated that the sentence of dismissal, no matter how it was inflicted, was to be communicated immediately to both the ordinary of the place of origin of the dismissed subject and to the ordinary of the place where the dismissed subject would live, or where it was judged that he would live. This prescription referred only to those dismissed after ordination. The permission of the Apostolic See was also demanded in this decree for the readmittance of a dismissed member into the order or congregation which dismissed him and also for admittance into another order or congregation.

Automatic dismissal appeared for the first time in universal legislation in this decree.[101] The grounds for such dismissal were the crimes of public apostasy from the Catholic faith, apostasy from the religious order or institute unless the religious returned within three months, flight from the monastery with a woman and finally the attempt or contraction of marriage even the so-called civil marriage.[102] This new institute of automatic dismissal was wholly incorporated into the schemata of the Code in 1914 and 1916, but in the edition of the Code one form of automatic dismissal was omitted, namely apostasy from an order or religious institute.[103] Vermeersch was of the opinion that automatic dismissal did not apply to women who had professed solemn vows, because the law was silent on the point.[104]

[99] Vermeersch, "Annotationes,"—*Periodica,* VI (1912), 47-50.

[100] Vermeersch, *op. cit.*, p. 47, note II, 52.

[101] Cf. Tabera, "De Dimissione Religiosorum,"—*CpR,* XI (1930), 411.

[102] S. C. de Rel., decr. *Quum singulae,* 16 maii 1911, n. 18—*AAS,* III (1911), 237.

[103] Tabera, *op. cit.*, p. 412.

[104] "Annotationes,"—*Periodica,* VI (1912), 53.

Part II

Canonical Commentary

CHAPTER IV

THE RECKONING OF CANONICAL STATUS

Article I. Moment of Dismissal

The dismissal of religious after perpetual profession is brought about in various ways. The legal modes of dismissal are dismissal which is automatic upon the commission of certain stated crimes, dismissal by the juridical sentence of a religious tribunal, dismissal by decree of the Holy See, dismissal by decree confirmed by the Holy See, dismissal by decree of the local ordinary and dismissal in extraordinary cases by the major superior, or by the major superior with the consent of his council. In the last case, i. e., where dismissal is the act of the major superior, if there is danger in delay and if there is no time to have recourse to the major superior, provision is found that the religious may also be dismissed by the local superior with the consent of his council, or by the local superior with the consent of his council and the consent of the local ordinary. Since by dismissal the religious is initiated into a new canonical status, it is necessary to know at what moment the legal effects of his new condition come into being. Each of the above modes of dismissal will be treated with a view to determine the moment in which the religious enters the canonical status of religious dismissed after perpetual profession.

A. *Automatic Dismissal*

Religious are considered as lawfully dismissed automatically if they publicly apostatize from the Catholic faith, or if they run away with a person of the opposite sex, or if they attempt or contract marriage, even the so-called civil marriage. In these cases it suffices that the major superior with his chapter or council makes a declaration of the fact in the manner prescribed by the constitutions.[1] After the promulgation of the Code, many disputes arose concerning the canonical status of religious who were dismissed automatically when the major superior had not yet made the required declaration, or when the major superior entirely neglected to do so. The Code Commission settled the question on July 30, 1934. It stated that those who commit the crimes mentioned in canon 646 are to be considered as legitimately dismissed even though the declaration of the fact is not made by the superior.[2] The declaration then, is not a declaratory sentence, but simply a declaration of a fact.[3] The religious therefore, is bound by the canons stating the condition of dismissed religious after perpetual profession, immediately upon the commission of the crimes stated in canon 646. The law itself produces these effects automatically.[4]

Since the declaration is not made to produce the effects of dismissal, its purpose is merely to show in the external forum that sufficient proofs of the crime have been evinced and to induce the full execution of dismissal in the external forum.[5] For this purpose the declaration should be made in writing and ought to be kept in the archives of the major superior with the proofs of the crime.[6]

[1] Canon 646.

[2] P. C. I., 30 iul. 1934, ad I—*AAS,* XXVI (1934), 494; cf. Maroto, "Annotationes,"—*CpR,* XV (1934), 352-356.

[3] Tabera, "De Dimissione Religiosorum,"—*CpR,* XI (1930), 419; Goyeneche, "Consultationes,"—*CpR,* XIII (1932), 103; Schaefer, *De Religiosis* (3. ed., Romae: Typis Polyglottis Vaticanis, 1940), n. 576, note 27; Bastien, *Directoire Canonique a l'Usage des Congrégations à Voeux Simples* (3. ed., Bruges: Beyaert, 1923), n. 211 (hereafter to be cited as *Directoire Canonique*); Cappello, *Summa Iuris Canonici in Usum Scholarum Concinnata* (2 vols., Romae: Apud Aedes Universitatis Gregorianae, 1928), II, n. 632, 3° (hereafter to be cited as *Summa Iuris Canonici*); Palombo, *De Dimissione Religiosorum,* n. 198.

[4] Tabera, *op. cit.,* p. 413.

[5] Tabera, *op. cit.,* pp. 417, 419; Palombo, *De Dimissione Religiosorum,* n. 198; Maroto, "Annotationes,"—*CpR,* XV (1934), 356; Schaefer, *De Religiosis,* n. 576.

[6] Bastien, *Directoire Canonique,* n. 211; Berutti, *Institutiones Iuris Canonici* (6 vols., Taurini, Romae: Marietti, 1936), III, *De Religiosis,* n. 158, B (hereafter to be cited as *De Religiosis*).

Since automatic dismissal has a certain similarity to a penalty inflicted *latae sententiae* [7] and since there is question of a law automatically introducing a status of dismissal, the principles of canon 2232 can be evoked. Thus all the canonical effects of dismissal bind the guilty party from the moment of the perpetration of the crime, both in the internal and in the external forum, if he is conscious of his offense. However, before the declaration of the fact is made according to canon 646, § 2, the dismissed religious would be excused from the observance of the external canonical effects, whenever he cannot observe them without the loss of his reputation. No one can demand that he observe the canonical effects in the external forum unless the offense is notorious. When the declaration is made all the canonical effects would have a retroactive effect to the moment in which the crime was committed.[8] The reason for the principle of canon 2232 is that since it is a great hardship for a delinquent whose offense is still occult to observe a prescribed automatic penalty if he, on that account, publicly betrays his guilt or arouses suspicion against himself, canon law does not demand of the culprit that he execute the penalty on himself. In such cases the culprit is permitted to act in public as though he had not incurred the penalty until the competent authority has issued the declaratory sentence. These same reasons for the principle of canon 2232 concerning penalties should be applied to the canonical effects of automatic dismissal.

Interpreting this mode of dismissal by the terms of the decree *Quum singulae,*[9] certain authors place an added obligation on the superior at the time of the declaration. They state that if there is question of a religious in holy orders the superior should then reveal the fact of dismissal to the ordinary of origin, and to the ordinary of the place where the dismissed religious will live or to the ordinary of the place where it is assumed that he will live.[10] However there is

[7] Berutti, *op. cit.*, p. 338.

[8] Cf. canon 2232; Maroto, "Annotationes,"—*CpR,* XV (1934), 354; Coronata, *Institutiones,* n. 646; cf. Goyeneche, "Annotationes,"—*Apollinaris,* VIII (1935), 552.

[9] S. C. de Rel., decr. *Quum singulae,* 16 maii 1911, n. 19—*AAS,* III (1911), 235-238; *Fontes,* n. 4409.

[10] Prümmer, *Manuale Iuris Canonici* (5. ed., Friburgi Brisgoviae: Herder, 1927), Q. 257; Pejška, *Ius Canonicum Religiosorum* (3. ed., Friburgi Brisgoviae:

now no obligation imposed by law of following this procedure,[11] but institutes may have such an obligation, arising from their approved constitutions.[12]

B. *Dismissal by Sentence of a Religious Tribunal*

A canonical trial is required by law for the dismissal of male religious with solemn vows or with perpetual simple vows in exempt clerical organizations.[13] The supreme head of the organization or monastic congregation, with his council or chapter, issues the sentence of dismissal.[14] However this sentence cannot be executed unless it is confirmed by the Sacred Congregation of Religious, to which the president of the tribunal is obliged to forward as soon as possible, the sentence and all the acts of the process.[15] Therefore without the confirmation of the Sacred Congregation, the sentence of the religious tribunal is not a final sentence *(sententia definitiva)*,[16] and on that account its execution cannot be demanded. Vermeersch-Creusen are of the opinion that the religious is truly dismissed by the unconfirmed sentence, because, as they state, the confirmation of the Sacred Congregation of Religious merely adds the force of execution or merely fulfills a condition required by law for execution.[17] However the opinion to be preferred is the opinion which Palombo holds as certain, namely that the guilty party remains united to the religious

Herder, 1927), p. 189; Coronata, *Institutiones*, n. 646; Schaefer, *De Religiosis*, n. 573, 3.

[11] The words of n. 19 of the decree *Quum singulae* were found in the schemata of the Code of 1913 and 1916 in this fashion, "Sequuta dimissio illico communicanda est Ordinario loci ubi dimissus moratur, aut sedem suam statuere velle dignoscatur." These words were omitted in the final edition of the Code.—Tabera, "De Dimissione Religiosorum,"—*CpR*, XI (1930), 420, note 34.

[12] Cf. *Constitutiones Ordinis Fratrum Minorum Sancti Patris Francisci Conventualium* (Romae, 1932), n. 800.

[13] Canon 654.

[14] Cf. canons 655, 667.

[15] Canon 666.

[16] Cf. canon 1868.

[17] *Epitome Iuris Canonici* (3 vols., Vol. I, 6. ed., 1937; Vol. II, 5. ed., 1934; Vol. III, 5. ed., 1936, Mechliniae-Romae: H. Dessain), I, n. 818 (hereafter to be cited as *Epitome*).

institute with all the rights and offices he enjoys until he is officially notified of the sentence confirmed by the Sacred Congregation.[18]

The unconfirmed sentence of the regligious tribunal then, has no effect until the Sacred Congregation confirms it. Only from the moment of official notification of the confirmed sentence does the religious become truly dismissed with all the effects of juridical dismissal. From that moment there is no remedy allowed against the sentence except recourse to the Roman Pontiff in virtue of canon 1569, § 1. If such recourse is taken the supreme moderator shall defer the execution of the confirmed sentence until it becomes evident whether the Roman Pontiff himself will take up the case or not.[19]

Indeed it may seem strange that a sentence made by a tribunal is subjected to the revision of a Sacred Congregation which is not a tribunal, and that a sentence which begins in a judicial way, is made final in an administrative manner, but so the legislator wills lest lawsuits be protracted in religious institutes.

It may be added that it is possible, although it happens very rarely, that the Sacred Congregtaion sanates a sentence which is in itself juridically null because of some defect in form, when it is evident that those things required by canon 664, § 2, are sufficiently proved. Also sometimes the Sacred Congregation approves a sentence juridically perfect, but commands the religious organization to keep the guilty party, especially if he is a priest, in some house of the religious institute until he finds a bishop willing to receive him. In this case, the guilty party is deprived of all the rights and offices of the religious institute and he is considered merely as a guest under the conditions and restrictions stated by the Sacred Congregation of Religious.

C. *Dismissal by Decree of the Holy See*

Concerning women religious who have made profesison of solemn vows [20] and women religious who have made profession of perpetual simple vows in institutes of pontifical approval, the Sacred Congregation of Religious issues the decree of their dismissal.[21] The can-

[18] *De Dimissione Religiosorum*, n. 144.

[19] Palombo, *loc. cit.*

[20] Canon 652, § 2.

[21] Canon 652, § 3.

onical effects of dismissal are binding in these cases from the moment of presentation of the decree of the Holy See. The only recourse allowed is recourse according to the norm of canon 1569, but this recourse does not entail suspensive effect.[22]

D. *Dismissal by Decree Confirmed by the Holy See*

In institutes of men religious which enjoy pontifical approval and which are not exempt clerical institutes, the decree of dismissal is issued by the supreme head of the organization, but in order to have effect it must be confirmed by the Holy See.[23] It must be stated then, that such religious are canonically dismissed from the moment of notification of the decree confirmed by the Sacred Congregation. After that moment, recourse with suspensive effect ceases.[24]

Before confirmation of this decree by the Sacred Congregation of Religious, the guilty party remains completely united to the religious institute with all the rights and obligations of a religious as was stated above.[25] Although in this instance the Code states nothing about recourse to the Holy See after the decree of dismissal, yet this cannot be doubted in view of an *a fortiori* argument taken from canon 647, § 2, n. 4.[26] Such action could also be allowed by canon 1569.

E. *Dismissal by Decree of the Local Ordinary*

In religious institutes of men of diocesan approval,[27] and in religious institutes of women of diocesan approval, after the profession of perpetual simple vows, the ordinary of the place in which the religious house of the guilty party in question is located has the right to issue the decree of dismissal. In both these cases the religious is considered as canonically dismissed from the moment in which he

[22] Palombo, *De Dimissione Religiosorum,* n. 187.

[23] Canon 650, § 2, n. 2.

[24] Palombo, *op. cit.*, n. 182; Coronata, *Institutiones,* n. 650; Schaefer, *De Religiosis,* n. 582.

[25] Section B, pp. 47-48.

[26] Fanfani, *De Iure Religiosorum* (2. ed., Taurini, Romae: Marietti, 1925), n. 505; Palombo, *De Dimissione Religiosorum,* n. 182; Schaefer, *De Religiosis,* n. 582.

[27] Canon 650, § 2, n. 1.

or she receives the communication of the local ordinary, unless the religious has recourse to the Holy See. The religious has this faculty to have recourse within ten days after the reception of the decree, and pending this action the dismissal has no juridic effect. Although in the Code, there is nothing said about this recourse, it cannot be doubted, for the recourse which is allowed to a religious in temporary vows,[28] *a fortiori* is conceded to a religious in perpetual vows in an institute of diocesan approval. After such recourse is taken by the religious, his or her canonical status depends upon the answer that will be forwarded from the Sacred Congregation of Religious.

F. *Dismissal in Extraordinary Cases*

1. Male religious of orders or of exempt clerical institutes are dismissed in extraordinary cases when immediate dismissal is required because of grave external scandal or of very serious, imminent harm to the community. Such dismissal is enjoined by the major superior. When there is danger in any delay whatsoever and time does not permit recourse to the major superior, the local superior with the consent of his council can also effect dismissal.[29] However in both cases juridic dismissal does not seem to be present before the sentence of the religious tribunal. Such religious cannot be placed in the juridic condition of dismissed religious after perpetual profession until the tribunal issues its sentence.[30]

In these cases, as also in the cases under the following paragraph it is true that the competent superiors can send the guilty party away from the religious house, but the canons use the words *"ad saeculum remitti"* very advisedly. These two canons 653 and 668 are the only places in the Code where that particular expression is found and this seems to show that only a provisional measure is authorized and not true juridical dismissal. The law further requires that in these cases the matter must be submitted without delay to the religious tribunal or to the judgment of the Holy See which seems to show again that there is question of a provisional measure to care for the

[28] Canon 647, § 2, n. 4.

[29] Canon 668.

[30] Palombo, *De Dimissione Religiosorum*, n. 148; Tabera, "De Dimissione Religiosorum,"—*CpR*, XI (1930), 278, note 11.

urgent necessity, present here and now, and that the juridical status of the dismissed must be settled by the religious tribunal or by the Holy See.

2. Men or women religious of all institutes which are not exempt clerical institutes can be dismissed in the circumstances just indicated by the major superior with the consent of his or her council. When there is danger in any delay whatsoever and time does not permit recourse to the major superior, the local superior with the consent of his or her council and also the consent of the local ordinary may dismiss the religious.[31]

However juridic dismissal does not seem to be present in these cases before the judgment of the Holy See for the reasons already given. Such religious are not bound by the canons affecting dismissed religious after perpetual profession until the Holy See settles their status.

Article II. Crimes Affecting the Status of Dismissed Religious

The reckoning of the canonical status of religious dismissed after perpetual profession by the crimes which they have committed and for which they have been dismissed is something new in law. This determination of the status by reason of the crimes has its basis in canons 670 and 671 and can be applied only to those religious who have received major orders. Therefore this entire article applies only to them.

The Code nowhere specifies what particular offenses are to be punished with dismissal, with the exception of the crimes of public apostasy from the Catholic faith, flight with a person of the opposite sex, and attempt of marriage or contraction of marriage, and these are punished by automatic dismissal.[32] The crimes intimated in canon 670 are not presented as causes for dismissal. The canon merely states that if dismissal has taken place because of the intimated crimes, a certain canonical status follows. The crimes mentioned in canon 646 and the crimes which are punished by common law with

[31] Canon 653.

[32] Canon 646, § 1.

infamy of law, deposition and degradation fall under the scope of canon 670.[33] It matters not whether the infamy of law involved takes place either automatically or by declaration. Deposition and degradation will always take place only after a trial and are never imposed automatically. Notice also that the infamy of law here mentioned is infamy branded as such by ecclesiastical and not by civil law.[34]

A. *The More Serious Crimes*

The terms "more serious" and "less serious" which are used in this division do not refer to moral culpability. They are used in a merely relative sense to distinguish between the crimes themselves. The crimes which come under the scope of canon 670 are those crimes committed by the following:

(1) Those who publicly apostatize from the Catholic faith.[35] (2) Those who run away with a person of the opposite sex.[36] (3) Those who attempt to contract marriage, even the so-called civil marriage.[37] (4) Those who are heretics and schismatics and who do not repent after they have been admonished.[38] (5) Those who have joined a non-Catholic sect or have publicly adhered to it.[39] (6) Those who cast away the Sacred Species or carry Them off or retain

[33] Canon 670. "Clericus in sacris qui aliquod delictum commisit de quo in can. 646, aut dimissus est ob delictum quod iure communi punitur infamia iuris vel depositione vel degradatione, perpetuo prohibetur deferre habitum ecclesiasticum."

[34] Cf. canon 2293, § 2. Such crimes as forgery and perjury are also declared infamous crimes by our civil laws. Also treason, felony, subornation of perjury, suppression of testimony by bribery, or conspiracy to procure the absence of a witness, or other conspiracy to accuse one of crime, and barratry are infamous crimes by our civil laws.—United States v. Block (U. S.) 24 Fed. Cas. 1174, 1175; United States v. Yates (U. S.) 6 Fed. 861, 863; United States v. Petit (U. S.) 11 Fed. 58, 60; Wick v. Baldwin, 36 N. E. 671, 672, 51 Ohio St. 51; Webb v. State, 29 Ohio St. 351, 358.

[35] Canon 646, § 1, n. 1.

[36] Canon 646, § 1, n. 2.

[37] Canon 646, § 1, n. 3.

[38] These are to be declared infamous and after renewed admonition they are to be deposed,—Canon 2314, § 1, n. 2.

[39] These incur infamy and also degradation after a fruitless admonition,—Canon 2314, § 1, n. 3.

Them for an evil purpose.[40] (7) Those who pretend to celebrate Mass or to hear confessions, if they are not yet priests.[41] (8) Those who violate the bodies or graves of the dead with a view to theft or any other evil purpose.[42] (9) Those who lay violent hands on the person of the Pope, Cardinals or Papal legates.[43] (10) Those who effectively procure abortion.[44] (11) The principals and their seconds in duels.[45] (12) Those who are guilty of the crime of homicide and those who in certain very grave circumstances are guilty of the abduction of minors of either sex; of selling a human being as a slave or for any other evil purpose; or usury, robbery, theft under aggravating circumstances changing the species of sin, as for instance, theft of sacred things, or even ordinary theft in a very grave matter; of incendiarism or malicious and very grievous destruction of things; of grave mutilation or wounding or violence.[46] (13) Those who commit a crime against the sixth commandment of the decalogue with minors under sixteen years of age, or those who have been guilty of adultery, rape, bestiality, sodomy, traffic in vice, incest with blood relatives or relatives by marriage within the first degree.[47] (14) Those who commit a specially grave crime of solicitation.[48] (15) Those who notoriously pass to a kind of life alien to the clerical state and who do not repent after a second warning.[49] (16) Those

[40] These crimes are punished with *ipso facto* infamy and with deposition,—Canon 2320.

[41] These crimes are punished with deposition,—Canon 2322, n. 1.

[42] These crimes are punished with infamy *ipso facto* and with deposition,—Canon 2328.

[43] These crimes are punished with infamy *ipso facto* and with degradation when violence has been used on the person of the Pope,—Canon 2343, § 1, n. 2, n. 3; § 2, n. 2.

[44] This crime is punished by deposition,—Canon 2350, § 1.

[45] This crime is punished with infamy *ipso facto*,—Canon 2351, § 2.

[46] These crimes may be punished with deposition and the crime of homicide is punished by degradation,—Canon 2354.

[47] These crimes are punished by the declaration of infamy, and in the more serious cases by deposition,—Canon 2359, § 2.

[48] This crime when especially grave may be punished with degradation,—Canon 2368, § 1.

[49] Three months from the second admonition these clerics shall be deposed,—Canon 2379.

who, in the more grievous cases, take possession of an ecclesiastical benefice, office or dignity on their own authority, or those who, after their election, presentation or nomination, take possession or interfere in the government or administration of the same, before they have received the necessary letters of confirmation or institution and shown them to the persons designated by law, and who refuse to retire from the possession, government or administration of the same office, benefice or dignity immediately upon being warned.[50] (17) Those who in the more grievous cases stubbornly persist in an office, benefice or dignity, notwithstanding legitimate privation or removal, or those who for the purpose of retaining possession unlawfully delay to withdraw, after they have been warned.[51]

B. *The Less Serious Crimes*

An adequate list of the crimes which are considered less serious would be too extensive to mention. The Code does not explicitly enumerate the crimes, but it merely presents norms for judging them in canons 649, and 656-662. In all events, the crimes must be certain and external. They must be grave delicts [52] for male religious and grave reasons for dismissal for women religious. In ordinary cases, the element of incorrigibility must always be present.[53] Canon 671 merely states that these crimes are any offenses causing dismissal which do not fall under the scope of the crimes intimated by canon 670. When dismissal has taken place because of the less serious crimes, the canonical status of the dismissed cleric is determined by the prescripts of canon 671.

[50] These crimes are punished by deposition,—Canon 2394, n. 2.

[51] These crimes are punished by deposition,—Canon 2401.

[52] In the sense of canon 2195, against the common law or against the particular law of the religious.

[53] Cf. Palombo, *De Dimissione Religiosorum,* nn. 38, 179; Coronata, *Institutiones,* nn. 650, 651, 655; Schaefer, *De Religiosis,* nn. 582, 590.

CHAPTER V

THE VOWS OF THE DISMISSED

Article I. The Three Vows of Religion

Canon 669, § 1. Professus qui vota perpetua emisit, a religione dismissus, votis religiosis manet adstrictus, salvis constitutionibus aut Sedis Apostolicae indultis quae aliud ferant.[1]

The religious who has professed perpetual vows, whether solemn or simple, is bound by those vows after dismissal from the religious organization, unless the constitutions of the institute or apostolic indults declare otherwise. The exceptions to the general principle of this canon, namely dispensation from the vows by virtue of the constitutions of the institute or by virtue of apostolic indults will be discussed later.[2] In the present chapter only the case of those religious who are still bound by the vows after dismissal will be treated.

These religious remain bound by the obligations of their vows because by dismissal the common good of the religious institute, not the private utility of the individual religious is directly desired.[3]

In those religious who are worthy of dismissal, there may be a longing to be free from the burdensome obligations of the vows and the Church grants no such premium to those who are guilty of serious faults. Also the religious superiors are not free to grant a dispensation in dismissal, since such dispensation is reserved to the Holy See,

[1] Canon 669, § 1. The religious who has made profession of perpetual vows and who has been dismissed from the Institute remains bound by his religious vows, except the constitutions or apostolic indults determine otherwise.—Authorized English Translation.

[2] Cf. *infra*, pp. 169-182.

[3] Cocchi, *Commentarium in Codicem Iuris Canonici* (5 vols. in 8, Vol. IV, *De Religiosis et Laicis* (2. ed., Taurinorum Augustae: Marietti, 1926), n. 157 (hereafter to be cited as *De Religiosis et Laicis*); Schaefer, *De Religiosis*, n. 596, 1; cf. *supra*, p. 8.

or the local ordinary when an institute of diocesan approval is involved.[4]

Since the promulgation of the Code, very little has been written about the obligations of the vows of the dismissed. The pre-Code authors treated this question, sometimes at great length and their opinions may still be followed *mutatis mutandis* in regard to simple vows. Before the promulgation of the Code, the obligation expressed in canon 669, § 1, was never incorporated into any universal enactment on dismissal. It was evident to all, considering the bond of religious profession, that the dismissed were not freed from their vows. The authors agreed unanimously that this was so.[5] Also in the ancient form of dismissal issued by the religious superior the fact that the religious was bound to the vows which he has professed was mentioned expressly.[6]

It is certain, and it was always maintained, that the obligations of the vows are not to be extended beyond the reasonable possibility of fulfillment in the new condition of the dismissed religious.[7] Fulfillment of certain obligations of the vows is no longer morally or even physically possible while the religious remains outside the community. Thus, when these obligations in any case would entail a grave *incommodum*, or would actually be incapable of fulfillment, the dismissed religious would be excused from them.[8]

A. *The Vow of Poverty*

It should be noted that every sin against the vow of poverty is necessarily a sin against the virtue of religion, in so far as it is the

[4] Cocchi, *loc. cit.*

[5] Barbosa, *Collectanea Doctorum in Jus Pontificium Universum*, Lib. III, tit. XXXI, c. XXIV, n. 10; Passerinus, *De Hominum Statibus*, Q. CLXXXIX, art. VIII, n. 597; Leurenius, Lib. III, tit. XXXI, q. DCCCLXII, n. 1; Reiffenstuel, Lib. III, tit. XXXI, n. 241; Schmalzgrueber, Lib. III, tit. XXXI, nn. 249, 254; Suarez, Tract. VIII, lib. III, c. V, n. 1; Bouix, *Tractatus de Iure Regularium*, Tom. II, pars VI, sec. IV, c. II, q. IV; Piatus Montensis, *Praelectiones Juris Regularis*, I, q. 244, 1°.

[6] Donatus, *Rerum Regularium Praxis Resolutoria*, Tom. I, pars II, tract. VIII, q. XVII.

[7] Coronata, *Institutiones*, n. 658, 1°.

[8] Coronata, *loc. cit.*

breaking of a promise made to God.[9] Moreover a religious also commits a sin of injustice if he disposes of property belonging to the religious community or to any other person, if he acts against the will of the owner. Furthermore unauthorized proprietary acts relative to property owned by an ecclesiastical person, such as a religious institute or a canonically erected house, are also "real" sacrileges.[10] Therefore, since the vow of poverty presents many difficulties after dismissal, it is generally because of this vow, rather than because of the others, that the dismissed religious is exposed to the danger of committing many sins.

In the first place it should be stated that the dismissed religious has no right to demand anything for the services he has in the past rendered to the community.[11] He would have no such right even though the religious institute is still profiting by his former work. He cannot therefore, on this account, deduct anything for himself from the goods which are owned by the religious institute and which he possesses while in the state of one dismissed. The reason for this conclusion is found in a provision of positive law. For, whatever a religious, either in simple or in solemn vows, acquires by his industry or by reason of the religious institute to which he is affiliated, he acquires to the religious organization or to the Holy See.[12] Therefore since he can acquire nothing to himself in this way, he can demand nothing in justice.[13] He can have no claim in justice, for persons who enter a religious organization know that they enter to give their services freely for the sake of a religious motive. Indeed in many cases, and it is to be highly recommended, the postulant makes a written declaration before he enters the institute, stating that he renounces any claim to wages for the work which he will do in the community.

In treating the vow of poverty distinction must be made between

[9] Vermeersch, "Poverty,"—*The Catholic Encyclopedia,* XII, 326; Turner, *The Vow of Poverty,* The Catholic University of American Canon Law Studies, n. 54 (Washington, D. C.: The Catholic University of America, 1929), p. 106.

[10] Turner, *loc. cit.*

[11] Canon 643, § 1.

[12] Canons 580, § 2, 582.

[13] Coronata, *Institutiones,* n. 641.

the solemn and the simple vow, not that in their essence they are different, but because the Church has introduced distinctions between them by adding to the solemn vows effects which are not attached to the simple vows.

For the dismissed, as well as for the religious in the community, the constitutions of the institute determine the obligations of poverty as he should observe them. As is evident, a religious does not profess the vow of poverty in general, but the vow of poverty as determined by the constitutions of his institute. The great variety of differences in the observance of poverty, found in the various religious organizations, is due to the various purposes of those organizations, as well as to the individual conceptions of their founders. The Code allows for this individuality by frequently referring to the constitutions of the individual religious institutes. In fact it obliges both superiors and subjects to observe faithfully and integrally the vow which they have professed.[14] To be ignorant of the legislation of the institute in the matter of poverty will not generally excuse from fault, although inadvertence may excuse.[15] Hence the dismissed religious cannot merely adopt the general principles as expounded by one author, but he must before all else consult the constitutions of his order or congregation.

1. The Simple Vow of Poverty

I. *Ownership and Acquisition.* Prescinding from particular constitutions,[16] the professed religious with simple vows has never relinquished his right to the ownership of goods,[17] and therefore he still retains the right after dismissal. He also enjoys the capacity to acquire goods at any time and in any legitimate way, with two exceptions, namely (a) when the constitutions place restrictions on the capacity to acquire [18] and (b) when the religious acquires goods

[14] Canons 569, 580, 581, 582, 593.

[15] Turner, *The Vow of Poverty*, p. 98.

[16] The Coadjutors of the Society of Jesus are incapable of having anything as their own.—Gregorius XIII, const. *Ascendente Domino*, 25 maii 1584, n. 11—*Fontes*, n. 153.

[17] Canon 580, § 1.

[18] Canon 580, § 1.

by his work or in consideration of his being a religious.[19] The dismissed religious who has professed simple vows can thus acquire goods by inheritance or legacy unless his constitutions forbid it. Concerning the second exception, it can be stated as a general principle that whatever arises from labor, mental or physical, or from the exercise of an art or a profession, or the priesthood, is included in the income from the "work" of a religious and therefore belongs to the religious institute.[20] When a religious is dismissed and obtains a position as a lecturer, teacher, stenographer, librarian, musician, laborer, etc., whatever he accepts in remuneration is acquired, not to himself, but to the religious institute. Such goods belong to the institute even though he has contracted for them in his own name. The same must be said of royalties paid to authors and also of the offerings given for the exercise of the holy ministry,[21] when such exercise is allowed after a certain period of emendation.[22]

The religious institute also acquires whatever is given to a dismissed member in consideration of his being a religious. Considering the common viewpoint of the laity, it is difficult to see how donations could be given to a dismissed religious *intuitu religionis*. Certainly if a dismissed member is not a cleric, or if he is a degraded cleric, in making the donation the person has no intention of considering the religious institute. Such a dismissed religious is dressed in the usual attire of a layman and he is recognized as such. Therefore such donations can be acquired by him in his own name. There is a possibility that donations given to those clerics who have been dismissed and who wear the cassock of the secular clergy, may be given in consideration of the religious institute, but in the majority of cases they will be given in consideration of the person. The presumption would be on this side, since there is no evident sign of attachment to the religious institute. These statements have been made because the acquisition of such donations depends above all on the intention of the donor. The further general principle also remains for the conscience of the dismissed religious, namely that when there is a

[19] Canon 580, § 2.

[20] Schaefer, *De Religiosis*, n. 270, d.; Turner, *The Vow of Poverty*, p. 147.

[21] Cf. Turner, *op. cit.*, p. 147.

[22] Canon 671, n. 7.

reasonable doubt about the intention of the donor and it is possible to have the intention determined, the religious is obliged to do so.

In view of these facts, the usual presumption in favor of the religious institute [23] when there is a doubt whether the institute is the final or motivating cause of the act by which property is acquired is not to be followed by the dismissed religious. This seems to be so also concerning unqualified donations which Turner says are to be presumed the property of the institute in the same way as the fruits of industry.[24] For the above presumption cannot be applied to the dismissed religious, because of the greater probability of the contrary intention of the donor, resulting from the status in which the dismissed is found.

II. *The Use and Administration of Goods.* It cannot be presumed that the religious superiors would dismiss a subject and deprive him of the support of the religious institute without granting permission for the use [25] and administration [26] of goods. Since the religious institute is obliged in justice to support no dismissed religious,[27] it is evident that the dismissed subject must provide for himself as regards food and the other necessities of life; and therefore it is certain that in his new condition he cannot observe poverty with the same rigor as in the religious house.[28] Thus some general permission must be allowed to the dismissed religious to prevent multiple sins against the vow of poverty while he is in the state of one dismissed. For this reason it was always admitted that the dismissed religious has permission for the use and administration of goods.[29] This permission

[23] Schaefer, *De Religiosis,* n. 270, d, arguing from canon 1536, § 1.

[24] *The Vow of Poverty,* p. 200.

[25] Use is the right of using a thing saving its substance.

[26] The general right to administer goods includes all acts which are necessary or useful, to keep the goods in proper condition, to make them productive, to derive benefit from them, to apply, pay out and use them for legitimate purposes.—Larraona, "Commentarium Codicis,"—*CpR,* XII (1931), 355-356.

[27] Cf. *infra,* pp. 139-140.

[28] Rotarius, *Theologia Moralis Regularium,* Tom. I, lib. III, c. II, punct. VI, n. 2.

[29] Reiffenstuel, Lib. III, tit. XXXI, n. 241; Schmalzgrueber, Lib. III, tit. XXXI, n. 250; Ferraris, *Prompta Bibliotheca,* s. v. "Ejecti a Religione," nn. 50, 58; Bouix, *Tractatus de Iure Regularium,* Tom. II, pars VI, sec. IV, c. II, q. IV; Appeltern, *Compendium,* Q. 143, 4°; *Schaefer, De Religiosis,* n. 596.

is not an explicit one, but an implicit [30] and general [31] permission given in the act of dismissal.

The question of the extent of this use and administration may be treated first. Passerinus [32] and Rotarius [33] held the opinion that the permission given for the use and administration of goods was absolutely indefinite and general, since no restriction had been placed on it by the superior. The majority of the authors however, are of the opinion that this use and administration extends only to those things which are necessary for the livelihood of the dismissed religious.[34] Such necessities would be food, clothing, habitation, medical care, reasonable recreation, etc. In the religious house the subject needs the permission of the superior for whatever he uses. Without permission it would be unlawful for him to take, accept, keep, borrow, buy, sell, exchange, loan, destroy, or use things for a purpose otherwise than that for which they were given. All of these acts may at times be necessary for the dismissed religious separated from the community and his superiors. For these reasons it is stated that an implicit, general permission is allowed in the act of dismissal to take care of the necessities of life of the dismissed religious.

It may now be asked if the cession of the use and administration of personal goods, which was made before profession, still binds the dismissed religious. The question is answered in the negative. However first, objections will be proposed to the recovery, at dismissal, of this use and administration of personal goods. It may be objected that canon 569, § 1, is very clear in stating that a novice before the profession of simple vows must cede the administration of his goods to someone else and must freely dispose of the use and usufruct [35] of them, and this *for the whole time in which he is bound by the*

[30] A permission is implicit when the act to be done is not directly allowed but is contained in another act expressly permitted.

[31] A permission is general if it is one given to place many acts, which require the permission of the superior, without applying for that permission each time an act is placed.

[32] *De Hominum Statibus*, Q. CLXXXIX, art. VIII, nn. 607-612.

[33] *Theologia Moralis Regularium*, Tom. I, lib. III, c. II, punct. VI, n. 4.

[34] Coronata, *Institutiones*, n. 658.

[35] Usufruct is the right of appropriating the fruits of goods to oneself, saving the substance of those goods.—Coronata, *Institutiones*, n. 593, 2°.

religious vows. It may be urged that the same cession of the use, usufruct and administration binds the religious when goods accrue to him after his profession.[36] On these grounds, since the religious is still bound by his vows after dismissal,[37] it might seem that the use and administration of the goods which he already has is not included in the permission given to the dismissed.

The same conclusion might be drawn from the following reasoning. In speaking of the formula which the novice should make in accordance with canon 569, § 1, Coronata states that it should be so drawn up as not to cease while the religious remains bound by the vows. He suggests these words, "I cede for the whole time in which I shall be bound by simple vows, etc." [38] Schaefer also suggests the same words [39] and adds that the words *"ad totum tempus"* of canon 569, § 1, mean "for as long a time as one remains a religious." [40] By fulfilling such suggestions in drawing up the formula of cession, the dismissed religious would seem to have no right after dismissal to reclaim the use, usufruct and administration of the goods which he owns, because after dismissal he is still bound by the vows.[41]

Another objection to the recovery of the use and administration of personal goods by the dismissed religious would seem to follow from canon 580, § 3. The said canon states that if a religious leaves the institute, the cession of the use, usufruct and administration of his goods which he has made according to canon 569 is canceled and loses all force. Since by dismissal a religious cannot be said to leave the institute in the strict sense,[42] it would seem that such cession remains intact after dismissal. Difficulties could certainly arise because of these arguments, especially when the religious has made the required cession of the use, usufruct and administration of his goods to persons outside the religious institute, since the cession is made in accordance with civil law.

These conclusions however are rejected for the following reasons.

[36] Canon 569, § 2.
[37] Canon 669, § 1.
[38] *Institutiones,* n. 587, 3.
[39] *De Religiosis,* n. 251, note 500.
[40] *De Religiosis,* n. 252.
[41] Canon 669, § 1.
[42] Cf. *supra,* pp. 1-4.

It is true that the novice makes the cession required by canon 569 for the whole time in which he is bound by the simple vows and that he is still under the obligation of the vows after dismissal. But canon 580, § 3, has been introduced into the Code to take care of the special emergency of dismissal. The crux of this assertion is the meaning of the word *"discessus"* in canon 580, § 3. Toso and Blat evidently accept the word in its strictest sense and therefore state that there is a real *"discessus"* only after the lapse of temporary vows or after a dispensation from the vows, temporary or perpetual, granted by the Holy See.[43] On the other hand, it is not correct to apply this *"discessus"* to dismissal as if dismissal were a departure wherein the juridical bond between the religious and the institute is completely and perpetually severed, so that the former religious is no longer in any sense a member of the organization.[44] This reason cannot be accepted and is canonically unsound.

The *"discessus"* of canon 580, § 3, should be interpreted broadly so as to include the departure of dismissal. Many authors apply the term to dismissal in their interpretation of this canon.[45]

The opinion that dismissal is included in the term *"discessus"* of canon 580, § 3, can be substantiated also from the canons on the status of dismissed religious. Canon 671, n. 5 states that a charitable subsidy should be provided by the religious institute for the necessities of a dismissed religious who has been ordained in major orders, unless the dismissed religious can provide for himself in any other way. Certainly he can provide for himself if he has goods in his own name. Thus Jansen states that if the dismissed religious cleric has personal property, the charitable subsidy need not be extended.[46]

[43] Toso, *Ad Codicem Iuris Canonici Commentaria Minora,* Lib. II, pars II (Romae: Jus Pontificium, 1927), p. 154 (hereafter to be cited as *Commentaria Minora*); Blat, *Commentarium Textus Codicis Iuris Canonici,* Lib. II, Partes II et III, *Ius de Religiosis et Laicis Iuxta Codicis Ordinem* (3. ed., Romae: Apud Angelicum, 1938), n. 464 (hereafter to be cited as *Ius de Religiosis*).

[44] Kealy regards dismissal as *"discessus"* for the reason indicated.—*Dowry of Women Religious,* The Catholic University of America Canon Law Studies, n. 134 (Washington, D. C.: The Catholic University of America Press, 1941), pp. 109-110.

[45] Schaefer, *De Religiosis,* n. 270; Larraona, "Annotationes,"—*CpRM,* XVII (1936), 342; Turner, *The Vow of Poverty,* p. 140.

[46] *Ordensrecht* (3. ed., Paderborn: Schöningh, 1931), p. 306.

There is no reason why the cession which was once made cannot be revoked because of dismissal. Canon 580, § 3, permits a change of this cession with the permission of the supreme Moderator of the institute. As Turner points out, although it is the intention of the Church that the cession of the use, usufruct and administration should remain in force as long as the individual is restricted by simple vows, it is also the intention of the Church that the cession be revocable for any good reason.[47] A sufficiently grave reason is present in the case of a dismissed religious. Since the cession which he had made is not absolutely irrevocable while he remains bound by his vows, there is no reason why it should not cease for the grave reason of dismissal.

Another argument is taken from the purpose of canon 583, n. 1. Speaking of the prohibition of this canon, forbidding a religious with simple vows to abdicate gratuitously the dominion of his goods by a voluntary deed of conveyance, Schaefer states that the purpose of this law is a provision for the personal sustenance of a religious in case of egress from the institute.[48] Since the dismissed has need of such sustenance after the egress of dismissal, the purpose of this canon is fulfilled by his recovery of the use, usufruct and administration of the goods which he owns.

It is well to point out here in conjunction with these arguments that great care should be taken in formulating the cession required by canon 569, §§ 1, 2. Difficulties may arise with the civil law if a dismissed religious, still bound by the vows, tries to recover the use, usufruct and administration of his goods, after he has explicitly ceded them *for the whole time in which he is bound by his vows.* The religious should take care that the cession would cease civilly if he should be dismissed by his superiors and this can be done most satisfactorily by mentioning dismissal in the cession. In religious institutes where dismissal entails automatic dispensation from the religious vows, of course no mention need be made of dismissal. The dismissal in such a case would be accompanied by a dispensation from the vows and the person concerned would come into full possession

[47] *The Vow of Poverty*, p. 126; cf. *Normae of 1901, arts.* 115, 117.

[48] *De Religiosis*, n. 271, note 178.

of his goods, even by the strictest interpretation of the formulae usually suggested.

Thus in conclusion to this matter, it is stated that the use, usufruct and administration of his own goods [49] are recovered by the religious at dismissal and the use, usufruct and administration of any goods which come into his possession after dismissal are permitted to him for necessities by an implicit and general permission granted in dismissal.

It may be asked if the permission for the use and administration of goods after dismissal is really effective, since to be so it must be both valid and licit. A permission is valid when the superior has the right to act in the matter and it is licit when there is a sufficient reason for granting the permission.[50] The superiors have the power to grant a general permission for the use and administration of goods for necessities as is sometimes done in religious communities in less important matters, and on a smaller scale. This power is evident for numerous practices in religious organizations. The extent of the general permission for use and administration depends entirely on the condition in which the religious concerned is placed. The licitness of the permission depends upon the reason for which it is given. The condition of the dismissed religious, in which he must take care of his material wants with the goods which he has or which he acquires and this without any assistance or guidance from the religious institute, certainly is sufficient reason for such a general permission. Therefore it is stated that the implicit and general grant accompanying dismissal is a licit and valid permission.

Concerning the recovery of the cession of the use, usufruct and administration of his goods which the religious has made at any time while he was affiliated with the religious organization, it has been stated that such cession becomes null and void at dismissal. Thus, if as a novice, or as a religious, one has ceded any of his goods to the institute as to their use, usufruct and administration, as he can legitimately do,[51] such goods should be restored to the dismissed religious in their entirety. If the dismissed religious originally ceded

[49] Coronata, *Institutiones*, n. 641.

[50] Turner, *The Vow of Poverty*, p. 102.

[51] Blat, *Ius de Religiosis*, n. 403; Turner, *The Vow of Poverty*, p. 139.

the usufruct of his goods to the institute, only the original capital should be restored, because the revenues accruing from that capital have been legitimately acquired by the religious institute. If he originally arranged that the interest accruing in time should be added to his capital, which practice is allowed in many religious institutes,[52] both the capital and the interest should be restored to him by the religious institute.

Since the permission which the dismissed religious receives concerns only things which are necessary for maintaining the standard of life which he has professed, the dismissed religious fails against the vow of poverty when he uses for illicit, superfluous or evil purposes any goods which are in his possession If the goods which the religious institute has acquired are concerned, by such acts the dismissed religious sins not only against the virtue of religion, but also against the virtue of justice If he uses for such ends the goods which he possesses in his own name he does not sin against the virtue of justice but only against the virtue of religion.

III. *Alienations.* Although the dismissed religious in simple vows can own things in his own name, he is forbidden to freely alienate or donate them after they have been acquired. The dismissed religious therefore, is not allowed to give away or make donations of his goods by gratuitous title.[53] Such forbidden practices would include the making of a present of part of his patrimony to a friend, or the canceling of a debt that is due to him under an onerous title or contract.[54] If a dismissed religious does make such donations, they are valid because the wording of the canon 583, n. 1 can be construed only as a prohibition.[55] In doing so, he fails against his vow of poverty, but not against justice, since he does not injure the rights of others or the rights of the institute.

Many authors point out that a partial alienation of the personal property of a religious with simple vows, which would not entail a great loss, and also a total alienation if the goods are of little moment,

[52] Vermeersch, "Quaestiones de Codice Canonico,"—*Periodica,* X (1922), (14); Turner, *The Vow of Poverty,* p. 128.

[53] Canon 583, n. 1.

[54] Blat, *Ius de Religiosis,* n. 475; Turner, *The Vow of Poverty,* p. 162.

[55] Coronata, *Institutiones,* n. 593; Schaefer, *De Religiosis,* n. 271, a.

would not seem to be prohibited by the above canon.[56] However these donations should not be of such frequency that they constitute a notable diminution of the capital.[57] It must be noted however that even such partial alienations are permitted only with the permission of the superiors to religious living in the community. The implicit and general permission for the use and administration of goods which a religious receives at dismissal is directed solely toward necessities. Therefore it would seem that he cannot make even such limited free gifts of his personal property by voluntary deeds of conveyance unless they can be determined as necessary in his status outside the community. However since such gifts can never be of very great frequency, certainly the dismissed religious could presume the permission of the superiors in particular cases, provided that he judges that the reason for the donation would be accepted as a legitimate reason by the superiors. He is also always free to approach his superior for explicit permission for things which are beyond necessities.

When the goods owned by the religious institute are concerned, donations of them are not permitted to the dismissed religious except for reasons which can be legitimately presumed to be included in the general permission given at dismissal. By law donations from the goods of the house, province or religious organization are not permitted except as alms or for some other just cause and with the permission of the superior and in accordance with the constitutions.[58] Certainly the permission to give alms to the poor, to make small donations for Church support or for the promotion of devotion or religion can be included in the general permission given at dismissal. If the dismissed however goes beyond these limitations and makes donations of the goods owned by the religious institute without just

[56] Vermeersch-Creusen, *Epitome,* I, n. 734; Coronata, *Institutiones,* n. 593; Augustine, *A Commentary on the New Code of Canon Law* (8 vols., Vol. III, 4. ed., St. Louis: Herder, 1929), III, 285 (hereafter to be cited as *A Commentary*); Papi, *Religious Profession* (New York, 1918), p. 64; Jansen, *Ordensrecht,* p. 195, 7; Gearin, "The Confessor and Vow of Religious Poverty,"—*AER,* LXI (1919), 148.

[57] Larraona, "De Paupertate Simplici,"—*CpR,* II (1921), 74-75.

[58] Canon 537.

cause, he sins not only against the vow of poverty, but also against the virtue of justice and each of his acts is a sacrilege.[59]

No dismissed religious can make large donations from any of the goods in his possession. If he does so the donation is valid when his own goods are concerned, but he fails against the vow of poverty, not however against justice. If he so donates the goods of the institute, the donation is invalid, and the dismissed religious fails against poverty and justice. In the latter case the donee has no right to the goods he has received and it remains his duty to make restitution to the religious institute when he becomes aware of the true owner of the property.

The permission that the dismissed religious has for the administration of goods will allow, at times, the making of contracts in his own name. This is not against the simple vow of poverty, because such a religious has the capacity to hold temporal goods in his own name, and with the permission of the superior he can also make contracts concerning the goods of the religious institute. Thus the dismissed religious has the right of making necessary contracts in his own name of any goods that he has in his possesion, whether he owns them or not, since this is a practical requisite for his livelihood in the world. Naturally in such cases the person cannot be said to be acting as an agent of the religious organization and therefore the organization cannot be held responsible for any of the contracts he makes.[60]

This is shown to be true also for another reason. Since the religious institute has no obligation in justice to support anyone after dismissal, certainly it has no obligation to answer for the contracts made by a dismissed religious. In one case only, the religious institute can be forced by action of an ecclesiastical court to fulfill a contract made by the dismissed religious. A charitable maintenance should be given to a dismissed clerical religious in major orders who is proving his amendment,[61] and if such a cleric makes a contract for his necessities in lieu of the charitable subsidy, the religious institute can be forced to meet the contract, provided it has not already ex-

[59] Schaefer, *De Religiosis*, n. 211.

[60] Canon 536, § 2; cf. Toso, *Commentaria Minora*, Lib. II, pars II, p. 85; Berutti, *De Religiosis*, n. 61.

[61] Canon 671, n. 5.

tended the subsidy and provided the dismissed cleric is still worthy of it according to the norms of canon 671. If a dismissed religious has no means to fulfill the contract he has made, he becomes an insoluble debtor.[62]

Religious of institutes of simple vows, as novices, freely dispose by last testament of the goods which they actually have and of the goods which they may obtain in the future.[63] Canon 583, n. 2, demands the permission of the Holy See, or at least the permission of the major superior or of the local superior in urgent cases, for a change in this will.

The state of the dismissed religious demands no change in this last testament which he has made. If he should change it as a dismissed religious, his action would be valid, but illicit.[64] If the dismissed wishes to change his will he must obtain the permission of the Holy See as other religious living in the community must do.[65] If the beneficiary of the testament of the dismissed religious should die before the testator, assuming that in the testament no provision was made for such an occurrence, the dismissed religious can without any recourse to the Holy See draft a second testament.[66] Otherwise, only after a dispensation from the vows and consequent complete separation from the religious institute is the dismissed religious entirely free to change the last testament which he has made.

2. The Solemn Vow of Poverty

I. *Ownership and Acquisition.* As a rule, the religious, after the profession of solemn vows, has no right to the proprietorship of goods.[67] It is said "as a rule" because it is possible under Apostolic

[62] Fanfani, *De Iure Religiosorum,* n. 166, B.

[63] Canon 569, § 3.

[64] Canon 583; Turner, *The Vow of Poverty,* p. 174; Schaefer, *De Religiosis,* n. 271, b.

[65] A petition for this permission should be addressed to, Congregatio Negotiis Religiosorum Sodalium Praeposita, Palazzo delle Congregazioni, Città del Vaticano, cf. *The Official Catholic Directory* (1943), p. 3.

[66] Cf. Turner, *The Vow of Poverty,* p. 175; Hannan, *The Canon Law of Wills,* The Catholic University of America Canon Law Studies, n. 86 (Washington, D. C.: The Catholic University of America, 1934), n. 347.

[67] Canon 581, § 1.

indult to profess the solemn vow of poverty and yet be able to own, retain, use or enjoy property with the permission of superiors [68] as has happened very often in the last century and as obtains today in some places in Europe.[69] Special indults that have been given by the Holy See to organizations professing solemn vows, allowing the members to retain title to property, are to remain in force.[70]

It is the common opinion of authors that when the religious, in anticipation of solemn profession, renounces the goods which he actually has, he may also renounce those goods which will come to him in the future, if he has a certain right to them at the time he makes the renunciation.[71] This right should be a certain right or a vested right as it is called in civil law. It must be noted that under the laws of the United States children have no vested right in the goods or property of their parents. At most they have a hope that their parents will give them a share in their goods or property by last will. Certainly there is a right of inheritance in the children in the possible case of the intestacy of the father, but whether that right will ever bring them anything depends on a contingency which may never happen, namely that the father die without a will.[72] Such a hope for future attainment cannot be renounced by the religious before solemn profession because, it remains merely a hope and is no certain right with a real money value.

[68] Canon 582; Turner, *The Vow of Poverty*, pp. 97-98.

[69] The regulars of the order of St. John of God in France have dominion of goods. Cf. Goyeneche, "Consultationes,"—*CpR*, II (1921), 46; Coronata, *Institutiones*, n. 593, b, note 4.

[70] Canon 581, § 1.

[71] Jardi, *El Derecho de las Religiosas según las Praescripciones Vigentes del Codigo Canonico y Civil* (2. ed., Vich: Serafica, 1927), n. 530 (hereafter to be cited as *El Derecho de las Religiosas*); Fanfani, *De Iure Religiosorum*, n. 261; Vermeersch-Creusen, *Epitome*, I, n. 736; De Meester, *Juris Canonici et Juris Canonico-Civilis Compendium* (nova ed., 3 vols. in 4, Brugis: Desclée, De Brouwer & Si, 1921-1928), n. 1011, note 2 (hereafter to be cited as *Compendium*); Larraona, "Consultationes,"— *CpR*, I (1920), 79-80; Woywod, *A Practical Commentary on the Code of Canon Law* (3. ed., 2 vols., New York: Wagner, 1929), I, n. 491 (hereafter to be cited as *Commentary*); Blat, *Ius de Religiosis*, n. 470; Turner, *The Vow of Poverty*, p. 185; Schaefer, *De Religiosis*, n. 274, b.

[72] Woywod, *loc. cit.*

In any event ordinarily, all goods which come to a solemnly professed religious after his profession are acquired not to himself, but to the order, or religious province or house according to the norms of the constitutions of the order,[73] providing such goods have not been legitimately renounced to other persons moral or physical by the religious before his profession.[74] This rule of acquired ownership by the order or the religious province or house is of course modified for those religious organizations which are incapacitated by special law of the church from holding legal title to property.[75] The goods which are obtained by the dismissed regular of such religious institutes are acquired by the Holy See.

Therefore a dismissed regular, as a rule, can never claim dominion of goods, no matter how they have come into his possession. If he obtains a position in the world, whatever he receives in remuneration is acquired by the order or religious province or house of his religious institute. This follows even though he has contracted for the goods in his own name. Acquisition accrues in a similar way as to all royalties paid to authors, offerings made for the exercise of the sacred ministry [76] and goods obtained by inheritance or legacy. If the civil law does not recognize such an acquisition by the religious institute, because it does not consider the order, or religious province or house a juridic person, the dismissed regular is obliged in conscience to execute a civil deed in his own name so that the order or religious province or house will acquire the goods.[77] While such a religious lived in the community, he would need the permission of the superior to execute such deeds, but the dismissed regular has that permission in the general, implicit grant for the administration of goods which he receives in dismissal.[78]

In cases where the religious has renounced goods to which he

[73] This is the adaptation to the new code of the pre-Code principle, *"Quidquid monachus acquirit, monasterio acquiritur."*

[74] Canon 582, n. 1.

[75] Only the houses of the Franciscan Friars and the Capuchins and Minor Observants are now forbidden to possess real property.—Conc. Trident., sess. XXV, *de regularibus*, c. 3.

[76] Cf. canon 671, n. 7.

[77] Coronata, *Institutiones*, n. 593; Turner, *The Vow of Poverty*, pp. 190-192.

[78] Cf. *infra*, pp. 72-73.

had a certain vested right before his profession, the dismissed regular cannot interfere with that renunciation when those goods are realized. The goods or property so renounced proceed to the designated party just as they would if the dismissed regular were still in the community. The reasons are that dismissal has no effect on the legitimate renunciation which the regular has made and it entails no right to own goods in his own name.

Concerning donations which are given to such a dismissed regular, the principle remains that they are acquired not to himself but to the order, or religious province or house. If the parents or friends of a dismissed regular, or of a dismissed nun with solemn vows give either of them money for use, formally excluding any acquisition by the institute, the religious would fail against poverty in accepting them and using them. If he uses them according to the intention of the donor, however, he would not fail against justice.

II. *The Use and Administration of Goods.* The religious dismissed after solemn profession has the same general and implicit permission for the use and administration of goods which is given to those dismissed religious who have made simple profession. The pre-Code authors almost unanimously stated that the dismissed regular had this permission.[79] Authors after the promulgation of the Code also follow this opinion,[80] and it is substantiated by the same reasons given in the preceding section on religious dismissed after the profession of simple vows.[81] Thus any goods which come into the possession of such a religious after dismissal can be used by him and administered for the supplying of those things which are necessary for the decent sustenance of life.[82] He can so use the money and goods which he possesses from donations of his parents and friends, from legacies, from remunerations of his work and from

[79] Reiffenstuel, Lib. III, tit. XXXI, n. 241; Schmalzgrueber, Lib. III, tit. XXXI, n. 250; Ferraris, *Prompta Bibliotheca,* s. v. "Ejecti a Religione," nn. 50, 68; Bouix, *Tractatus de Iure Regularium,* Tom. II, pars VI, sec. IV, c. II, q. IV; Appeltern, *Compendium,* Q. 143, 4; Passerinus, *De Hominum Statibus,* Q. CLXXXIX, art. VIII, n. 602.

[80] Cf. Schaefer, *De Religiosis,* n. 596.

[81] Cf. *supra,* pp. 60-61.

[82] Rotarius, *Theologia Moralis Regularium,* Tom. I, lib. III, c. II, punct. VI, n. 2.

any other legitimate method of acquisition, even though these goods belong to the order or religious province or house.

III. *Alienations.* The incapacity to place acts contrary to the solemn vow of poverty is not absolute, for solemn profession renders acts of proprietorship invalid only when the religious acts for himself, and in his own name, not when he acts with the permission of the superior.[83] The dismissed regular has permission from the superior to make those alienations which are necessary for his maintenance in the state of dismissal. Hence he can also give alms to the poor and make other small donations which can be construed as acts of virtue or merit.[84]

The dismissed regular cannot make large donations of the goods which he possesses. Such donations would be the exercise of proprietary acts and would be illicit and void by canon 579. If he should presume to make such donations, he would sin not only against his vow, but also against the virtue of justice. Certainly he can make contracts for the maintenance of his livelihood, for he has the right to administer the goods which come into his possession. However if he exceeds the standard of life which he professed and makes superfluous expenses his contract is certainly invalid and is rescindible in an ecclesiastical court. The civil court would bind such a dismissed regular to those contracts. The religious institute has no responsibility to meet such contracts as they are not made in the name of the religious institute and furthermore it has no obligation in justice to support the dismissed regular.

B. *The Vow of Chastity*

The vow of chastity binds the dismissed religious as strictly as it did when he lived in the community. The difference between the simple vow and the solemn vow remains unchanged. The former does not debar valid marriage but renders it illicit [85] whereas the

[83] Coronata, *Institutiones,* n. 593.

[84] Cf. *supra,* p. 67.

[85] Canon 1058, § 1.

latter renders an attempted marriage invalid.[86] Furthermore all those in major orders who attempt marriage do so invalidly.[87]

By presuming to contract marriage, even the so-called civil marriage, those religious who have professed simple perpetual vows automatically incur an excommunication reserved to the ordinary.[88] Clerics in major orders and regulars or nuns having professed the solemn vow of chastity, who presume to contract marriage, even by mere civil ceremony, automatically incur excommunication reserved simply to the Holy See.[89] Those religious who have professed the simple vow of chastity, conjoined with invalidating effect, do not incur the latter excommunication, unless they are in Holy Orders.[90]

The authors point out that if a religious who has professed simple vows enters an illicit but valid marriage, he can, and in fact must by an obligation of justice, render the marital rights, if the other party to the marriage asks for them. He can never ask for them himself unless he obtains a dispensation from his vow.[91] If the other party loses the right to ask for the use of conjugal rights, as for example by the commission of adultery, neither party can ask for or render those rights.[92] Therefore after the contraction of an illicit marriage the most expedient procedure is for the religious to petition immediately for a dispensation from the Holy See, lest he remain in constant danger of falling into sin. The usual dispensation granted in such cases is conceded only for the marriage which has been con-

[86] Canon 1073.

[87] Canon 1072.

[88] Canon 2388, § 2.

[89] Canon 2388, § 1.

[90] Iorio, *Theologia Moralis Iuxta Methodum Compendii Ioannis P. Gury et Raphaelis Tummulo* (6. ed., 3 vols., Neapoli: D'Auria, 1938-1939), II, n. 502 (hereafter to be cited as *Theologia Moralis*).

[91] Aertnys-Damen, *Theologia Moralis Secundum Doctrinam S. Alfonsi De Ligorio Doct. Ecclesiae* (13. ed., 2 vols., Taurini: Marietti, 1939), II, n. 700; Tanquerey, *Synopsis Theologiae Moralis et Pastoralis* (3 vols., Vol. I, *De Paenitentia, Matrimonio et Ordine,* 10. ed., Tornaci: Desclée, 1925), n. 939; Merkelbach, *Summa Theologiae Moralis ad Mentem D. Thomae et ad Normam Iuris Novi* (3. ed., 3 vols., Parisiis: Desclée de Brouwer, 1938-1939), III, n. 865; Iorio, *Theologia Moralis,* III, n. 1142.

[92] Iorio, *loc. cit.*; Tanquerey, *loc. cit.*

tracted.[93] Therefore if the other party dies and the ex-religious wishes to contract a new marriage, another dispensation from the Holy See is required.

While the religious is bound by his simple vow, he sins against the vow if he asks for the use of conjugal rights. The question arises whether the religious in so acting against his vow, sins against the virtue of religion and against the virtue of chastity, or sins merely against the virtue of religion. Coronata states that such a religious who validly contracts matrimony and uses the conjugal rights, in the absence of any malice against chastity, sins only against the virtue of religion in transgressing his vow.[94] Vermeersch-Creusen also seem to hold the same opinion.[95] Most canonists merely state that there is an infraction of the vow by such actions, but they do not treat the question discussed here. Several Moralists discuss the point concerned. Wouters [96] states that the question is disputed, but he does not cite any authors who claim that the infraction of the vow of chastity by the use of conjugal rights is also a sin against the virtue of chastity. The present writer has found no author who makes that explicit statement. St. Alphonsus,[97] Marc,[98] Sabetti-

[93] Gasparri, *Tractatus Canonicus de Matrimonio* (ed. nova, 2 vols., Civitate Vaticana: Typis Polyglottis Vaticanis, 1932), I, n. 430.

[94] "Religiosus a votis simplicibus matrimonium contrahens et illo utens, absente malitia contra castitatem, peccat solum contra religionem votum transgrediendo."—*Institutiones,* n. 604.

[95] "Validum quoque est matrimonium, cuius usus voto quidem, ac proin religioni, non autem castitati erit saepe contrarius."—*Epitome,* I, n. 733.

[96] "Qui violat votum castitatis peccat; contra religionem, ut patet . . . contra virtutem castitatis, saltem si actum in se illicitum perpetrat; disputatur, si exercet actum, per se licitum, ut si maritus factus religiosus denuo uteretur coniuge."—*Manuale Theologiae Moralis* (2 vols., Brugis [Belgii]: Carolus Beyaert, 1932), I, n. 1251.

[97] "Quod si conjuges mutuo consensu voveant castitatem aut religionem, nequeunt vota invicem irritare; quia virtualiter uterque cedit juri suo. . . . Conjuges isti, si post tale votum mutuo consensu emissum, revocent pactum et coeant; licet non peccent contra castitatem, peccant tamen contra votum, nisi a gravissima causa excusentur."—*Theologia Moralis,* Lib. III, n. 236.

[98] "Ex voto simplici castitatis, matrimonium subsequens prohibetur, sed non dirimitur; unde si religiosus, non obstante hoc voto nuptias iniret, unum duntaxat peccatum (nempe contra religionem) in petitione debiti conjugalis

Barrett,[99] Iorio,[100] and Vermeersch,[101] state that the actions concerned would be against the virtue of religion, but not against the virtue of chastity.

The perpetual vow of chastity is an absolute promise made to God of abstaining from all acts of venereal pleasure, whether internal or external. The object of this vow comprehends two classes of such acts, first, those which are forbidden to all by the natural and the divine law, and secondly, those which become licit by legitimate marriage. The efficacy of the vow is that those acts which are rendered licit by valid marriage become illicit to such a religious only because of his vow and he must avoid them only because of an obligation of religion. Those acts which are forbidden to all he must avoid because of an obligation of chastity and religion.[102]

To ask for the use of marital rights after valid marriage is not therefore a sin against the virtue of chastity. The religious possesses the right to those acts from the beginning of the valid marriage, but the use of those rights is restricted because of the vow which he has made to God. Thus in asking for the use of the rights, he sins and sins grievously, not because he acts against the virtue of chastity, but because he acts against the virtue of religion. In such circumstances therefore the religious violates the vow of chastity without violating the virtue of chastity.

committeret."—*Institutiones Morales Alphonsianae* (19. ed. [4. ed. post Codicem], 2 vols., Lugduni: Emmanuel Vitte, 1934), II, n. 2160.

99 "Si quis enim voto simplici castitatis ligatus matrimonium contraheret, unicum peccatum, scilicet contra religionem, in usu conjugii patraret. Potest igitur quandoque violari votum, quin ipsa virtus laedatur."—*Compendium Theologiae Moralis* (8. ed. post Codicem, Neo Eboraci: Frederick Pustet Co., 1939), n. 617.

100 "Si quis enim voto simplici castitatis ligatus matrimonium contraheret, unicum peccatum, scilicet contra religionem, in usu conjugii patraret. Potest igitur quandoque violari votum, quin ipsa virtus laedatur."—*Theologia Moralis*, II, n. 1203.

101 "Qui voto simplici ligatur, illicite sed (salva peculiari exceptione) valide nuptias contrahit. Si iisdem utatur, votum quidem sed non virtutem castitatis laedet."—*Theologiae Moralis Principia, Responsa, Concilia* (ed. altera, 3 vols., Brugis: Charles Beyaert, 1926-1928), III, n. 135.

102 Cf. Iorio, *Theologia Moralis*, II, 1201.

C. *The Vow of Obedience*

The dismissed religious is bound by the vow of obedience to obey the superiors of his religious institute. This obligation is present whether the religious has made a profession of solemn or of merely simple vows. That the dismissed religious is not freed from this obligation has always been the common opinion of canonists.[103] Hence he must obey the precepts of the religious superiors by virtue of the vow of obedience.[104] Also when a grave matter is concerned, a formal command under the vow of obedience can be imposed on the dismissed religious.[105] The superiors can command in the same manner the return of the dismissed to the religious institute.[106] Without doubt they have this power to command return to the religious institute, even though the dismissed religious has not yet corrected himself,[107] but the religious superior will very rarely impose this precept, otherwise the very purpose of dismissal would be defeated.

Moreover the Roman Pontiff has the power to impose precepts on the dismissed religious by reason of the vow of obedience.[108] This power of the Pope is based upon the ordinary, full and universal power vested in him in virtue of which he is the highest superior of all religious. Usually the Roman Pontiff exercises his power over religious through the Sacred Congregation of Religious. Wherefore the dismissed religious may receive certain injunctions from that Sacred Congregation and must obey them by reason of his vow.[109]

In all the above cases, namely in reference to the authority of the Pope, or the Sacred Congregation of Religious, or the religious superiors, it is evident and fundamental that by reason of the vow

[103] Passerinus, *De Hominum Statibus,* Q. CLXXXIX, art. VIII, n. 615; Schmalzgrueber, Lib. III, tit. XXXI, n. 250, 3; Piatus Montensis, *Praelectiones Juris Regularis,* I, q. 244.

[104] Coronata, *Institutiones,* n. 658; Augustine, *A Commentary,* III, 410.

[105] Goyeneche, *Iuris Canonici Summa Principia, De Religiosis* (Romae: Tip. Pol. "Cuore di Maria," 1938), n. 126 (hereafter to be cited as *De Religiosis*).

[106] Goyeneche, *loc. cit.*; Schaefer, *De Religiosis,* n. 596.

[107] Donatus, *Rerum Regularium Praxis Resolutoria,* Tom. I, pars II, tract. VIII, q. XXIV, n. 4.

[108] Canon 499, § 1.

[109] Vermeersch-Creusen, *Epitome,* I, n. 613; De Meester, *Compendium,* n. 947; Berutti, *De Religiosis,* n. 22, II.

no command can be given which goes beyond the rules and constitutions which the dismissed religious has promised to obey. The religious has the intention in his profession to bind himself no farther than the limits assigned by his rule and constitutions, and therefore where the rule and constitutions stop there the vow of obedience also ceases and even the Roman Pontiff cannot go beyond it. It should also be noted that where there is question of a formal command, it should be made evident by the superior that it is such a command.

The authors do not agree on the obligation of the dismissed religious to obey the ordinary of the place where he lives after dismissal. Certainly he is bound to obey the local ordinary by reason of subjection to him, as other laymen and as other ecclesiastics are bound to obey him. It is evident, too, that a dismissed religious is bound by the vow of obedience to obey a particular ordinary if he and the other religious of his institute obliged themselves in their profession of vows to obey him as their religious superior. However, even where such an obligation does not arise by reason of the rules and constitutions of particular institutes, some authors claim that a dismissed religious is bound to obey the ordinary of the place where he lives by reason of his vow.[110] These authors seem to place under this obligation all religious. They do not distinguish between male religious and women religious and therefore both classes seem to be included in the general term.

Some pre-Code authors [111] argued to this point of view in considering the status of dismissed regulars. They gave as their reason that the vow of obedience cannot be understood except in reference to some prelate. Since the dismissed religious was not under the subjection of the regular superior, they stated that he was so bound to the ordinary of the place where he lived. In reference to the dismissed religious, they stated, this ordinary should take the place of the religious superior.

[110] Berutti, *De Religiosis,* n. 177; Prümmer, *Manuale Iuris Canonici,* Q. 264; Raus, *De Sacra Obedientiae Virtute et Voto* (Lugduni: Apud Emmanuelem Vitte, 1923), n. 118, b; Larraona, "Commentarium Codicis,"—*CpR,* VI (1925), 183, note 77.

[111] Cf. *supra,* pp. 18, 25-26.

It is true that the vow of obedience cannot be understood except in reference to some prelate or superior, either outside[112] or within the religious institute.[113] Yet, although the vow of obedience is suspended in many things, because of the condition of the dismissed religious, and although he is *de facto* separated from the guidance of his religious superiors, nevertheless, he is still subject to the superiors of his religious institute. Thus, as has been shown, they can command the dismissed subject by reason of the vow and can impose upon him the precept of returning to the religious institute. Therefore the dismissed religious cannot be said to be obliged by his vow without reference to any prelate or superior.

Raus maintains the view that all religious dismissed after perpetual profession seem to come under a special law, by which they are obliged to obey the ordinary of the place by reason of the vow of obedience. As the basis of his contention, Raus cites canon 669, § 1, which states that the dismissed religious is bound by the obligation of his vows and canon 671, n. 4, which states that the dismissed religious with major orders is bound to obey the injunctions of the ordinary of the diocese assigned to him by the Holy See.[114]

The opinion of Raus can be applied at most only to dismissed religious who have received major orders. Canon 671, n. 4, treats of such religious clerics and not of dismissed religious in general. Therefore this opinion cannot be applied to all dismissed religious. As regards dismissed religious in major orders, it cannot be pointed out from canon 671, n. 4, that their obligation of obedience to the assigned ordinary is anything more than the obligation of other clerics, belonging to the secular clergy. It is a fundamental principle that a religious is bound by the vow of obedience to obey only those to whom he has promised obedience according to the norms of the rules and constitutions of his particular religious institute. In most cases, the religious has never vowed obedience to the local ordinary. If the obligation of the vow is to be extended to other superiors in certain circumstances, it seems evident that the extension should be an explicit one by common law, and until that

112 Canon 639.

113 Cf. Raus, *op. cit.*, n. 113.

114 Raus, *De Sacra Obedientiae Virtute et Voto*, n. 118, b.

explicit extension is made, the religious would be bound under his vow only to those superiors to whom he has promised obedience. An explicit extension of the vow is found in canon 639 in reference to religious who have received an indult of exclaustration, but no explicit extension is found anywhere in the Code concerning religious dismissed after the profession of perpetual vows. Therefore no special law can be advanced which would demand of the dismissed religious obedience *by reason of his vow* to the ordinary of the place where he stays.

Larraona also seems to agree with the contention of Raus and reaches that conclusion by a comparison of canon 639 and canon 671, n. 4. Canon 639 states explicitly that those who have obtained an indult of exclaustration from the Holy See are subject to the local ordinary of the place where they stay by reason of the vow of obedience, in place of the superiors of their own religious institute. Larraona, noting the similarity of cases between this canon and canon 671, n. 4, states that for this reason and also by reason of pre-Code law, that the dismissed religious is bound to obey the ordinary of the place where he stays under the vow of obedience.[115] Again, the opinion of Larraona is applicable only to religious clerics in major orders who are dismissed after the profession of perpetual vows. There certainly is no basis from the canons cited to apply the obligation to all religious. That there is a similarity of cases between a religious who has received an indult of exclaustration and a religious in major orders who has been dismissed after perpetual profession cannot be denied, but the similarity cannot be shown to extend to the obligation of the vow of obedience. Canon 639 and canon 671, n. 4, both treat of the obligation of the religious in certain circumstances to obey the local ordinary. In the former case obedience by reason of the vow is explicitly mentioned and in the latter case no mention is made of the vow. Therefore the similarity cannot be extended in this matter, since as was stated, the extension of the vow ought to merit an explicit statement.

Larraona does not state his argument from a pre-Code *law,* but merely states that there was such a law. The present writer has

[115] "Commentarium Codicis,"—*CpR,* VI (1925), 183, note 77.

found no such law in pre-Code history. At most there was pre-Code opinion in favor of Larraona's view. It is true that several pre-Code authors proposed the view which Larraona accepts, but it should be noted that their opinion was against the practice of the whole Church in regard to dismissed religious. Thus Molina [116] in the sixteenth century, and Rotarius,[117] in the early eighteenth century, pointed out that the practice of the Church was in favor of the opinion which stated that the dismissed religious was obliged to obey the local ordinary, but not under the vow of obedience. They stated that the bishops nowhere devised a special method of life for the dismissed religious, but rather ruled them according to the manner of other ecclesiastics in their dioceses, exhorting and correcting them as they would their diocesan clerics and punishing them in the same manner when it was necessary. After the eighteenth century nothing can be found in canonical history which definitely shows a change in this practice. Therefore the sole argument that is available from pre-Code practice is that the dismissed religious was bound to obey the ordinary of the place where he stayed, not by reason of the vow of obedience, but by reason of subjection to that ordinary in the manner of the diocesan clergy. The extrinsic authority of many authors who wrote both before and after the promulgation of the Code can also be cited in favor of this opinion.[118] Therefore it is stated here that the dismissed religious has no obligation *by reason of his vow* to obey the ordinary of the place where he stays.

Though the dismissed religious is bound by the vow of obedience, its execution is suspended in many things, until he returns to the religious institute. The reason for this is that there is present a defect of the matter of the vow, and that *de facto* the dismissed religious has not the guidance of the religious superior.[119]

[116] *De Iustitia,* Tom. I, disp. 140.

[117] *Theologia Moralis Regularium,* Tom. I, lib. III, c. II, punct. V, n. 5.

[118] Barbosa, *Collectanea Doctorum in Jus Pontificium Universum,* Lib. III, tit. XXXI, c. XXIV, nn. 10, 11; Rotarius, *Theologia Moralis Regularium,* Tom. I, lib. III, c. II, punct. V, n. 5; Piatus Montensis, *Praelectiones Juris Regularis,* I, q. 250; Goyeneche, *De Religiosis,* n. 126, note 3; Coronata, *Institutiones,* n. 658; Schaefer, *De Religiosis,* n. 596.

[119] Cf. Donatus, *Rerum Regularium Praxis Resolutoria,* Tom. I, pars II, tract. VIII, q. XXIV, n. 3.

ARTICLE II. ADDITIONAL VOWS MADE IN PARTICULAR INSTITUTES

In certain religious orders and congregations special vows, over and above the three essential vows of the religious life, are professed on entrance into the religious institute. Thus the members of the Order of Minims of St. Francis of Paula profess a fourth solemn vow of perpetual abstinence from all flesh and white meats. The Mercedarians or the members of the Order of Our Lady of the Redemption of Captives vow that in case of necessity they will exchange their own person for the redemption of captives.[120] The members of the Order of St. John of God, called the Brothers Hospitallers, make a fourth vow of serving the sick for life in their hospitals.[121] Certain professed priests in the Society of Jesus take a fourth solemn vow of special obedience to the Pope in the matter of missions, undertaking to go wherever they may be sent without even requiring money for the journey. They also profess certain additional, but non-essential vows in the matter of poverty and the refusal of external honors.

After dismissal the obligation of the observance of such additional vows is a disputed point. It is true that additional vows are not dispensed with merely by the action of dismissal, unless the constitutions or a particular papal indult state otherwise. However many pre-Code authors, expressing the more common opinion stated absolutely that the obligations of these vows were suspended after dismissal.[122] Some authors after the promulgation of the Code have also proposed this milder opinion.[123]

[120] Pejška, *Ius Canonicum Religiosorum,* p. 145.

[121] Pejška, *loc. cit.*

[122] Barbosa, *Collectanea Doctorum in Jus Pontificium Universum,* Lib. III, tit. XXXI, c. XXIV, n. 12; Leurenius, Lib. III, tit. XXXI, q. DCCCLXV; Schmalzgrueber, Lib. III, tit. XXXI, n. 251; Appeltern, *Compendium Praelectiones Juris Regularis,* Q. 143, 2°.

[123] Goyeneche, *De Religiosis,* n. 126, note 2. Schaefer also holds this opinion for he states, "Etsi nominatus Religiosus votis suis teneatur, ab aliis tamen obligationibus, quae non se referunt ad vota communia, liberatus manet.—*De Religiosis,* n. 596.

The reasons which have been proposed for this assertion are the following. First, a religious in professing such vows cannot be presumed to have willed the obligation of them, if he should be dismissed from the communal life of the religious institute, with the necessity of living outside of the religious house where the observance of them would be very difficult and much more burdensome. Secondly, the additional vows are merely annexations and accessories to the religious life and since the same authors state a dismissed religious is free from the obligations of the religious life, they declare that they are also free from the obligations of such vows, because of the principle, *"accessorium sequitur principale."* [124] Thirdly, these vows were professed merely to preserve the state of the religious institute and therefore they would endure only as long as the professed lives within the body of the religious institute. Fourthly, such vows do not constitute one a religious, and are not necessarily connected with the profession of the three essential vows.

Even though this opinion has some probability, the opinion which obliges the dismissed to the obligations of these vows is more probable. This contention is held for the following reasons. First, strong arguments are available in opposition to the reasons given above in support of the milder opinion. If the dismissed religious is to be freed from the obligations of such vows because there is no presumption that he had the intention of binding himself to them, while a dismissed religious when their obligation would be more difficult, he should be freed also from the observance of the obligations of the three essential vows, *i. e.*, the vows of poverty, chastity and obedience. The additional vows are made perpetually and without limitation as are the essential vows. Concerning the reason which states that these vows are merely annexations and accessories to the religious life and that therefore dismissal would free from the obligation arising from them, it is pointed out that these vows are rather annexations and accessories of the religious profession, introducing a religious into a particular institute. The dismissed religious is still a member of his institute, and therefore since the *principle* of a particular religious profession still remains, so should the *accessories*. To the further reason, stating that these vows are

[124] Cf. Schmalzgrueber, Lib. III, tit. XXXI, n. 251.

professed merely for the preservation of the state of the religious institute, Rotarius has already proposed an answer. He stated that this reason confuses the additional vows and the rules of the religious institute. The rules, he stated, are truly intended in religious profession for the preservation of the state of the religious institute and moreover they are not primarily intended, but only as means for advancement to perfection and for order in the religious life. This cannot be said of the additional vows which are primarily and *per se* intended in religious profession. The vows are not therefore intended as means to facilitate life in the religious community, but are promises *per se* vowed. Moreover, the further reason that such vows do not constitute one a religious, since they are not necessarily connected with the three essential vows, seems to insinuate that the dismissed religious is merely in the religious state with no reference to a particular religious institute. It has been pointed out that the dismissed religious is still a member of his religious institute and therefore, as a member, he should be bound by the obligations of all the vows which he made in the institute.

A second argument for the opinion which is here regarded as more probable is the argument taken from the status of religious who have been elevated to an ecclesiastical dignity. It is the common opinion that such religious are not freed from the obligations of the particular vows which they have professed over and above the three essential vows.[125] Certainly then, the dismissed religious should not be freed from them, since by dismissal he would be gaining from his crimes an advantage which is not given to religious who have been highly honored by the Church. This opinion was also sponsored by many pre-Code authors [126] and has been proposed by authors writing after the promulgation of the Code.[127]

It should be noted that these additional vows are usually public vows in so far as they are accepted by the legitimate superior in

[125] Schaefer, *De Religiosis,* n. 493; Fanfani, *De Iure Religiosorum,* n. 466; Vermeersch-Creusen, *Epitome,* I, n. 786; Pejška, *Ius Canonicum Religiosorum,* p. 179; cf. canon 626, § 3.

[126] Donatus, *Rerum Regularium Praxis Resolutoria,* Tom. I, pars II, tract. VIII, q. LI; Rotarius, *Theologia Moralis Regularium,* Tom. I, lib. III, c. II, punct. VI, n. 11; Ferraris, *Prompta Bibliotheca,* s. v. "Ejecti a Religione," n. 51.

[127] Augustine, *A Commentary,* III, 410; Blat, *Ius De Religiosis,* n. 714.

the name of the Church. Therefore in religious institutes of pontifical approval, only the Roman Pontiff can dispense from such vows, unless the constitutions state otherwise.[128] In religious institutes of diocesan approval the bishop can dispense from such vows. Moreover, according to the general principles of vows, such vows would cease or would be totally suspended if there were after dismissal a substantial change in the matter promised, or if the final cause of the vow ceased.

The dismissed religious, then, must observe the obligations of the additional vows which he has professed and such vows are suspended only in those particular cases where they cannot be fulfilled because of the state of the dismissed religious.[129] Finally, concerning those obligations which arise from particular promises made under oath at the time of profession, it is analogically apparent that the dismissed religious is also obliged to their observance.[130]

Article III. Private Vows

Any private vows which have been legitimately dispensed with by the local ordinary, or by religious superiors of exempt clerical organizations or by persons who have received the delegated faculty from the Holy See,[131] do not revive after dismissal from a religious institute. The same is also true of vows which have been annulled by religious superiors in such a manner that their obligations will never revive.[132]

Before the Code, it was certain that all private vows previously made were wiped out by solemn profession. This doctrine was based on the law of the Decretals of Gregory IX.[133] Simple profession did not remove or suspend the obligation of previous vows, unless the laws of a particular organization gave such force to its

[128] Blat, *loc. cit.*

[129] Cf. Ferraris, *loc. cit.*

[130] Cf. Donatus, *Rerum Regularium Praxis Resolutoria,* Tom. I, pars II, tract. VIII, q. LVI.

[131] Canon 1313.

[132] Canon 1312, § 1.

[133] C. 4, X, *de voto et voti redemptione,* III, 34.

simple vows.[134] The Code modifies the former law in two points. First, it denies to any religious profession, solemn or simple, the power to annul permanently all former vows. Secondly, it extends the suspension of private vows to the religious profession of both solemn and simple vows.

Canon 1315 states that vows which were made before profession in a religious institute are suspended as long as the person remains in the religious organization. Do such suspended vows revive after dismissal? Augustine holds the affirmative opinion,[135] but such vows do not revive, but remain suspended after dismissal because the dismissed religious is still a member of the religious institute. Goyeneche has stated that such vows remain suspended for a religious called to military service, even though at the same time the religious vows cease.[136] His reason is that such a religious remains a member of the religious institute and must be called a religious, as was explicitly declared by the Sacred Congregation of Religious in these words, "*. . . perdurante militari servitio, alumnus, quamvis votis religiosis non sit ligatus, tamen membrum religionis esse perseverat, sub auctoritate suorum Superiorum qui de eo curam habere debent forma praescripta in Decreto Inter reliquas, nn. IV, V.*" [137] The argument proposed by Goyeneche can be applied *a fortiori* to dismissed religious. Besides being a member of the institute, the dismissed religious has a closer union with it than the religious in military service, for the dismissed person is still bound by the religious vows. Thus, the dismissed religious is not obliged to observe the private views which he made before his religious profession, for the suspension of such vows, as stated in canon 1315 still endures.

Moreover Fanfani [138] and others state that such private vows revive only when the religious vows cease. Usually the religious vows have not ceased in dismissal [139] and therefore the suspension

[134] Cf. Woywod, *Commentary*, n. 1336.

[135] *A Commentary*, VI (2. ed., St. Louis: Herder, 1923), 309.

[136] "Consultationes,"—*CpRM*, XVIII (1937), 89.

[137] S. C. de Rel., 15 iul. 1919—*AAS*, XI (1919), 322; decr. *Inter reliquas*, 1 ian. 1911—*AAS*, III (1911), 37-39.

[138] *De Iure Religiosorum*, n. 218, A.

[139] Canon 669, § 1.

of the private vows according to canon 1315 still endures. Concerning the private vows which were taken after religious profession, the dismissed religious must observe them as far as his condition after dismissal allows. Such vows would be validly made in so far as the obligations arising from them do not conflict with the obligations arising from religious profession. The superiors of both men and women religious can annul such private vows at will. Such action is always valid and is also licit if there is a just cause for the annulment.[140] The same superiors have this power over such vows even after dismissal, until such time as the dismissed obtains a dispensation from the religious vows and ceases to be a religious.

[140] Canons 501, § 1; 1312, § 1.

CHAPTER VI

JURIDIC CONDITION COMMON TO ALL DISMISSED RELIGIOUS

Article I. The Obligations of the Rule

Canon 593 states that all religious, both superiors and subjects, must not only faithfully keep the vows which they have professed, but must also live according to the rules and constitutions proper to the individual organizations and in this manner strive for religious perfection. The observance of this obligation of living according to the particular rules and constitutions after dismissal is treated mainly by the pre-Code authors.

It is evident that certain obligations enjoined by the rule cannot be observed by the dismissed religious and therefore he is entirely free from them.[1] Thus any obligations which have the nature of social acts or which can be performed only in cooperation with a community cease to bind after dismissal. The dismissed religious then, is evidently not bound to choral recitation of Divine Office, to the observance of a specific cloister, to presence at chapter, to participation in common penances, etc.

Before the promulgation of the Code, it was the opinion of the greater majority of authors that the dismissed religious was not bound to observe any of the rules and constitutions.[2] Few authors have treated the question after the promulgation of the Code, but certain ones have also followed this mild opinion.[3] Schaefer certainly sponsors it, for he states that the dismissed religious is free from all the obligations which do not refer to the common vows.[4] In

[1]Suarez, Tract. VIII, lib. III, c. VI, n. 10.

[2] Barbosa, *Collectanea Doctorum in Jus Pontificium Universum,* Lib. III, tit. XXXI, c. XXIV, nn. 12, 14; Leurenius, Lib. III, tit. XXXI, q. DCCCLXV, n. 2; Rotarius, *Theologia Moralis Regularium,* Tom. I, lib. III, c. II, punct. VI, n. 10; Schmalzgrueber, Lib. III, tit. XXXI, n. 248; Suarez, Tract. VIII, lib. III, c. VI, nn. 10-13; Piatus Montensis, *Praelectiones Juris Regularis,* I, q. 244, 3°.

[3] Berutti, *De Religiosis,* n. 177.

[4] *De Religiosis,* n. 596.

agreeing with the opinion of Schaefer, Blat states incorrectly that by legitimate dismissal the bond contracted in religious profession is broken, and the dismissed religious is separated from his religious institute and therefore Blat concludes that the dismissed is freed from the obligations of his religious profession with the exception of the vows.[5] Without stating his reasoning on the point and relying on the mild opinion of certain pre-Code authors, Augustine absolves the dismissed religious from the obligations of saying Divine Office and of observing the fasts imposed by the rule.[6] In like manner Geser frees dismissed Sisters from the obligation of saying Office.[7]

The reasons proposed by the pre-Code adherents of this opinion are the following. A religious binds himself to keep the rules and constitutions in so far as he lives within the community, in a religious house, where without doubt there is a certain adaptability and facility in their observance.[8] Therefore when the common life and union with the religious community cease, so do the obligations of the rule and constitutions. Again, just as a citizen of a state is not obliged to the rules of that state when he is away from it, so the religious after dismissal is not bound to the rules and constitutions. Furthermore, the dismissed religious admittedly does not enjoy the privileges of the institute and therefore he should not be obliged to the burden of the religious rules.[9] If such a burden were placed on the religious after dismissal, in addition to the further obligations of his new condition, it would place him in a state dangerous to his general welfare and for this reason he is free from the observance of the religious rules.

Despite these reasons of notable authors, it is the opinion of the present writer that the dismissed religious is bound to the observance of the rules and constitutions of his religious institute. It

[5] *Ius de Religiosis,* n. 714.

[6] *A Commentary,* III, 410.

[7] Geser, *The Canon Law Governing Communities of Sisters* (St. Louis: Herder, 1938), n. 1212.

[8] Leurenius, *loc. cit.*; Suarez, Tract. VIII, lib. III, c. VI, n. 11; Piatus Mentensis, *loc. cit.*

[9] Suarez, *loc. cit.*

is evident that if particular rules conflict with the life which the dismissed religious must lead in his new condition, he is excused from the observance of those rules on that account. But this by no means warrants a general liberation from the observance of all the rules. The work done by a dismissed religious may excuse him from the observance of the rules of rising at a certain hour, of fasting and abstaining, of choosing or excluding certain foods, and of doing certain corporal and spiritual works of mercy. In like manner his life in the world will excuse him in most cases from the rules of silence. It may be safely stated then that he is bound to all the rules which do not demand the presence of a community, in so far as he can observe them in his new condition.

The reasons proposed by the authors for the opposite opinion are not convincing. A religious, in his profession, does not bind himself to the observance of the rules and constitutions in so far as he will be present in a community or in so far as he is allowed to remain in the communal life. No such intention can be presumed. A religious promises in his perpetual profession to observe all the rules of his institute for life, unless he is excused from any particular injunction for a legitimate reason. If the proposed reason favoring freedom were a valid argument, a religious bishop would certainly be freed from all the rules of his religious institute.[10] But formerly, by the common opinion of authors,[11] and at present by precept of common law,[12] such is not the case. The obvious difficulty in observing the rules and constitutions outside of the religious community cannot be advanced as an argument for freedom from the religious observances, for the dismissed religious has voluntarily placed himself in the unfavorable condition.

Concerning the argument derived from a comparison with a citizen absent from his state, it should be noted that the similarity is a weak one. It presupposes the argument treated above, that a religious promises to obey the rules only in so far as he remains

[10] Piatus Montensis, *Praelectiones Juris Regularis,* I, q. 244, 3°.

[11] Donatus, *Rerum Regularium Praxis Resolutoria,* Tom. I, pars II, tract. VIII, q. LII, n. 8; Ferraris, *Prompta Bibliotheca,* s. v. "Ejecti a Religione," n. 51.

[12] Canon 627, § 1.

in the community. This is not the case, as has been stated. Furthermore the condition of an absent citizen is to be judged by the state in which he is found, but the condition of a dismissed religious is to be judged by the state into which he was introduced by his perpetual profession, for after dismissal he still remains a religious and a member of his particular organization. Therefore the proposed similarity cannot give rise to a convincing argument.

Neither does the fact that the dismissed religious is deprived of the privileges of the religious institute argue to his freedom from the observance of the rules and constitutions. The privation of the privileges arises in punishment for his crime or crimes and certainly the same reason cannot be advanced for freedom from the religious observances, since no one should be rewarded for the commission of sins or crimes.[18] Dismissal is inflicted partly to urge the repentance of the dismissed religious and certainly liberation from the obligations of the religious institute will not tend toward that end.

If the burden of religious observances proves a danger to the general welfare of the dismissed religious, it is admitted that he is excused, not from all the rules and constitutions, but merely from those particular ones which cause the danger. Certainly some religious observances will not in most cases prove dangerous. Certain religious observances as the injunctions to offer certain vocal and mental prayers, to sleep on certain material, to observe silence, to fast, to keep vigils and to perform certain penances may often be dispensed with because of the new condition of the dismissed religious, but this is by no means a general liberation from all of the religious rules and constitutions.

Concerning the opinion of Blat, it should be noted that the only bond that is broken by legitimate dismissal after the profession of perpetual vows is the bond of communal life. On this account the dismissed religious is freed only from those observances that necessitate the presence of a community. The incorrect argument of Blat cannot be applied to all the observances of the rule, because by

[18] Donatus, *op. cit.*, Tom. I, pars II, tract. VIII, q. LII, n. 5; Reiffenstuel, Lib. III, tit. XXXI, n. 242; Ferraris, *Prompta Bibliotheca*, s. v. "Ejecti a Religione," n. 51.

legitimate dismissal there is no further interference with the obligations contracted in religious profession than the one mentioned above.

Certain authors as Donatus,[14] Passerinus,[15] Reiffenstuel,[16] and Ferraris [17] held this stricter opinion before the promulgation of the Code. They stated as the obligation of the dismissed religious that he should observe the rules and constitutions of his institute in so far as he could in his new condition.

As for the obligation of reciting Divine Office, the small Office of the Blessed Virgin, the Office of the Dead, or the seven penitential psalms, which may be required by the rules of the calendar of a religious institute, the dismissed religious has the same obligation as he had when he lived within the community in regard to extrachoral recitation. Therefore the general statement of Augustine which excuses from all recitation of Divine Office, except when the obligation arises from Holy Orders,[18] is too broad and liberal. It need not be mentioned that the dismissed religious is still strictly bound to the recitation of Divine Office if the obligation arises from Holy Orders.

Just as in the community, the religious does not always sin in acting contrary to the rule, so the same must be said of the dismissed religious. Sin is involved only in the infractions of rules which fall under a common precept, or in infractions of the rules which involve contempt.[19] Nevertheless although the rules may not oblige under pain of sin, if one frequently or as a general rule, violates the rules of his religious institute it is difficult to excuse him from sin.

Finally moralists speak of the obligation of every religious to strive after the perfection of his state of life and they declare that it is an additional obligation, distinct from the duty of keeping the vows and of observing the rule and constitutions. The dismissed

[14] *Rerum Regularium Praxis Resolutoria,* Tom. I, pars II, tract. VIII, q. LII, nn. 5, 8, 9.

[15] *De Hominum Statibus,* Q. CLXXXIX, art. VIII, n. 624.

[16] Lib. III, tit. XXXI, n. 242.

[17] *Prompta Bibliotheca,* s. v. "Ejecti a Religione," n. 51.

[18] *A Commentary,* III, 410.

[19] Fanfani, *De Iure Religiosorum,* n. 294.

religious can certainly fail seriously against this obligation. Thus for example if he commits many grave sins, he shows a frame of mind set against the love and desire of perfection and by this he certainly sins seriously.[20]

Article II. Obligation of Putting Aside the Religious Habit

Nothing is mentioned concerning the obligation of putting aside the religious habit in the canons treating the condition of religious dismissed after perpetual profession. However, it has been the constant practice in religious institutes that a dismissed religious should not wear the religious habit. This same practice was introduced into the first universal legislation on dismissal, enacted under Pope Urban VIII.[21] It is also the unanimous opinion of authors that the dismissed religious ought to put aside his religious habit, not only if he is freed from the religious vows, but also if he is still bound to them according to the norm of canon 669, § 1.[22]

This obligation can be reasoned to from canons 653 and 668, which treat of provisional dismissal in cases of grave exterior scandal and of imminent harm to the community. These canons state that the religious who is sent into the world should immediately put aside the religious habit. If such is the case in provisional dismissal, certainly it follows also when the religious is more definitely excluded from the communal life by the normal process of dismissal.

Also it is pointed out that those who obtain an indult of exclaustration are bound by the common law to put aside the religious habit,[23] thus showing that the religious habit is a sign of union with the communal life of a religious institute. That religious bishops are permitted to wear the religious habit is allowed rather as a mark of honor which the ecclesiastical dignity brings to the religious institute.

[20] Cf. Berutti, *De Religiosis,* n. 108, II.

[21] S. C. C., dec. *"Sacra Congregatio,"* 21 sept. 1624, § 7: "Sic vero eiecti, quandiu non redierint ad Religionem, in habitu clericali incedant"—*Fontes,* n. 2454.

[22] Fanfani, *De Iure Religiosorum,* n. 518, C; Pejška, *Ius Canonicum Religiosorum,* pp. 195-196; Berutti, *De Religiosis,* n. 178, II, A.

[23] Canon 639.

Furthermore Suarez [24] has pointed out that if the dismissed subject were allowed to wear the religious habit, it would bring infamy to the religious institute and harm to its good name. The wearing of the religious habit is in the common conception and impression a sign of good standing and union with a religious community and such a signification would be a falsehood in the dismissed religious. It may also be added that the wearing of the religious habit would place the dismissed religious in circumstances very unfavorable to his good name, for it would then be evident to everyone that he remains separated from his community for serious reasons.

The obligation of clerics to wear the ecclesiastical garb may not be affected in dismissal, but that particular obligation will be treated under the sections devoted to dismissed religious clerics.[25]

Finally, Berutti, in confirmation of the obligation that the dismissed religious has to put aside the religious habit, quotes canon 492, § 3, which states that the religious habit cannot be assumed by those not legitimately belonging to the religious organization, or by any new organization.[26] This canon is not well applied, for the dismissed religious undoubtedly legitimately belongs to the religious organization. Therefore the dismissed religious should put aside the religious habit for the reasons given above and not by virtue of canon 492, § 3.

Article III. Loss of Suffrages and Privileges

The loss of the right to the suffrages and privileges of the religious institute is not afflicted on the dismissed religious by the Code. However, by the nature of dismissal, the loss of these favors is evident. It does not seem fitting that suffrages and privileges should be extended to members who have been separated from the community because of their evil conduct, to those who have been a hindrance, rather than a help, toward the end for which the community was founded. Thus Coronata [27] and Fanfani [28] point out

[24] Tract. VIII, lib. III, c. VI, n. 14.

[25] Cf. *infra*, pp. 115, 118, 129.

[26] *De Religiosis*, n. 178, II, A.

[27] *Institutiones*, n. 658.

[28] *De Iure Religiosorum*, n. 519, C.

that the religious has no right to suffrages if he dies outside of the community before he has amended and before he has been re-admitted. Fanfani [29] also follows the opinion of certain authors [30] who wrote before the promulgation of the Code, in stating that the dismissed religious has no right to the privileges of his institute.

Canon 614 states that all religious, even lay members, enjoy the clerical privileges enumerated in canons 119-123. These canons treat of the privilege of the canon, the privilege of forum, the privilege of personal immunity, and the privilege in case of insolvency. Vermeersch-Creusen [31] are of the opinion that the religious loses these clerical privileges at dismissal. However, ordinarily no reduction to the lay state in contradistinction to the religious state takes place in dismissal. The dismissed person ordinarily still remains a religious. Therefore it seems that he would still retain the clerical privileges until he ceases to be a religious. Of course, it is certain that those religious who have been ordained in major orders enjoy the clerical privileges after dismissal, unless they have been deprived of them for some crime which is punished by reduction to the lay state or by perpetual deprivation of the ecclesiastical garb.[32]

Article IV. The Obligation to Amend and to Return to the Religious Institute

Since one of the purposes of dismissal tends toward the final correction of a delinquent subject, it is evident that the dismissed religious is obliged to amend his life. In his religious profession the delinquent promised to live perpetually according to his vows and according to the rules of his institute and thus to strive after perfection. This promise obliges him at every moment and therefore even immediately after dismissal. The perpetual bond established in religious profession becomes completely severed only by dispensation from the religious vows or by transfer to another religious institute.

[29] *Loc. cit.*

[30] Rotarius, *Theologia Moralis Regularium,* Tom. I, lib. III, c. II, punct. VI, n. 10; Suarez, Tract. VIII, lib. III, c. VI, n. 11.

[31] *Epitome,* I, n. 772.

[32] Canon 213.

Besides this obligation of amendment, is the dismissed religious bound to correct himself and to manifest his change of dispositions with a view to re-entrance into the religious institute? Is the dismissed religious in all cases bound to return to his religious institute? Such an obligation could arise from two sources, namely, from the prescripts of canon law or from the contract of his religious profession. This obligation of returning to the religious institute will now be treated from both these standpoints.

A. *The Obligation from Canon Law*

Canon 672, § 1. Dimissus, votis in religione emissis non solutus, tenetur ad claustra redire; et si argumenta plenae emendationis per triennium dederit, religio tenetur eum recipere; quod si graves obstent rationes sive ex parte religionis sive ex parte religiosi, res iudicio Sedis Apostolicae subiiciatur.

§ 2. Quoties vero vota in religione emissa cessaverint, si dimissus Episcopum benevolum receptorem invenerit, sub eius iurisdictione et speciali vigilantia maneat, servato praescripto can. 642; secus res ad Sanctam Sedem deferatur.

Only in this canon does the Code treat of the obligation by which the dismissed religious must return to his religious organization. The greater majority of authors apply this canon to all dismissed religious, whether lay or clerical religious.[38] It would seem

[38] Bouuaert, *Selecta Capita Codicis Iuris Canonici Analytica Proposita et Brevi Commentario Adaucta* (Gandae: Siffer, 1919), n. 247 (hereafter to be cited as *Selecta Capita Codicis Iuris*); Cocchi, *De Religiosis et Laicis*, n. 159; Chelodi, *Ius de Personis iuxta Codicem Iuris Canonis* (2. ed., a Sac. Ernesto Bertagnolli recognita et aucta, Tridenti: Libr. edit. Tridentum, 1927), p. 294 (hereafter to be cited as *Ius de Personis*); Prümmer, *Manuale Iuris Canonici*, Q. 264, 5; Toso, *Commentaria Minora*, Lib. II, pars II, p. 276; Vermeersch-Creusen, *Epitome*, I, n. 823; Oesterle, *Praelectiones Iuris Canonici*, Vol. I (Romae: In Collegio S. Anselmi, 1931), p. 377; Gerster, *Ius Religiosorum in Compendium Redactum* (Taurini: Marietti, 1935), p. 162 (hereafter to be cited as *Ius Religiosorum*); Palombo applies this canon to both lay and clerical religious, not however to all dismissed clerical religious.—*De Dimissione Religiosorum*, n. 209;

that this opinion is the more probable in so applying this canon for the following reasons:

(1) It enjoys the extrinsic authority of many authors.

(2) As paragraph one of canon 672 is worded, it seems to speak in a general way of all dismissed religious, and therefore because general words are to be understood in a general way,[34] this paragraph should be applied to all religious, both to men and women religious,[35] and to lay and clerical religious.[36]

(3) This paragraph is only a necessary consequence to canon 669, § 1, which canon without doubt binds all religious.[37]

(4) The same reasons are present for including both lay and clerical religious under this paragraph.[38]

(5) Both canons 672 and 669 are very similar to the prescripts of other canons of the Code which are common to all religious members and religious institutes; as for example, canon 640, on secularized religious; canon 645, on apostates and fugitives from religious institutes; and canon 648, on religious dismissed after the profession of temporary vows. Both canons 672 and 669 are placed under the general inscription of the Code, "*De Religiosis dimissis qui vota perpetua nuncuparunt.*" It does not seem to be evident why, contrary to the general inscription, the discipline referring to such religious should not be applied to all, both to clerical and lay religious, since as has been pointed out, the discipline of the Code is common for all secularized and exclaustrated religious, for all apostates and fugitives from religious institutes and for all religious dismissed after the profession of temporary vows.

Creusen in the second edition of his *Religieux et Religieuses*

Berutti, *De Religiosis,* n. 177; "Sat mirum videtur canonem 672 non inveniri in versione autorizata partis Codicis quae spectat religiones laicales."—De Meester, *Compendium,* n. 1063; Raus, *Institutiones Canonicae* (2. ed., Lugduni: Typis Emmanuelis Vitte, 1931), nn. 207-208.

[34] Michiels, *Normae Generales Juris Canonici* (2 vols., Lublin in Polinia: Universitas Catholica, 1929), I, 410; Cicognani, *Commentarium ad Librum I Codicis* (Romae: ex Schola Typographica "Pio X," 1925), p. 127.

[35] Cf. canon 490.

[36] Oesterle, *Praelectiones Iuris Canonici,* p. 377.

[37] Palombo, *De Dimissione Religiosorum,* n. 209.

[38] Toso, *Commentaria Minora,* Lib. II, pars II, p. 276.

(1921), first proposed the doubt about the general application of this canon. Larraona, in the following year, defended the proposition that canon 672, § 1, does not apply to lay religious, or to those who have been laicized in dismissal, but only to clerical religious in major orders and only to those clerical religious in major orders who are comprehended in canon 671, namely, those who have been dismissed for the less serious crimes.[39] The former section of the proposition will be treated first, namely, the proposition that canon 672, § 1, refers only to dismissed clerical religious in major orders and not to lay religious. This opinion of Larraona is accepted by the present author. The reasons for the opinion are taken mainly from Larraona who has treated the question profusely in *Commentarium pro Religiosis.*

This opinion has been adopted for the following reasons: (a) Strong arguments can be advanced in opposition to the reasons given by the sponsors of the more common opinion. (b) A consideration of the context of canon 672 shows that the canon refers only to dismissed religious who are clerics. (c) An argument is taken from the omission of canon 672 in the vernacular versions of the Code, edited for the use of the lay religious. Each of these reasons will now be discussed at length.

(a) Strong arguments can be advanced in opposition to the reasons given by the sponsors of the more common opinion.

In opposition to argument (1).[40] As for the contrary extrinsic authority of the authors, it must be noted that many do not mention the opinion of Larraona. Such authors as Cocchi,[41] Chelodi,[42] Gerster,[43] Prümmer,[44] Berutti,[45] Raus,[46] and Vermeersch-Creusen,[47] cannot be convincingly cited as opposing the opinion which Larraona has advanced, since they refer only to the words of the canon and

[39] "Quaestio Canonica circa Canonem 672, § 1,"—*CpR,* III (1922), 318-329.

[40] Cf. *supra,* p. 97.

[41] *De Religiosis et Laicis,* n. 159.

[42] *Ius de Personis,* p. 489.

[43] *Ius Religiosorum,* p. 182.

[44] *Manuale Iuris Canonici,* Q. 264, 5.

[45] *De Religiosis,* n. 177.

[46] *Institutiones Canonicae,* nn. 207-208.

[47] *Epitome,* I, n. 823.

do not show in any way that they have considered his opinion, even though they wrote after his proposition was published. Bouuaert,[48] who holds the same general opinion of the above cited authors, wrote before Larraona published his opinion. Hence although when a point is seriously discussed by the authors, the opinion of the majority may be followed in practice, it should not be concluded in this matter until it can be shown that all the cited authors have considered this well substantiated opinion.

Toso[49] and Oesterle[50] have considered this opinion and have rejected it, but their reasons have been given among the general reasons for the view which they maintain, and those reasons will be treated immediately. Fanfani[51] and Blat[52] have agreed with the opinion of Larraona; and Goyeneche[53] considers it as solidly probable. Both Coronata[54] and Schaefer[55] extend to it some probability.[56] Palombo states that it seems probable although he accepts the contrary opinion as more probable.[57]

In opposition to argument (2).[58] It is certain and admitted that general words are to be understood in a general way. This principle stands until the contrary is apparent from the context or in some other way. Canon 18 states that ecclesiastical laws are to be interpreted according to the proper meaning of the terms of law *considered in their context.* Here the literal general meaning of the word *"dimissus"* is not accepted because restriction of the word seems apparent from the context, as will be shown later.

Moreover, the Pontifical Commission for the Interpretation of

[48] *Selecta Capita Codicis Iuris,* n. 247.

[49] *Commentaria Minora,* Lib. II, pars II, p. 276.

[50] *Praelectiones Iuris Canonici,* p. 377.

[51] *De Iure Religiosorum,* n. 519.

[52] *Ius de Religiosis,* n. 721.

[53] *De Religiosis,* n. 130; "Consultationes,"—*CpR,* XIII (1932), 105.

[54] *Institutiones,* n. 658, 2°, note 6.

[55] *De Religiosis,* n. 598.

[56] Geser mentions the dispute about this canon and then states advisable norms from the prescriptions of the canon in regard to women religious of simple vows. He does not actually apply canon 672, § 1 to such lay religious.—*The Canon Law Governing Communities of Sisters,* n. 1214.

[57] *De Dimissione Religiosorum,* n. 209.

[58] Cf. *supra,* p. 97.

the Code has already shown to a certain extent that the word "*dimissus*" of canon 672, § 1, is not to be understood in an absolutely general sense, for it has stated that this canon does not apply to those who have been dismissed under canon 646.[59]

In opposition to argument (3).[60] This canon 672, § 1, understood in a general sense, could indeed be considered as a necessary consequence to canon 669, § 1, which canon undoubtedly refers to all religious. But it should be noted that this argument does not serve very well for practical interpretation, because from it can be concluded practically nothing except that the legislator who applied to lay religious canon 669, § 1, *could* or *ought* to apply to them this canon, but from this the fact that he did, or did not apply it, is not proved.

In opposition to argument (4).[61] The juridic reason why the prescripts of canon 672 were enacted is not extended to lay religious or to those who by dismissal are reduced to the lay state. There was little difficulty in enacting legislation for the exclusion of lay religious from the religious communal life in comparison with the difficulties arising from the exclusion of religious who are clerics. Accordingly it was ordained for lay religious in the preparatory schema of the Code, even until the last edition of it, that dismissal itself would produce dissolution of the vows, both for those professed with temporary vows and for those professed with perpetual vows. The contrary principle was received into the promulgated edition, which includes also lay religious of perpetual vows under the principle which is now stated in canon 669, § 1. This was done lest the Code seem to favor dismissals. Moreover, it offers an opportunity for penance for those in whom there is hope of amendment.[62] Besides, a dispensation from the vows is readily granted by the Holy See to lay religious in the dismissal itself. The law apparently shows no concern about the sustenance of such lay religious, if one excepts what canon 643, § 2, states generally about religious women

[59] P. C. I., 30 iul. 1934—*AAS*, XXVI (1934), 494.

[60] Cf. *supra*, p. 97.

[61] Cf. *supra*, p. 97.

[62] Cf. Larraona, "Quaestio Canonica circa Canonem 672, § 1,"—*CpR*, III (1922), 322.

who leave the religious institute. Neither does the law show any concern about their amendment, about their place of living or about the maintenance of vigilance over them. Neither does it place any obligation on the bishop of the place where they live. The lay religious can live what he wants. He does not wear the religious habit and therefore he can occupy himself in any type of labor.

On the contrary, all of these provisions are the concern of canon 671 in reference to religious in major orders who have been dismissed for the less serious crimes. A special subjection to a bishop, a charitable maintenance and a gradual rehabilitation depending on their amendment is definitely prescribed for them. These points are determined so that the cleric may not wander about and bring dishonor to his state and scandal to the faithful, so that he may live a life worthy of a cleric, so that he may more surely amend, so that his amendment can be proved and so that he may finally be readmitted to the religious institute.. Therefore an identical reason why canon 672 should include lay as well as clerical religious is not present. The Code merely continues consistently after canon 671 and states in canon 672 what must be done for the reception of the dismissed religious cleric mentioned in the preceding canon, after the whole process of preparation for that reception has been treated. Since that process is not outlined for the lay religious, it can hardly be said that the same reason is present for the inclusion of both classes of religious in canon 672.

Moreover, whether the legislation of canon 672, § 1, seems necessary for the lay religious or not, whether the same reason could be given for that necessity or not, would not prove it as a fact that its provisions actually include dismissed lay religious.

For the above reasons Larraona states that if one reads attentively the fourth chapter of the sixteenth title of the Code, the connection between the canons is very apparent. Canon 669, § 1, treats of all professed religious with perpetual vows and § 2 treats of those religious who before dismissal were clerics in minor orders, but who by dismissal were reduced to the lay state. In the following canons lay religious are not considered, nor are those who by dismissal were reduced to the lay state, but only clerics who after dismissal remain clerics, namely clerics in Holy Orders. This is expressly stated in canon 670 and in canon 671 it is supposed from the citation of canon 670. In canon 672 the matter continues to deal only with those who were the concern of the preceding canon.[63]

In opposition to argument (5).[64] It is true that canon 640 on the indult of secularization, canon 645 on apostates and fugitives from religious institutes, and canon 648 on religious dismissed after the profession of temporary vows, are common to all religious and these canons have some relation with canon 669 which is also common to all religious. As for canon 672, on the contrary, as the canon stands, it does not seem certainly to be applied by the legislator to lay religious.[65] After considering the arguments for the more common opinion, the writer may now proceed with positive arguments for his view.

(b) A consideration of the context of canon 672 shows that the canon refers only to dismissed religious who are clerics.

The scope or extent of paragraph one can be defined from a comparison with paragraph two, for each one is placed as a member of one disjunctive proposition. In the beginning of paragraph two, without limiting the extent of the subject of paragraph one, the first member of the disjunction, the second number is presented and expounded. An example of this disjunction is given in canon 669, § 1, namely, *either* the *dismissed religious,* according to the general rule of law, remains bound by the religious vows after dismissal, *or* the *dismissed religious,* by exception, is freed from the vows by dismissal. Certainly in the text of canon 672 there is a double hypothesis which is disjunctive, namely, *either* those dismissed religious who remain bound by the vows after dismissal . . . , contained in paragraph one, *or* those dismissed religious who are freed from their vows . . . , contained in paragraph two. Note that in paragraph two, or in the second hypothesis, the text certainly treats only of dismissed clerical religious in major orders. This is so apparent from the words," . . . *si dimissus Episcopum benevolum receptorum invenerit. . . .*" Therefore also in the first hypothesis, or in paragraph one, the matter must be understood of dismissed clerical

[63] Quaestio Canonica circa Canonem 672, § 1,"—*CpR,* III (1922), 321.

[64] Cf. *supra,* p. 97.

[65] Cf. *infra,* (b).

religious in major orders and therefore it must be so interpreted from canon 18.

(c) An argument is taken from the omission of canon 672 in the vernacular versions of the Code, edited for the use of lay religious.

In all the versions of the legislation of the Code treating of lay religious, which were made in the vernacular with special permission and which were edited in the Vatican Printing Office, this canon 672, and also canons 670 and 671 are omitted. From the fourth chapter of the sixteenth title of the Code only canon 669 is included. Now even though these versions, as has been expressly declared by the Sacred Congregation of Religious, cannot be considered as official,[66] yet without doubt they have great authority. This authority is derived from the canonists who drew up the translations and also from the circumstances of the translations, from which it can be conjectured, there is some approval and approbation. In the present case, the argument has greater weight because the point under discussion concerns a rather lengthy omission which would be observed very easily in revisions. Moreover, this omission is common to all the versions. It is also added that this omission is found in the more recent editions which were published after the above cited response of the Sacred Congregation of Religious in which it was commanded that those things which did not agree with the Code, be corrected in the vernacular versions.[67]

The second member of the proposition proposed by Larraona is that canon 672, § 1, refers only to those clerical religious who have been dismissed for the less serious crimes and not to those who have been dismissed for the crimes intimated in canon 670. Immediately it is noted that the Pontifical Commission for the Interpretation of the Code has already decided that the prescripts of canon 672, § 1, are not to be extended to religious who have been dismissed automatically by virtue of canon 646.[68] The matter is definitely settled

[66] S. C. de Rel., resp., 2 apr. 1919—*AAS*, XI (1919), 179; "Although this translation has been specially authorized by the Holy See, it has not the official character of the Latin text."—Foreword of *Authorized English Translation* in editions of 1918 and 1919.

[67] Larraona, "Quaestio Canonica circa Canonem 672, § 1,"—*CpR*, III (1922), 321, note 14.

[68] P. C. I., 30 iul. 1934—*AAS*, XXVI (1934), 494.

then, for such dismissed clerics, but a question remains about those clerical religious dismissed for the other crimes intimated in canon 670.

The above opinion of Larraona is also commonly opposed for the following reasons:

(1) The opposite opinion enjoys the extrinsic authority of the majority of authors.

(2) An argument is deduced from the text. No distinction is made in canon 672, § 1, between clerics who have been dismissed because of more serious, or because of less serious crimes. The canon treats in a general way of them all. Therefore it is arbitrary to restrict it to those clerics who have been dismissed for the less serious crimes. Further, this general interpretation of canon 672 can be confirmed from a comparison with the preceding canons 670 and 671, for in them the legislator, since he wished to, distinguished between dismissal for the more serious crimes and dismissal for the less serious crimes. If therefore, in this canon 672, immediately following, he does not distinguish, it is clear that he did not wish to make a distinction.

(3) An argument is advanced from the reason of the law. The reason for which this law was enacted applies in the same manner, perhaps even in a more urgent manner, to those dismissed because of the more serious crimes.

Nevertheless, the proposition of Larraona is accepted by the present writer as a more probable opinion for the following reasons: (a) The arguments of the contrary opinion can be opposed. (b) An argument is proposed from the context. (c) An argument may be advanced from the nature of the case juridically considered. (d) An argument is deduced from the difficulties created by the stricter opinion. Each of these arguments will now be discussed.

(a) The arguments of the contrary opinion can be opposed. In opposition to argument (1).[69] It is noted again that many authors show in no way that they have at all considered this particular point. Therefore their general statements referring canon 672, § 1, to all dismissed religious cannot be convincingly cited in oppo-

[69] Cf. *supra*, p. 1.

sition to this view. Choupin [70] has entirely agreed with this proposition and Goyeneche [71] states it as a probable opinion. What Palombo states can also be shown to agree with this opinion.[72]

In opposition to argument (2).[73] As has been stated before, the general connotation of words should be accepted until good reasons are proposed for certain restrictions. From the arguments that follow, it seems that the apparent general sense of canon 672, § 1, should be restricted also with regard to dismissed clerics.

In opposition to argument (3).[74] Larraona claims that the need for which this discipline was introduced ceases for a twofold reason in the cases concerned in canon 670. First, such dismissed religious are perpetually forbidden to wear the ecclesiastical garb, whence scandal is in great part averted. Secondly, the crimes for which this dismissal is incurred are of such a nature that the reason for the law can scarcely be believed to be present because of the fear of

[70] Apud Coronata, *Institutiones*, n. 658, p. 886, note 6.

[71] *De Religiosis*, n. 130.

[72] Palombo holds that all dismissed religious both lay and clerical are bound by the obligation to return which is expressed in canon 672, § 1. At the same time he states that the injunction of canon 672, § 1, obliging the religious institute to accept a dismissed religious who has amended, is not to be applied to those dismissed clerics who are mentioned in canon 670 or to those dismissed clerics who are mentioned in canon 671, n. 6. Such clerics, he states, must have their juridic condition determined by the Holy See in each case, even though they have amended. If a particular section of canon 672, § 1 does not apply to such religious, how can the remainder of the paragraph be applied to them since the canon itself leaves no room for distinction? Palombo states that even for such dismissed clerics, the general principle remains, namely, that they are bound to return to the religious institute *because of their religious vows.* Here he does not trace the obligation to canon 672, § 1. Larraona's proposition is not contrary to what Palombo has proposed, for all that it states is that the positive legislation of canon 672, § 1 does not apply to such religious. It is apparent that Palombo in his argumentation has agreed with this point. Larraona explicitly states that, in his proposition, he is not treating of the obligation arising from religious profession, but merely of the obligation arising from the positive legislation of canon 672, § 1.—"Quaestio Canonica circa Canonem 672, § 1,"—*CpR*, III (1922), 329. Therefore what Palombo states agrees with the restriction of canon 672, § 1 which is here accepted.—*De Dimissione Religiosorum*, n. 209, p. 255, note 1.

[73] Cf. *supra*, p. 104.

[74] Cf. *supra*, p. 104.

further scandal on the part of the dismissed religious who has already given very serious scandal and has incurred the most grave penalties. Having opposed the reasoning of the contrary view, the writer may now advance positive arguments in favor of his opinion.

(b) An argument is proposed from the context. Canon 672 appears sufficiently clear in connection with canon 671. In the latter canon the procedure imposed on religious who have been dismissed because of the less serious crimes is stated, namely, where they should live, by whom they should be supported, when they can be absolved from the suspension and how their rehabilitation can be gradually procured. After the legislation so indicates to the dismissed cleric the way to emendation, it can logically treat of the obligation of returning to the religious institute and of the obligation of the religious institute of receiving him. Each obligation supposes emandation in the mind of the legislator.

On the contrary canon 672 has no relation with canon 670 and with the dismissed religious there treated. Concerning the dismissed religious of canon 670, after the Code states that they are perpetually forbidden to wear the ecclesiastical garb, it does not seem to be further solicitous about them. It states nothing about their lot, nothing about their place of dwelling or sustenance, nothing about the vigilance of bishops over them or about their gradual rehabilitation. Therefore there is no reason why afterwards the Code should treat of an obligation to return or of an obligation to receive them, since not even hypothetically did it consider their emandation before.

(c) An argument may be advanced from the nature of the case juridically considered. Those dismissed for the more serious crimes and those dismissed for the less serious crimes cannot be made equal in reference to canon 672. Neither can the circumstances of this canon be put on a par for both cases, as to the same time, as to the same cautions for amendment, etc. Those dismissed for the more serious crimes deserve the perpetual prohibition of wearing the ecclesiastical garb inflicted by the Code itself. Juridic reasoning then urges that a diversity of degree has been admitted in the punishment of dismissal, since by law the causes of dismissal seem to separate the subject farther, in some cases than in others, from the religious communal life. Those religious mentioned in canon 670 meet from the law with the greatest degree of punishment given in dismissal or in penal separation from religious communal life, since they are forever forbidden to wear the ecclesiastical garb. The causes for their dismissal are also, in some cases, causes for infamy, deposition, and degradation. Therefore from the nature of the crimes and from the penalties which the law inflicts on them the dismissal of such clerics appears more grave and qualified, more severe and harsh than simple dismissal because of ordinary crimes. How then can the injunctions of canon 672 be said to bind in the same manner those dismissed because of the more serious crimes and those dismissed because of the less serious crimes?

(d) An argument is deduced from the difficulties created by the stricter opinion. Infamy of law, deposition, and degradation are perpetual vindictive penalties reserved to the Roman Pontiff, which can be taken away only by a dispensation *ex gratia*. This papal dispensation, because it proceeds *ex gratia* and because it concerns very serious penalties, is such that it cannot be demanded juridically, nor can the obtaining of it be supposed with certainty after a fixed and determined time, especially if this time is rather brief. Moreover, it must be added that the cited penalties involve irregularity, incapacity for exercising legitimate ecclesiastical acts and at times privation of the clerical privileges and reduction of clerics to the state of the laity.[75] Certainly no one affirms that the dismissed subject, still bound by these penalties, must be received into the religious institute. Therefore, because by law, a dispensation from these penalties cannot be supposed after an amendment of three years, it must be affirmed that canon 672, § 1, which absolutely imposes the obligation of receiving the dismissed religious after an amendment of three years, does not state anything about those dismissed for the more serious crimes.

It seems strange to demand for these two categories of dis-

[75] Chelodi, *Ius Poenale et Ordo Procedendi in Iudiciis Criminalibus iuxta Codicem Iuris Canonici* (Tridenti: Libr. Edit. Tridentum, 1925), nn. 50, 52, 53 (hereafter to be cited as *Ius Poenale*); Sole, *De Delictis et Poenis Praelectiones in Lib. V Codicis Iuris Canonici* (Romae: Pustet, 1920), nn. 289-296, 272-280 (hereafter to be cited as *De Delictis et Poenis*).

missed religious, categories which are expressly distinguished in the Code, the same period for amendment. The law is not solicitous concerning the amendment of the religious referred to in canon 670, since it does not prescribe anything for them concerning the place of dwelling, concerning special subjection to a local bishop, concerning absolution from the censures and dispensation from the penalties, concerning the precautions to be exercised and the material assistance to be given during the time of their probative penance. All these things which are preparations for readmittance into the religious institute are advanced and provided for in canon 671 in referance to those dismissed for the less serious crimes. From the omission of those things which can be considered as necessary, it can be justly conjectured that the Code does not treat further concerning those dismissed because of the more serious crimes intimated in canon 670, after their dismissal has been effected. The law does not suppose amendment or consider penance so probable that the matter should be important and practical enough to be treated specially in universal legislation. When an individual case arises, the legislator implies that it will be specially provided for.

In conclusion then, it is stated that the obligation to return which is expressed in law, refers only to dismissed clerical religious in Holy Orders, and that furthermore, it is also more probable, that this obligation does not refer to those clerical religious in Holy Orders who have been dismissed because of the crimes intimated in canon 670.

The legal obligation to return to the religious institute binds immediately upon dismissal. The fact that the religious institute is not obliged to accept the dismissed cleric before the expiration of a period of three years does not argue to the opinion that on his side the religious has no obligation of returning in the meantime. His amendment from the beginning is directed toward the end of his return and only grave reasons can excuse him from that obligation. The nature of those grave reasons will be treated immediately.[76]

B. *The Obligation Arising from the Bond of Religious Profession*

Dismissed religious who are still bound by their vows retain a permanent bond with their religious institute. By the profession of

[76] Cf. *infra*, p. 112.

vows, this bond between the religious institute and the individual religious was established *in perpetuum.* By this bond which still persists after dismissal, the religious has a certain obligation to return to his religious institute and to put himself in the proper dispositions for the observance of the vows which he has professed. This obligation refers to all classes of dismissed religious, whether clerical religious or lay religious whether men religious or women religious. Therefore despite what has been stated concerning the absence in the Code of a precept imposing an obligation to return, in regard to certain classes of religious, it cannot be said that any class of dismissed religious with perpetual vows has no obligation to return.

In view of the bond which is established in the profession of perpetual vows, the principle is stated that all dismissed religious are bound to return to their religious institute if they can.[77] The last phrase "if they can" is added because sometimes the obligation cannot be fulfilled due to serious reasons on the part of the religious institute or on the part of the individual dismissed religious.

For dismissed clerical religious in Holy Orders, who are mentioned in canon 671, there is a twofold obligation, one from positive law and one from the bond of their religious profession. For them the whole process of amendment with a view to return is outlined in law and nothing further need be said.

For dismissed clerics in Holy Orders who were dismissed because of the crimes intimated in canon 670, the obligation from the bond of religious profession remains. The Pontifical Commission has stated that canon 672, § 1, is not to be applied to those religious who have been dismissed for the crimes mentioned in canon 646. Moreover, as has been stated, those who have been dismissed for the other crimes intimated in canon 670, with greater probability, are not included under canon 672, § 1. Nevertheless from these facts it cannot be concluded that such dismissed religious are entirely free from the obligation to return. From them, one can admit at most that there is no obligation from positive law. Goyeneche,[78]

[77] Cf. Larraona, "Quaestio Canonica circa Canonem 672, § 1."—*CpR,* III (1922), 320.

[78] "Annotationes,"—*Apollinaris,* VIII (1935), 554.

Vermeersch [79] and Maroto [80] state that after the response of the Pontifical Commission it seems that such religious who have been dismissed because of the crimes mentioned in canon 646 are not bound to return. Otherwise, they state, what would be the force of the obligation if the dismissed religious could not attain its effect? It should be noted that from the response of the Pontifical Commission the effect of this obligation cannot be attained even after a three-year period of amendment. However, it seems that it would be too extensive an interpretation of the response to state that because of it, this obligation could never attain its effect. The Pontifical Commission has merely stated that the prescript of canon 672, § 1, does not apply to such religious. As a consequence, the above mentioned authors have reasoned that there seems to be no obligation to return for such religious. It has been stated, because of the reasons given in the previous section, that canon 672, § 1, does not apply to lay religious, yet as a consequence it cannot be said that lay religious have no obligation to return to the institute. In view of the bond of perpetual profession, it is evident that such religious are obliged to return. Likewise it seems that the above response has not absolved the religious dismissed because of the crimes of canon 646 from the obligation to return which arises from perpetual profession. The same obligation persists in all the dismissed religious here concerned and therefore also in those dismissed religious who are referred to in canons 646 and 670. Since with regard to such religious there is no prescription stated in the Code, concerning the obligation to return and circumstances directed to that end, the best mode of procedure is for such clerics to have recourse immediately to the Holy See.[81] If the Holy See considers their crimes and the scandal which they have caused as grave reasons against return to the religious institute, it will in time grant a dispensation from the religious vows. If it is discerned that there is hope of final amendment, the religious must proceed according to the instructions which he will receive.

When lay religious are concerned, whether they have been dis-

[79] "Annotationes,"—*Periodica,* XXIII (1934), 147.

[80] "Annotationes,"—*CpR,* XV (1934), 356.

[81] Cf. Palombo, *De Dimissione Religiosorum,* n. 209, p. 255, note 1.

missed automatically or by action of the religious superiors, the authors advise almost unanimously that in most cases a dispensation from the vows be sought directly.[82] This advice can in all charity be given by religious superiors, spiritual directors and confessors, even though the bond of religious profession obliges to return to the religious institute. Considering the difficulties of such return and the unworthiness of the religious vocation which the dismissed has shown, it is well to suggest and advise that he immediately seek a dispensation from the religious vows and then strive to lead a worthy life in the world.

Toso points out that the question of return is largely theoretical, for in practice it will be rather rare that a delinquent religious would wish to return to the institute which dismissed him and also that a religious institute which dismissed a subject would very willingly receive him.[83] Some authors mention that the return, even of clerical religious is a rare occurrence.[84] However, if a dismissed religious judges before God that his place is in the religious institute and if he is willing to amend thoroughly so that he may return, he cannot be obliged to seek a dispensation. If there are grave reasons against his return on the part of the religious institute, the Holy See will decide his status. When there is question of a lay dismissed religious who wishes to fulfill his obligation to return, he should be careful to so act that he can prove his amendment to the religious superiors. Thus he should either make known his intentions to the religious superior and follow his instructions or he should place himself under the guidance of his pastor or of some other cleric who will be able to testify and prove his amendment to the superior.

Grave reasons against the return of a dismissed religious can be present either on the part of the dismissed religious or on the part

[82] Vermeersch-Creusen, *Epitome,* I, n. 822; Wernz-Vidal, *De Religiosis,* n. 452; De Meester, *Compendium,* n. 1063; Prümmer, *Manuale Iuris Canonici,* Q. 264; Jardí, *El Derecho de las Religiosas,* n. 1071; Creusen-Garesché-Ellis, *Religious Men and Women in the Code* (3. English ed., Milwaukee: Bruce, 1940), n. 364.

[83] *Commentaria Minora,* Lib. II, pars II, p. 276.

[84] Creusen-Garesché-Ellis, *Religious Men and Women in the Code,* n. 364; Toso, *loc. cit.*

of the institute. When either party is conscious of such a cause, the Holy See should be approached in all cases. With regard to dismissed clerics in major orders who are referred to in canon 671, the obligation arises from canon 672, § 1. With regard to those dismissed clerics referred to in canon 670, the Holy See should always be approached for it alone can deal with them. With regard to all dismissed lay religious, if a grave reason against return is present, the case should be taken to the Holy See, for it alone can decide in the matter, either by dispensing from the religious vows, or by settling the question in some other way. One theoretical exception may be proposed. If this question concerns a diocesan institute and a subject dismissed after the profession of perpetual vows, the bishop could adequately settle the question. The matter is theoretical because in dismissal from such an institute the bishop would hard ever dismiss the subject without dispensing him from the religious vows.

Grave reasons against return on the part of the dismissed religious would be reasons such as a realization that the religious life is too strict for him, constant difficulties with the superiors, the contraction of a valid though illicit marriage and all other causes which can move a religious to petition for an indult of exclaustration or an indult of secularization.[85]

NOTE—It may be asked if the dismissed religious can acquire a domicile or quasi-domicile while he is outside the religious community. Since the promulgation of the Code, the authors generally, but not unanimously, follow the opinion that the religious acquires a legally necessary domicile or quasi-domicile in the religious house to which he has been assigned.[86] However, it may be well disputed if the religious has in any place a domicile or quasi-domicile in the strict sense. In reference to religious the Code uses a different formulary concerning the juridic effects that ordinarily follow upon the acquisition of a domicile or quasi-domicile. Thus in treating of the reception of Holy Viaticum and of Extreme Unction,[87] and

[85] Palombo, *De Dimissione Religiosorum*, n. 207.

[86] Cf. Michiels, *Principia Generalia de Personis in Ecclesia* (Lublin in Polonia: Universitas Catholica, 1932), pp. 143-145; Schaefer, *De Religiosis*, n. 598.

[87] Canon 514, §§ 1, 3.

in determining the proper *forum* [88] and the rights of ecclesiastical burial,[89] the Code refers to the house to which the religious is assigned, or at least to the place in which that house is situated. With reference to other members of the faithful, such matters depend upon the acquisition of a domicile or quasi-domicile.[90]

Since the dismissed religious has been separated from the religious house, he must acquire either a domicile or a quasi-domicile in the place in which he stays. Whether or not this is a voluntary domicile is a further question. Certainly those who live under religious obedience to their superiors ordinarily are incapable of having a voluntary domicile or quasi-domicile, whether diocesan or parochial.[91] The dismissed religious who is assigned to a certain place while he is outside the religious community, *e. g.*, a dismissed cleric, acquires a domicile or quasi-domicile in the place of penance, but it can hardly be said that he acquires a voluntary domicile in that place. However, in most cases the dismissed religious may acquire a voluntary domicile.

Therefore the general juridic effects of an acquired domicile or quasi-domicile, whether diocesan or parochial, would follow for such religious. Hence their reception of Holy Viaticum and Extreme Unction would be regulated by the norms of canons 850 and 938. If they should die outside the religious community, they would be comprehended in the general norms for ecclesiastical burial and not in the particular norms for the ecclesiastical burial of religious in good standing.

Something further may be stated about the ecclesiastical burial of dismissed religious. The Code states nothing explicitly about this matter. The general prescript of common law whereby a perpetually professed religious who dies outside the religious home is to be transferred to the church or oratory of his religious house, or at least to some house of his organization,[92] can hardly be applied to dismissed religious. It would hardly be in accordance with the com-

[88] Canon 1563.

[89] Canon 1221, § 1.

[90] Holy Viaticum and Extreme Unction—Canons 850, 938; ecclesiastical burial—Canons 1216-1220, 1223; and proper *forum*—Canon 1561.

[91] Schaefer, *De Religiosis*, n. 598.

[92] Canon 1221, § 1.

mon good of the religious institute which prompted the dismissal to allow to such a religious ecclesiastical burial from the religious house, or interment in the cemetery for religious. This statement is in full accord with the pre-Code practice and the opinions of pre-Code authors concerning this matter.[93]

It is added that dismissal in itself is no cause for the deprivation of ecclesiastical burial. However, the crimes that warranted the dismissal may cause this effect if no probable and positive sign of repentance has been given by the dismissed.

[93] Cf. *supra,* p. 42.

CHAPTER VII

JURIDIC CONDITION PECULIAR TO THOSE IN HOLY ORDERS

Article I. Religious in Minor Orders

If a religious cleric in minor orders is dismissed after the profession of perpetual vows, he is automatically reduced to the lay state.[1] Whether the cleric is automatically dismissed because of the crimes mentioned in canon 646 or whether he is dismissed by the legitimate action of superiors; whether he is automatically freed from the obligations of the vows, or whether he is bound by them according to the norm of canon 669, § 1, this reduction to the lay state is always incurred. This is one of the cases referred to in canon 211, § 2, for it is an instance in which a minor cleric is automatically reduced to the lay state for a cause explicitly stated in law. The reasons for such reduction are mainly punishment for the crimes of the cleric and honor and reverence for the clerical state. The latter reason urges the reduction lest the delinquent cause further scandal as a cleric after his dismissal.

From this reduction, it follows that the cleric is not only deprived of the right to wear the religious habit,[2] but also of the right to wear the ecclesiastical garb.[3] Moreover, as a cleric the religious loses his title to the clerical privileges.[4] However, as a religious it seems that he would still retain them.[5] From the moment of dismissal such a religious is considered and is dealt with merely as a dismissed lay religious. All that is said concerning dismissed lay religious applies without exception to him.

If such a dismissed religious should be readmitted to his own institute after dismissal, Goyeneche states that it seems he would

[1] Canon 669, § 2.

[2] Cf. *supra*, pp. 93-94.

[3] Canon 213, § 1.

[4] Canon 123.

[5] Cf. *supra*, p. 95.

be automatically restored to the clerical state.[6] However, a difficulty may arise in the following case. When the superior readmits a dismissed subject and when it is that superior's duty and right to promote to Orders,[7] readmission to the institute may be on the condition that the religious remain in the status of a choral member. The superior judges that because of proved amendment, the dismissed religious is worthy of readmittance to the religious life, but because of the former crimes and incorrigibility, he is not worthy to be promoted to orders. Even though the members of clerical institutes are *per se* generally classed as lay brothers and as priests or those aspiring to the priesthood, a third class of members may arise *per accidens*. A good reason may arise why a perpetually professed religious living in the community should not aspire to holy orders, yet the reason may be in no way a legitimate cause for dismissal. In such a case, the religious could hardly be forced to leave the institute, unless the constitutions stated something explicitly concerning the matter. Hence there is a possibility of such a class of members even in clerical organizations. If a dismissed religious were received back on the understanding that he would not be promoted to orders, he would remain a choral member of the institute without aspiring to orders. Certainly such a religious is not restored to the clerical state by this conditional reception. Berutti has well stated that readmittance into the clerical state demands the special permission of the major superior,[8] and this seems to be the better opinion. It is true that one who was formerly a minor cleric and who is unconditionally received back among the brethren aspiring to Holy Orders would have implicit permission for readmittance into the clerical state. Certainly the superiors would not receive him back in such a manner without considering his future life in the institute. However, the general principle of Goyeneche stating that readmittance into the community entails readmittance into the clerical state seems too broad in the light of the possible conditional reception stated above.

Canon 212, § 1, states that if a cleric in minor orders has for

[6] *De Religiosis,* n. 127.

[7] Canon 964, nn. 1, 2.

[8] *De Religiosis,* n. 178.

any reason returned to the state of the laity, he may again be admitted to the clergy with the permission of the ordinary into whose diocese he was incardinated by ordination. The ordinary, the canon continues, shall grant the permission only after a diligent inquiry into the life and character of the individual, and after a test, the length of which is to be determined by the judgment of the same ordinary. Concerning this matter, nothing is stated explicitly in law with reference to religious clerics in minor orders who have been reduced to the lay state. From analogy of law,[9] it would seem that for them the right of readmittance to the clerical state pertains to the religious superior who possesses the right to ordain his subjects to minor orders,[10] to the major superior of clerical exempt organizations,[11] or, when the ordination of the religious was governed by the laws for seculars,[12] to the particular bishop who had the right to ordain the religious. Therefore these superiors may use this right when the religious returns to the community. By the same token the inquiry and probative test demanded by canon 212 should not be neglected by these superiors. It is an obligation over and above the obligation of ascertaining that the religious has amended in such a manner that he merits readmittance into the religious community.

Finally, if a religious in minor orders is dismissed, is dispensed from his religious vows and later aspires to the ranks of the secular clergy, he cannot be admitted into a seminary until the ordinary confers with the Sacred Congregation of Studies and Universities.[13] Moreover, the said ordinary can admit the ex-religious to the clerical state only after he has complied with the prescripts of canon 212.

Article II. Religious in Major Orders

Particular prescripts on the juridic condition of dismissed religious in major orders are stated in canons 670, 671 and 672. In view

[9] Canon 20.

[10] Canon 964, § 1.

[11] Canon 964, § 2.

[12] Canon 964, § 4.

[13] S. CC. de Religiosis atque de Seminariis et Studiorum Universitatibus, decr. *Consiliis initis,* 25 iul. 1941—*AAS,* XXXIII (1941), 371.

of canons 670 and 671, the juridic condition of such clerics depends in great part upon the type of crime which they have committed and for which they have been dismissed. Therefore, before determining the status of a dismissed cleric in major orders, it is always necessary to know what crime urged his dismissal from the religious institute. This knowledge is not as decisive a factor in regard to dismissed lay religious or to those who have been laicized in dismissal. However, it is necessary also in reference to these religious, especially when there is question of amendment and of a desire to return to the religious institute.

A. *Those Dismissed for the More Serious Crimes*

Canon 670. Clericus in sacris qui aliquod delictum commisit de quo in can. 646, aut dimissus est ob delictum quod iure communi punitur infamia iuris vel depostione vel degradatione, perpetuo prohibetur deferre habitum ecclesiasticum.

The crimes intimated by this canon have already been listed in the second article of chapter IV. If a major cleric with perpetual vows has been dismissed for any of those crimes, he is comprehended by this canon and not by canon 671. It is mentioned again that the crimes concerned are not referred to as causes for dismissal. The canon merely states that if dismissal has taken place because of those crimes, the dismissed cleric is perpetually forbidden to wear the ecclesiastical garb. Whether dismissal takes place automatically or according to the legitimate action of superiors, this prohibition is effective by the very fact of dismissal. It is a measure that acts automatically since it is here imposed by common law.[14]

A question arises concerning the nature of this prohibition. Can it be said that the prohibition of canon 670 is identical with the vindicative penalty of canon 2304? Coronata notes a difficulty in explaining how the perpetual prohibition to wear the ecclesiastical

[14] Palombo, *De Dimissione Religiosorum,* n. 202; cf. *Index Analytico-Alphabeticus Codicis,* s. v. "Habitus clericalis," where it states, "quinam eo ipso iure prohibetur, 670."

garb as identical with the penalty of canon 2304 can be applied in canon 670, for he states that the infliction of that penalty seems to suppose previous deposition.[15] In answer to the difficulty Palombo states that the deprivation of the ecclesiastical garb does not necessarily suppose previous deposition.[16] Findlay proposes the opinion that the perpetual prohibition of canon 670 is an administrative measure rather than a penal sanction.[17] However, most canonists state that the perpetual prohibition to wear the ecclesiastical garb mentioned in canon 670 is the particular penalty mentioned in canons 2298, n. 11 and 2304.[18] Palombo refers to the Index of

[15] "Difficultas in explicando modo quo prohibitio deferendi habitum ecclesiasticum applicari possit; talis enim poenae inflictio depositionem praeviam supponere videtur. At forte difficultas solvitur dicendo in casu tribunal qui dimissionem decernit, debere simul ex connexione causarum primo depositionem et deinde etiam habitus privationem decernere."—*Institutiones*, n. 660.

[16] "Cfr. Coronata qui non recte putat inflictionem poenae privationis habitus ecclesiastici supponere praeviam depositionem: datur etiam ad aggravandam depositionis poenam (cfr. c. 2304, § 1), sed non praesupponit eam absolute."—*De Dimissione Religiosorum*, n. 202, p. 247, note 1.

[17] "It is an administrative measure rather than a penal sanction, a necessary precautionary measure to prevent scandals. This is evident from the fact that the prohibition is extended to include those who are dismissed for delicts punished by the common law with degradation. If besides the decree of dismissal a sentence of degradation has been passed against the religious, then the prohibition of the canon would no longer serve any purpose. In aggravated deposition as well as in degradation there is involved not merely a perpetual *prohibition* which forbids the wearing of the ecclesiastical garb but a perpetual *privation* of the right to wear it. Accordingly, if and when these penalties are inflicted upon the aforementioned religious in conformity with the sacred canons, he will not only be forbidden to wear the ecclesiastical garb but will be deprived of the right to do so. Only then is he forever deprived of the clerical privileges, an effect nowhere attributed in law to a prohibition, even perpetual, of wearing the ecclesiastical garb."—*Canonical Norms Governing the Deposition and Degradation of Clerics*, The Catholic University of America Canon Law Studies, n. 130, (Washington, D. C.: The Catholic University of America Press, 1941), p. 175.

[18] Berutti, *De Religiosis*, n. 178; Cocchi, *De Religiosis et Laicis*, n. 158; Palombo, *De Dimissione Religiosorum*, n. 202; Blat, *Ius de Religiosis*, n. 716; Schaefer, *De Religiosis*, n. 597; Coronata, *Institutiones*, n. 660, 2°, note 10; Chelodi, *Ius de Personis*, n. 294; Fanfani, *De Iure Religiosorum*, n. 517; Goyeneche, *De Religiosis*, n. 128; Beste, *Introductio in Codicem*, p. 453; Gerster, *Ius Religiosorum*, p. 161; Larraona, "Quaestio Canonica circa Canonem 672, § 1,"—*CpR*, III (1922), 325, note 23, 326-327; Smith, *The Penal Law for Religious*,

the Code under *"Habitus clericalis"* where the term *prohibition* which is used in canon 670 is also used in reference to the canonical penalty.[19]

As a result the effects of the canonical penalty of the perpetual privation of the right of wearing the ecclesiastical garb are applied to the religious clerics referred to in canon 670. These effects are the deprivation of the clerical privileges and the cessation of any charitable subsidy from the religious institute or from the local ordinary.[20] This latter effect can also be based on the traditional consequences of dismissal and on a consideration of the charitable subsidy for dismissed religious as it is found in the Code. It is evident from pre-Code history that the religious institute was in no way obliged to support the dismissed cleric. The lack of sustenance was one of the punishments of dismissal and was intended to urge speedy amendment and return to the religious institute. Also the Code in speaking of dismissed clerical religious mentions the obligation of a *charitable* subsidy only once, and that reference is to those who have been dismissed for the less serious crimes.[21] The obligation to supply the charitable subsidy for such a religious is not imposed absolutely. It is conditioned on the amendment of the dismissed cleric and it endures only for a short period, usually for a period of not more than a year.[22] Wherever the Code states nothing about the charitable subsidy, there is no obligation on the religious institute to supply anything. Neither is the local ordinary obliged in this matter. When such clerics amend and have recourse to the Holy See instructions will be forwarded concerning their support, if they are again received into the clerical state. It need not be mentioned that it is certainly in accordance with the charity of the religious life for the superiors to take care that such clerics are not left in a state of extreme want. However, there is present no obligation in justice or in positive law.

The Catholic University of America Canon Law Studies, n. 98 (Washington, D. C.: The Catholic University of America, 1935), p. 91.

[19] *De Dimissione Religiosorum*, n. 202, p. 246, note 1.

[20] Cf. canon 2304, § 2.

[21] Canon 671, n. 5.

[22] Cf. canon 671, n. 7.

The authors are unanimous in stating that clerics dismissed for the more serious crimes are suspended even though the Code states nothing expressly about the matter. Some authors trace the suspension to the penalty of the perpetual deprivation of the right of wearing the ecclesiastical garb.[23] Some trace it to the individual crimes committed by the delinquent,[24] or derive it from an *a fortiori* argument from canon 671, n. 1.[25] Others merely state that such clerics incur a suspension without referring to its source.[26] Palombo has considered the variant opinions of the authors and has concluded that the best explanation is that suspension is present because of the penalty of the perpetual privation of the ecclesiastical garb. Although this penalty is distinct from the penalty of suspension, it is a greater and more stringent penalty and comprehends the effects of suspension.[27]

The canonical status of the clerics referred to in canon 670 depends greatly upon the canonical penalties which will be inflicted for their crimes. These penalties are found in the fifth book of the Code. Each of the classes of dismissed clerics referred to in canon 670 will now be treated with a view to determining which canonical penalties are imposed.

With regard to clerics who have been automatically dismissed, it should be noted again that the full effects of such dismissal can be demanded in the external forum only after the declaration of the fact has been made by the competent superior. The same must be said concerning the effects of the canonical penalties which they have incurred automatically on the commission of the specified crimes.

Those who have publicly apostatized from the Catholic faith incur an automatic excommunication.[28] If they have been admonished and do not repent they shall be deprived of any benefice, dig-

[23] Coronata, *Institutiones*, n. 660; Schaefer, *De Religiosis*, n. 597.

[24] Goyeneche, *De Religiosis*, n. 128.

[25] Prümmer, *Manuale Iuris Canonici*, Q. 264, 4; Jansen, *Ordensrecht*, p. 306; Beste, *Introductio in Codicem*, p. 453.

[26] Vermeersch-Creusen, *Epitome*, I, n. 822; De Meester, *Compendium*, n. 1064, 2°; Chelodi, *Ius de Personis*, n. 294.

[27] Palombo, *De Dimissione Religiosorum*, n. 202.

[28] Canon 2314, § 1, n. 1.

nity, pension, office or other position which they may hold in the Church and they shall be declared infamous. Finally, after renewed admonition, they shall be deposed.[29] If such clerics join a non-Catholic sect, or publicly adhere to it, they automatically incur infamy and if an admonition to repent is fruitless, they shall be degraded.[30] By public apostasy from the Catholic faith, any office held by the cleric automatically becomes vacant without any declaration. The law considers this crime as a tacit renunciation of all offices.[31]

Those clerics who have taken flight with a woman, in so far as they may be fugitives and not apostates from the religious institute, incur an automatic suspension reserved to their proper major superior and also an automatic privation of any office which they might have in the religious institute.[32]

Those who presume to attempt to contract marriage, or who contract a civil marriage,[33] incur an automatic excommunication reserved simply to the Holy See. When they have been admonished by their ordinary and do not repent within the specified time, determined according to the circumstances of the case, they shall be degraded.[34] Attempted marriage also automatically effects the vacancy of any office held by the cleric, because the law considers this crime as a tacit renunciation.[35] It is added that usually the crimes causing automatic dismissal are accompanied by the crime of apostasy from the religious institute. When this is actually the case the cleric incurs an excommunication reserved to his proper ordinary.[36] In clerical exempt organizations, the proper ordinary is the major superior, whereas in non-exempt organizations the proper ordinary is the ordinary of the place where the religious stays.[37]

[29] Canon 2314, § 1, n. 2.

[30] Canon 2314, § 1, n. 3.

[31] Canon 188, n. 4.

[32] Canon 2386.

[33] "Vinculum civile est ea coniunctio quae in facie civilis legis matrimonium putatur."—Schaefer, *De Religiosis*, n. 576.

[34] Canon 2388, § 1.

[35] Canon 188, n. 5.

[36] Canon 2385.

[37] *Ibid.*

Such a cleric is also deprived of the right to place legal ecclesiastical acts and he is deprived of all the privileges of his religious organization.[38] Moreover, when the crime of apostasy has been committed, the law itself states that after the religious has returned to his institute, he is forever deprived of the right of voting and the right of being voted for. Furthermore, he should be fittingly punished by the superior.[39]

The crimes causing automatic dismissal may sometimes lack the element of apostasy from the religious institute. The intention is the principal factor in this crime.[40] This intention consists in the will of perpetually deserting one's religious institute. Hence there would be no apostasy from the religious institute if the religious committed these crimes with the intention of later returning to his institute. In such a case the religious would certainly be dismissed, even though he returns and is living in the religious house.[41]

Clerics who have incurred automatic infamy of law are burdened with that infamy from the moment of the commission of the crime, even though they are not yet dismissed. Such infamy would be incurred, for example, by a religious cleric who would cast away the Sacred Species or carry Them off or retain Them for an evil purpose,[42] or by a religious cleric who would violate the bodies or graves of the dead with a view to theft or any other evil purpose.[43] The declaration of infamy of law is made by an ecclesiastical judge, but it can be inflicted only for the specified crimes fixed by common law. The same must be said concerning automatic infamy of law.[44] Those clerics who are burdened with infamy of law become irregular from defect.[45] Moreover, they are incapacitated from obtaining

[38] Canon 2385.

[39] *Ibid.*

[40] Blat, *Ius de Religiosis*, n. 649; Vermeersch-Creusen, *Epitome*, III, n. 589; Riesner, *Apostates and Fugitives from Religious Institutes*, The Catholic University of America Canon Law Studies, n. 168 (Washington, D. C.: The Catholic University of America Press, 1942), p. 62.

[41] Coronata, *Institutiones*, n. 646; Schaefer, *De Religiosis*, n. 576.

[42] Canon 2320.

[43] Canon 2328.

[44] Canon 2293, § 2.

[45] Canon 984, n. 5.

benefices, pensions, offices and ecclesiastical dignities, from the exercise of legitimate acts,[46] from the execution of any ecclesiastical right or duty and finally from the exercise of the ministry in sacred functions.[47] If it is publicly known that a cleric is burdened with infamy of law, he must be refused Holy Communion until his repentance and amendment has been established and satisfaction has been made for the public scandal which he has given.[48] This infamy of law ceases only by a dispensation granted by the Holy See.[49]

The vindicative penalty of deposition effects a suspension from office and a deprivation of all ecclesiastical offices, dignities, benefices, pensions and functions which the cleric has, even though he was ordained on the title of them. Moreover he is incapacitated to obtain them in the future.[50] This penalty is never imposed automatically, but must be inflicted by a tribunal of five ecclesiastical judges,[51] for certain crimes determined by common law. A deposed cleric is not rejected from the clerical state, nor is he deprived of the clerical privileges. Also, he is still bound by the obligations arising from sacred orders.

Finally, the cleric who merits the sentence of degradation is completely excluded from the clerical state. This penalty contains in itself deposition, the perpetual privation of the ecclesiastical garb and reduction to the lay state.[52] As was stated about deposition, this penalty can be inflicted only by a tribunal of five ecclesiastical judges for certain crimes specified in common law.[53]

When there is question of inflicting canonical penalties after dismissal, the matter of juridical competence may be raised. If there is question of dismissal from an exempt clerical institute, and if the dismissed cleric has not yet subjected himself to the obedience and vigilance of any local ordinary, is the major superior of an exempt clerical organization competent to inflict further penalties,

[46] Canons 2256, n. 2; 765, n. 2; 766, n. 2; 795, n. 2.

[47] Canon 2294, § 1.

[48] Canon 855, § 1.

[49] Canon 2295.

[50] Canon 2303, § 1.

[51] Canon 1576, § 1, n. 2.

[52] Canons 213, § 2; 2305, § 1.

[53] Canon 1576, § 1, n. 2.

or must the case be referred to the local ordinary? A practical example would be the case of a priest who after perpetual profession attempts marriage. The Code states that if such a cleric is admonished by his ordinary, and if he does not repent within the time specified according to the circumstances of the case, he should be degraded.[54]

Even after the declaration of the fact of dismissal made according to law,[55] such a cleric remains bound by his religious vows, unless his constitutions or apostolic indults declare otherwise. While he remains bound by his vows, he continues to be a religious and a member of his religious institute. He is therefore still under the jurisdiction of his religious superiors because that jurisdiction embraces all the members of the religious institute except those who have been withdrawn from it by common law.[56] Therefore the dismissed religious would still be under the judicial power of the immediate major superior of the religious house from which he was dismissed.[57] It is evident also that the canon which demands the degradation of such a cleric refers to the major superior of clerical exempt institutes.[58] The canon speaks of three classes of persons as incurring excommunication, namely, clerics, regulars and women religious who have professed solemn vows. It then provides for an admonition to clerics by their ordinary. Since it mentions clerics and regulars, they and their respective ordinaries must be included. Therefore if the cleric concerned does not obey the admonition of his major superior, the superior should establish the tribunal to issue the sentence of degradation.

It may be asked if the admonition referred to may ever be omitted. Sometimes the dismissed cleric may either personally or

[54] Canon 2388, § 1.

[55] Canon 646, § 2.

[56] Canons 627, 639.

[57] Cf. Oesterle, "De Reductione ad Statum Laicalem,"—*CpR,* XX (1929), 95. However Wernz-Vidal state, "Etiam S. C. de Religiosis tractat causas illorum qui iam e Religione dimissi sunt, tamquam causas proprias."—*Ius Canonicum* (Vol. VI, *De Processibus,* 1927), n. 57.

[58] Canon 2388; cf. Keene, *Religious Ordinaries and Canon 198,* The Catholic University of America Canon Law Studies, n. 135 (Washington, D. C.: The Catholic University of America Press, 1942), p. 11.

by letter inform the superior that he will never again return to the religious life or to the sacerdotal ministry and that he intends to remain in his sinful union. This reason would not be sufficient to omit the admonition. The law states that an admonition must precede the extreme penalty of degradation.[59] Therefore the major superior should approach the dismissed cleric or send a registered letter, informing him that he must within a specified time, *e.g.* within fifteen days, dismiss his sinful companion and determine to have no relations with her in the future and that otherwise he will incur the penalty of degradation. If after the lapse of that time, the cleric has not conformed to the mandates of the admonition, he shall be degraded. It is added that in this matter one admonition suffices.[60] In this matter it is apparent that the ordinary of the place of the house from which the cleric was dismissed is a competent judge in case of members of institutes which are non-exempt.[61] The ordinary of the place where the crime was committed is also a competent judge in such cases.[62] Though the religious cleric has left the diocese after committing the crime, the competent ordinary has the right to serve the admonition and to see that the sentence is decreed.[63]

Such action is required by canon law, but in practice it is not observed in some localities. Danger of scandal would arise if law suits were resorted to concerning the validity of marriages which are recognized by the state. If the admonition were found by the wife of the civil marriage, or if she could prove that the admonition was given personally, she might take action in the civil courts against the ecclesiastical authorities. The same action might be taken in bad will by the cleric after he has received the admonition. For these reasons at times the admonition and the penalty of degradation are not imposed in some localities.

[59] Canon 2388.

[60] Oesterle, "De Reductione ad Statum Laicalem,"—*CpRM,* XX (1939), 96; Cappello, *Tractatus Canonico-Moralis De Censuris Iuxta Codicem Canonici* (3. ed., Romae: Marietti, 1933), n. 35 (hereafter to be cited as *De Censuris*).

[61] Canon 1563.

[62] Canon 1556, § 1.

[63] Canon 1556, § 2.

B. *Those Dismissed for the Less Serious Crimes*

All priests, deacons and subdeacons who have been dismissed from the religious communal life, for crimes less serious than those intimated in canon 670 are subject to the prescriptions of canon 671. The less serious crimes are those which are not punished with infamy of law, deposition or degradation and which do not cause automatic dismissal from the religious institute. This division of crimes, made in canons 670 and 671, considers the perpetrated crimes objectively and not subjectively, *i. e.*, not on the basis of the dispositions of the delinquent. The distinction is made stressing the quality of the delicts, more than their quantity.[64]

The Code is most solicitous for the amendment and return of the clerics who have been dismissed for the less serious crimes. A complete method of reinstatement is outlined for them alone. This fact is due primarily to a profound respect and reverence for Holy Orders and to a consideration of the particular delinquency in such cases. The law here evidently considers that there is still hope of amendment and therefore it shows itself solicitous for the final correction of the clerics concerned. The same cannot be said concerning the clerics referred to in canon 670, for the legislator seems to have considered that in reference to them hope for amendment has, morally speaking, vanished. On this account, he did not judge that norms for their reinstatement deserved a place in universal legislation.

From the moment of dismissal, clerics who have been guilty of the less serious crimes must put aside the religious habit, the outward sign of union with the religious institute.[65] However, they are bound to wear the clerical garb under an obligation arising at the time of their first tonsure.[66] Consequently, lest scandal would ensue, if they should wander about far from their immediate superiors, the legislator is careful to point out the steps which must be taken for a resumption of the religious life, or at least for establishment in the sacred ministry among the secular clergy. The particular

[64] Cf. canon 2196.

[65] Cf. *supra*, pp. 93-94.

[66] Canons 108, § 1; 136, § 1; cf. Fanfani, *De Iure Religiosorum*, n. 298.

laws directing the life of these clerics while they are outside the religious community will now be treated.

1. *The Automatic Suspension.* These clerics are automatically suspended at the moment of dismissal,[67] and they remain so until they have obtained absolution from the Holy See. It is apparent from canon 671, n. 1, that no other superior has the power to absolve from this suspension, no matter how praiseworthy the delinquent's dispositions may be. It is a true censure, since it is referred to as such later in the same canon.[68] Therefore it comprehends all the effects of an absolute suspension. Consequently, these dismissed clerics are forbidden to make use of any right of election, presentation or nomination. They are incapable of acquiring dignities, offices, benefices, ecclesiastical pensions or any position in the Church and they cannot be promoted to Orders.[69] If they exercise their Orders in violation of this suspension, they incur an irregularity.[70]

This suspension has a certain peculiarity as a censure. Suspensions as censures cease by absolution after the delinquent party recedes from his contumacy. The same cannot be said of the cessation of a suspension which is a vindicative penalty. A vindicative penalty ceases whether by expiation or by a dispensation granted by the competent superior.[71] In the case of suspension a vindicative penalty is present when the suspension is perpetual or when it is inflicted for a fixed time, or when it is inflicted at the will of the superior.[72] The cessation of a suspension as a vindicative penalty does not depend upon the dispositions of the delinquent, but the cessation of it as a censure always looks primarily to his dispositions.

[67] Cf. *supra*, pp. 47-50.

[68] "Ordinarius eius preces apud Sanctam Sedem commendabit pro absolutione a censura suspensionis. . . ."—Canon 671, n. 7; cf. Toso, *Commentaria Minora*, Lib. II, pars II, p. 274; Cipollini, *De Censuris Latae Sententiae iuxta Codicem Iuris Canonici* (Taurini: Marietti, 1925), p. 220 (hereafter to be cited as *De Censuris*); Palombo, *De Dimissione Religiosorum*, n. 203; Goyeneche, *De Religiosis*, n. 129; Chelodi, *Ius Poenale*, n. 45; Cocchi, *De Religiosis et Laicis*, n. 158; Beste, *Introductio in Codicem*, p. 453; Coronata, *Institutiones*, n. 660; Schaefer, *De Religiosis*, n. 597; Blat, *Ius de Religiosis*, n. 718.

[69] Canons 2265, 2282, 2283.

[70] Canon 985, n. 7.

[71] Canon 2289; cf. Vermeersch-Creusen, *Epitome*, III, n. 491.

[72] Canon 2298, n. 2.

As a vindicative penalty, suspension is directed toward the chastisement of the offender, or toward the upholding of the social order, whereas suspension as a censure is directed toward the correction of the delinquent.

It is evident that the suspension of canon 671, n. 1, does not cease immediately when the delinquent cleric recedes from his contumacy, or when he determines to lead a worthy religious or a worthy clerical life. This fact would seem to show that the suspension concerned must be a vindicative penalty. On the other hand, one is forced by the Code itself to admit that it is a censure.[73] The peculiarity of the penalty as a censure may be explained for the most part. Despite the reference of the canon to a year's probation under suspension, the cessation of the censure depends to a great degree on the dispositions of the delinquent cleric. This can readily be seen from a study of the canon itself. It must also be inferred from the canon that such clerics are to be considered as juridically contumacious until they are judged truly amended by the Holy See.[74] Cipollini states that this censure is a peculiar penalty inflicted after the manner of a censure, for it is directed toward the proved amendment of the delinquent and is remitted by absolution.[75]

A dismissed religious cleric who incurs the suspension of canon 671, n. 1, may receive the Sacraments, provided he is truly contrite for his crimes and provided he desists from his contumacy. This statement stands even though the censure is reserved to the Holy See, so that the confessor cannot absolve it.[76]

2. *Amendment in the Assigned Diocese.* Immediately upon dismissal, the Sacred Congregation of Religious, if it judges it expedient, will command the dismissed cleric to live in a particular diocese,[77] wearing the clerical garb and will communicate the causes of dismissal to the ordinary of that place.[78] In all cases of institutes

[73] Canon 671, n. 7.

[74] Blat, *De Religiosis*, n. 718.

[75] *De Censuris*, p. 220.

[76] Canon 2250, § 1.

[77] When the Sacred Congregation does not assign the dismissed cleric to any particular diocese, he should prove his amendment in some house of penance or monastery established or used for that purpose.

[78] Canon 671, n. 2.

of pontifical approval the Holy See will have reviewed the causes for dismissal of these clerics, before making the decision. With the return of the confirmed sentence, or of the confirmed decree, the Holy See may issue the command to the dismissed cleric. At the same time, the particular ordinary will be informed about the matter and about the causes of dismissal. Although the Holy See has the power to command a particular local ordinary to permit a dismissed religious to remain in his diocese during the term of probation, yet it seems that it would hardly do so without having first consulted him. In practice, the Holy See is aware of houses of penance for clerics in certain dioceses and the appointment of the particular diocese for the residence of the cleric may be based on that knowledge.

In institutes of diocesan approval the ordinary has the right of dismissal.[79] If he employs this power in reference to the religious clerics mentioned in canon 671, it seems that he could provide a place of penance for them in his own diocese, if he wished to do so. It seems that in such a case there would be no necessity to have recourse to the Holy See until the cleric proves that he is worthy of absolution from the censure which he incurred at dismissal.

When a dismissed cleric has received a command from the Holy See, he should proceed immediately to the determined diocese. From that time on he is under the guidance and direction of the ordinary of that place as regards his amendment and mode of life. The designated ordinary shall either send the dismissed religious to a house of penance or shall commit him to the care and vigilance of a holy and prudent priest.[80] This appointment shall be based on the knowledge that the ordinary has received concerning the crimes for which the cleric was dismissed. In making the appointment the ordinary shall issue certain injunctions concerning the manner of life that the delinquent shall live. It is within his power to enjoin that the cleric remain within a certain district. If he assigns the cleric to the care and vigilance of a priest, he may command that the delinquent should not go out without the permission of the assigned priest.

[79] Canon 650, § 2, n. 1.

[80] Canon 671, n. 4.

When the delinquent has been committed to the care and vigilance of a priest of the diocese, it is not necessary that the said priest receive all the information which has been given to the ordinary. Only such information should be communicated to him as will aid in the proper execution of his office. It will be the duty of this priest to report to the ordinary at regular intervals, concerning the dismissed cleric's obedience to the injunctions which have been imposed and concerning the life which the delinquent is living.

If the delinquent cleric shows himself disobedient after dismissal, he may incur further penalties. If he refuses to obey the command of the Holy See to live in a certain diocese wearing the garb of the secular clergy, he is by that very fact automatically deprived of the right of wearing the ecclesiastical garb.[81] After such conduct the religious institute is not obliged to render him any pecuniary aid. The canon does not demand that the Holy See should be informed of this further exhibition of incorrigibility, but certainly the religious superior should take great care to collect proofs of the cleric's disobedience, to state the penalties which have been incurred and to preserve the documents in the archives of the religious institute.

Schaefer points out that the automatic privation of the right of wearing the ecclesiastical garb incurred by this disobedience is not a perpetual privation.[82] Other authors state that the privation is a perpetual one and that it entails the full effects of the penalty of canon 2304.[83] The opinion of Schaefer is the correct one. In accordance with the strict interpretation which penal laws demand,[84] his opinion should be accepted, for there is no mention of a *perpetual* privation in the canon. Moreover, if the penalty were a perpetual privation, there would be no need to state, as the canon does, that the charitable subsidy of the religious institute should cease. If the privation were perpetual, that effect would be understood since it is an essential part of the penalty of canon 2304. The privation here concerned is a penalty which will endure as long as the delinquent

[81] Canon 671, n. 3.

[82] *De Religiosis,* n. 597, note 151.

[83] Blat, *Ius de Religiosis,* n. 718; Creusen-Garesché-Ellis, *Religious Men and Women in the Code,* n. 366.

[84] Canon 19.

continues in his bad dispositions and until he is reinstated. In the meantime he is deprived of the clerical privileges,[85] but apparently this privation signifies no more than their penal suspension.[86] The privation of the clerical privileges must be so understood for their penal loss is incurred only by degradation[87] or by the perpetual deprivation of the right of wearing the ecclesiastical garb.[88] When the cleric repents of his conduct, he must have recourse to the Holy See for a dispensation from the penalty incurred by his disobedience.

If after obeying the command of the Holy See and proceeding to the designated diocese the cleric then refuses to take up residence in the place determined by the assigned ordinary, he also incurs the identical penalty of automatic privation of the right of wearing the ecclesiastical garb. Again the religious institute is not obliged to continue the charitable maintenance.[89] The obedience, here concerned, is that which is shown to the initial injunctions of the assigned ordinary. It refers to the ordinary's designation of the place of penance or to the assignment of the priest who will assume the care and vigilance of the delinquent. Once the cleric has started to live in the assigned place, the law does not directly punish his disobedience, but it demands that the ordinary do so. The automatic penalty concerned here can be incurred only before the cleric goes to the place assigned. If he refuses outright to obey the assignment, or if accepts it and then deliberately never appears at the place, the penalty is incurred. These distinctions about the incurrence of the penalty are evident from a study of canon 671. After the penalty has been incurred the ordinary should then inform the religious superior and proof of the delinquent's disobedience and a statement of the penalties which he has incurred should be kept in the archives of the religious institute. There seems to be no obligation here of immediately informing the Holy See of this matter.

All that has been stated about the penalty incurred by the cleric

[85] Canon 2300.

[86] De Meester, *Compendium*, n. 1795, note 6; Findlay, *The Deposition and Degradation of Clerics*, p. 173.

[87] Canon 2305.

[88] Canon 2304.

[89] Canon 671, n. 4.

who has disobeyed the commands of the Holy See also applies here. The penalty is identical, since the canon states it only once,[90] and later makes reference to it.[91]

When the cleric has shown himself obedient both to the commands of the Holy See and to the initial injunctions of the ordinary, he is to continue to live in the assigned place. After he has resided there for a year, the ordinary must come to a decision about his future status.[92] Since the amendment under the assigned ordinary is the meaning of canon 671, n. 6, the year should begin only when the cleric has taken up his residence in the house of penance and not on the day of dismissal. Hence the starting point of the year is determined implicitly by law. It follows then, that the year is to be taken as it is in the calendar.[93] The starting point will hardly coincide with the beginning the day, so the first day will not be counted in the reckoning of the time. The year will expire when the day of the same date in the particular month of the following year is completed.[94] Thus if the cleric arrived at the house of penance during the day of November 4, 1942, the ordinary must settle his future status on November 5, 1943.

If during the year, the cleric has led so worthy a life that he can justly be considered amended, the ordinary shall recommend to the Holy See the cleric's petition for an absolution from the censure. It is solely the ordinary's place to decide whether the cleric should be considered truly amended. As long as the cleric has striven to lead a worthy life during the time of probation, he may proceed to draw up his petition to the Holy See. However, since the law demands that the petition be recommended by the ordinary, the cleric should first consult him on the advisability of the petition. It is possible that the ordinary may judge that, by special merit in a particular case, the cleric should petition for the absolution before the close of the year,[95] but it is evident that the initiative in such a case will be taken by the ordinary and not by the dismissed cleric.

[90] Canon 671, n. 3.

[91] Canon 671, n. 4.

[92] Canon 671, nn. 6, 7.

[93] Canon 34, § 3, n. 1.

[94] Canon 34, § 3, n. 3.

[95] Cf. *infra*, pp. 163-165.

Up to this point of amendment, all clerics, whether priests, deacons or subdeacons, referred to in canon 671 prove their amendment in the same manner.[96] If there is question of a deacon or subdeacon, mention should be made of the fact in the petition for absolution from the suspension.[97] When the absolution is returned from Rome, the Holy See will include special directions for these cases.

Once absolution has been granted by the Holy See, the religious priest has the right to offer the Holy Sacrifice, but only within the restrictions set by the ordinary. This much is allowed to the cleric by common law. Therefore the assigned ordinary cannot without a just cause entirely forbid him the celebration of Holy Mass in the diocese, but the ordinary can and should impose restrictions. The reason for this is that unless the Sacred Congregation of Religious expressly states otherwise for particular cases, the dismissed cleric becomes fully capable of exercising his Holy Orders only if he is finally received into his religious institute, or if he finds a bishop willing to receive him, and the Holy See is willing to grant a dispensation from his vows. It depends entirely on the free discretion and prudence of the ordinary whether the dismissed cleric should be allowed further exercise of the sacred ministry. An ordinary would be legally justified if he merely allowed the dismissed religious to celebrate Mass with certain restrictions and if he did not permit the cleric any other exercise of the ministry. Certainly in most cases the ordinary will be more liberal, especially if certain administrations of the cleric can be used to the good advantage of the faithful of the diocese.

At this point of amendment the charitable maintenance which the religious institute has been furnishing through the ordinary of the place may in cases entirely cease.[98] This would be so, if the cleric becomes able to support himself by the income which accrues from Mass stipends and from any other exercise of the sacred ministry.

[96] Cf. Jansen, *Ordensrecht*, p. 307; Palombo, *De Dimissione Religiosorum*, n. 205, b; Blat, *Ius de Religiosis*, n. 718.

[97] Canon 671, n. 7.

[98] Cf. canon 671, n. 7.

If the dismissed religious has not led a life worthy of a cleric during the year of his probative amendment, the ordinary may dismiss him from the place of penance and may deprive him of the charitable maintenance and of the right of wearing the ecclesiastical garb.[99] Considering the drastic effects of such action, it is apparent that serious delinquency is in question. However the new offenses of the religious during the time of penance, should not be considered merely in themselves in reference to these penalties. The offenses must be judged in reference to the previous conduct and life of the cleric, e. g., in the light of his repeated offenses, of the frequent admonitions of superiors, of the fruitless effects of previous penalties, of the dismissal from the religious institute, and of the efforts of the assigned ordinary to direct his amendment. The Code states that these penalties shall be inflicted if, in the judgment of the ordinary, the religious is not leading a worthy clerical life. If that is the ordinary's judgment after a year, he must inflict the penalties. Before the lapse of a year, he may inflict them if he judges that the seriousness of the case demands it.

No special process is demanded for the infliction of these penalties, for the Code leaves the matter entirely to the judgment of the ordinary.[100] Palombo states that these penalties are already contained implicitly and quasi-conditionally in the sentence or decree of dismissal. Moreover he states that there is no process required here as can be deduced *a pari* from the privation of the right of wearing the ecclesiastical garb, which is inflicted on clerics who are disobedient to the commands of the Holy See or of the assigned ordinary.[101]

It should be said that these penalties can hardly be connected with the decree of dismissal. First those who have the power to issue *merely* a decree of dismissal may have no external ecclesiastical jurisdiction and therefore cannot even implicitly include a canonical penalty in the decree. Secondly it cannot be said that the Holy See implicitly supplies that element to the decree by its confirmation, for the mind of the Holy See is expressed in canon

[99] Canon 671, n. 6.

[100] Cf. Beste, *Introductio in Codicem*, p. 454.

[101] *De Dimissione Religiosorum*, n. 205.

671. It should be sought in that canon, unless an additional penalty is expressly threatened in the confirmed decree of dismissal. On this account, it should rather be said that the concerned penalties have their source in the common law without reference to the decree or sentence of dismissal. Furthermore, concerning the infliction of these penalties, no argument is justified from the manner of imposition of the penalties discussed in the previous numbers of the canon. The wording of canon 671, n. 3 and n. 4, which impose the penalty upon clerics who have been disobedient to the Holy See or to the initial injunctions of the assigned ordinary, shows without doubt that the penalty takes effect automatically by intervention of law. In the present case, the wording of canon 671, n. 6, shows that the penalty has no automatic effect, but must be imposed by the ordinary, at his own judgment.[102] It must be said then, that no process is necessary in these cases, because by common law the ordinary himself is commanded to impose them according to his own judgment as to whether the dismissed cleric's actions warrant them.

Again the penalty concerned here is not the perpetual privation of the right of wearing the ecclesiastical garb. The penalty is the identical sanction mentioned in two of the previous numbers of the same canon.[103] Although Schaefer states expressly in the two former instances that the penalty is not perpetual, he is of the opinion that the penalty concerned here is a perpetual privation for he refers to canon 2304.[104] It seems evident that the three penalties of the privation of the right of wearing the ecclesiastical garb mentioned in this canon are identical. This is stated not concerning their mode of infliction, but concerning their effects. Certainly the religious who has attempted amendment for a time and who has shown himself to be unworthy can hardly be said to be more guilty than the religious who did not attempt to amend at all. Moreover there is nothing stated in the canon that would show that a per-

[102] ". . . iudicio ordinarii, privetur caritativo subsidio, eiiciatur e domo poenitentiae eique auferatur ius deferendi habitum ecclesiasticum ab ipso ordinario. . . ."—Canon 671, n. 6.

[103] Canon 671, nn. 3, 4.

[104] *De Religiosis*, n. 597.

petual privation is meant. Why then, should the penalty be made more severe with regard to the cleric which the ordinary dismisses after attempted amendment than with regard to one who made no attempt at all? It should, therefore, be stated that the penalty which such a cleric incurs is not the perpetual privation of the ecclesiastical garb, any more than the penalties previously mentioned in the canon.

CHAPTER VIII

THE OBLIGATIONS OF THE RELIGIOUS INSTITUTE AND OF THE ASSIGNED ORDINARY

Article I. The Obligations of the Religious Institute

Since the bond between the institute and the dismissed religious still persists as long as the religious is not dispensed from the vows, the institute is not entirely free of all obligations toward the dismissed religious. Superiors then, in accordance with Christ-like zeal will endeavor to keep in touch with their dismissed subjects, at least until they are dispensed from their religious vows. They should spur them on to prove their amendment, if there is hope for return to the institute. If the latter supposition is not possible, the religious superiors will urge them to take the proper measures for establishment outside the religious life, so that they may strive after perfection according to their new state.

Despite the fact that the Holy See is immediately aware of the dismissal in some cases, through its confirmation of the decree or of the sentence, yet the religious institute must report on the fact of dismissal in its quinquennial report. This concerns the report that must be made by the General Moderators, both men and women, of institutes of pontifical approval whose members profess simple vows.[1] In the official questionnaire,[2] the following points are included:

> "32. Have the prescriptions of the Sacred Canons and the Constitutions of the Institute been always observed, according to the circumstances of each case, in the dismissal of members.
>
> "33. Has any one (except in the case of urgency treated of in canons 653 and 668) been dismissed or left the Institute:

[1] S. C. de Rel., decr. *Sancitum est,* 8 mart. 1922—*AAS,* XIV (1922), 161-163.

[2] S. C. de Rel., instruc., 25 mart. 1922—*AAS,* XIV (1922), 278-286. There is also an official English Translation of the questionnaire, S. C. de Rel., instruc., 1 sept. 1923—*AAS,* XV (1923), 459-466; also in *IER,* XXII (1923), 653-660.

"(a) before having received from the Holy See, in the case of perpetually professed men, the confirmation of the sentence or decree; or, in the case of perpetually professed Sisters, before having received the decision of the same Apostolic See;

"(b) pending appeal to the Holy See, in the case of those temporarily professed;

"(c) without first having obtained a dispensation, asked for by the religious himself, from the vows made." [3]

It may now be asked if the religious institute is obliged in any way to support the dismissed religious. The Code states nothing about pecuniary assistance from the funds of the religious institute, except in two canons, namely in canon 643, § 2, which refers to a charitable subsidy for women religious, and in canon 671, n. 5, which refers to the charitable maintenance of dismissed clerics who are proving their amendment. No other dismissed religious has a legal right to demand any assistance from the religious institute.[4] Lack of sustenance or support is one of the punishments involved in dismissal. It is meant primarily as an incentive to urge the dismissed subject to repent and to return.

Concerning dismissed men religious in particular, the Code makes no mention of any pecuniary assistance for them even for the journey from the convent after dismissal. The only exception in this matter is the charitable maintenance which is to be given to dismissed clerics who are obedient to the commands of the Holy See and who wish to prove their amendment.[5] With all other dismissed clerics and with all dismissed men religious who are not clerics, dismissal may possibly leave them in a state of extreme want. Those especially who have taken solemn vows will likely have no means of support as they will ordinarily have no property of their own. Clerics dismissed after perpetual profession will have no benefices outside the religious institute. Benefices they formerly possessed became vacant one year after the first profession was made, if they were parochial benefices. All other benefices became vacant three years after the first profession.[6] Certainly it is equitable then that

[3] Official English Translation—*AAS*, XV (1923), 461.

[4] Goyeneche, *De Religiosis*, n. 126; Fanfani, *De Iure Religiosorum*, n. 519; Pejška, *Ius Canonicum Religiosorum*, p. 197; Schaefer, *De Religiosis*, n. 596.

[5] Canon 671, n. 5.

[6] Canon 584.

the religious institute should not retain any of the existing goods which the religious has brought to the institute with him.[7] It is also to be recommended out of charity and prudence that sufficient funds be given to such religious, who have no means of support, to enable them to return home safely and properly and to establish themselves outside the monastery. Whether there is an obligation in equity in regard to such funds may well be disputed, considering the serious offenses of the religious and his incorrigible infractions of the contract made at profession to live according to the rules and constitutions of the institute. Some religious institutes of men have considered this matter in their constitutions. Certain constitutions state that members departing from the institute should be provided with what is necessary for a safe journey home,[8] and for proper maintenance during a certain period,[9] unless they have sufficient money from other sources. Sometimes constitutions merely demand that the institute give back to departing subjects such goods as they brought with them, but without interest.[10] The obligations of extending a charitable subsidy and a charitable maintenance and the obligation of restoring the dowry will now be treated under separated headings.

A. *The Restoration of the Dowry*

Canon 551, § 1. Dos religiosae professae sive voto rum sollemnium sive votorum simplicium quavis de causa discedenti integra restituenda est sine fructibus iam maturis.[11]

[7] Prümmer, *Manuale Iuris Canonici,* Q. 254.

[8] *Constitutiones Congregationis Missionariorum de Mariannhill* (1936), nn. 94, 111; *Constitutions of the Institute of the Brothers of the Sacred Heart* (Metuchen, N. J., 1928), n. 243; *Regulae ac Praescriptiones a variis Capitulis generalibus praesertim a decimo exaratae accedit Statutum pro Missionibus* (Congregatio Sacerdotum a Sacro Corde Jesu), (Romae: apud Curiam Generalitiam, 1934), n. 292; *Constitutions of the Institute of the Marist Brothers of the Schools or Little Brothers of Mary* (Belgium, 1935), Art. 110.

[9] *Constitutions of the Institute of the Brothers of the Sacred Heart, loc. cit.*

[10] *Constitutions of the Brothers of Christian Doctrine* (New Jersey, 1936), Part I, n. 70.

[11] Canon 551, § 1. If, from whatever cause a professed religious with either

The words *"quavis de causa discedenti"* of canon 551, § 1, certainly include the departure of dismissal. It is evident from the purpose of this law that the above clause should be interpreted broadly and not restricted to absolute and complete departure as would follow from a dispensation from the religious vows. Thus the authors state that there would be a departure according to this canon whether a woman religious leaves voluntarily or under compulsion.[12]

The opinion that dismissal after profession of perpetual vows is a departure wherein the juridical bond between the religious and the institute is completely and perpetually severed, so that the religious is no longer in any sense a member of the organization, has been advanced as a reason why dismissal is included in the general wording of this canon.[13] Certainly this reason cannot be upheld for the juridical bond between the religious and the institute is not completely and perpetually severed in dismissal. The dismissed religious is certainly still a religious and also a member of his organization.[14]

As Kealy well remarks, it is not apparent that the expression *"quavis de causa discedenti"* of this canon presupposes a juridical dissolution of the bond.[15] The reasons advanced then, for the inclusion of dismissal in the above cited canon are the following. The dowry is a definite sum of money, or its equivalent, paid by the postulant to a convent in which she wishes to make her profession. The dowry is destined primarily for her support as long as she re-

solemn or simple vows leaves the institute, her dowry must be returned to her intact, but not the interest already derived therefrom.—Authorized English Translation.

[12] Toso, *Commentaria Minora,* Lib. II, pars II, p. 111; Fanfani, *De Iure Religiosorum,* n. 171; Vromant, *De Bonis Ecclesiae Temporalibus ad Usum praesertim Missionariorum et Religiosorum* (Louvain: Desbarax, 1927), n. 256 (hereafter to be cited as *De Bonis Ecclesiae Temporalibus*); Chelodi, *Ius de Personis,* n. 267; Gerster, *Ius Religiosorum,* p. 88; Kealy, *Dowry of Women Religious,* p. 109; Larraona, "Commentarium Codicis,"—*CpRM,* XXI (1940), 146.

[13] Kealy, *op. cit.,* pp. 109-110.

[14] Cf. *supra,* p. 1-4.

[15] *Op. cit.,* pp. 113-115.

mains in the institute.[16] The purpose of the dowry therefore ceases in case of dismissal, for the dismissed woman religious no longer enjoys the support of the religious institute, but is burdened with the obligation of self-support.

Another argument is taken from related canons in the Code. It is expressed in canon 652, § 3, that the charitable subsidy mentioned in canon 643, § 2, must be extended to a woman religious who has been dismissed after profession of solemn vows, or of simple perpetual vows, in institutes of pontifical approval. From an *a pari* argument a charitable subsidy must also be extended to women religious dismissed from institutes of diocesan approval, even though canon 652 states nothing explicitly about a charitable subsidy in reference to them.[17] Nothing is said in canon 652, § 3, about the woman religious being dispensed from the vows in dismissal. Now it is evident that the legislator is here treating of an obligation which is over and above the obligation of returning the dowry. Therefore, *a fortiori* the dowry should be returned to the dismissed. For these reasons it is stated that the general wording of canon 551, § 1, includes *dismissed* women religious as being entitled to the return of their dowry. Hence Larraona includes under the general clause of this canon as a title for the return of the dowry not only a departure which is complete and absolute because of the cessation of the religious vows, but also dismissal, whether in that dismissal the cessation of the vows is accomplished or not.[18] And all the authors consistently adhere to this opinion, many explicitly including dismissal under the general clause of canon 551, § 1.[19]

[16] Battandier, *Guide canonique pour les constitutions de instituts à voeux simples* (6. ed., Paris, 1923), n. 173; Cappello, *Summa Iuris Canonici*, II, n. 604; Vromant, *De Bonis Ecclesiae Temporalibus*, n. 251; Chelodi, *Ius de Personis*, n. 267; Beste, *Introductio in Codicem*, p. 367; Vermeersch-Creusen, *Epitome*, I. n. 698; De Meester, *Compendium*, n. 436; Prümmer, *Manuale Iuris Canonici*, Q. 208; Augustine, *A Commentary*, III, 224; Wernz-Vidal, *De Religiosis*, n. 267; Coronata, *Institutiones*, n. 577; Kealy, *Dowry of Women Religious*, p. 1; Fanfani, *De Iure Religiosorum*, n. 167.

[17] Palombo, *De Dimissione Religiosorum*, n. 188.

[18] "Commentarium Codicis,"—*CpR*, XXI (1940), 146.

[19] Fanfani, *De Iure Religiosorum*, n. 171; Palombo, *De Dimissione Religiosorum*, n. 188; Pejška, *Ius Canonicum Religiosorum*, p. 197; Blat, *Ius de Religiosis*, n. 341; Farrell, *The Rights and Duties of the Local Ordinary Regarding*

It may be noted here that the dowry should not be restored in the case of provisional dismissal,[20] until the matter has been settled by the Holy See.[21] In the meantime the religious institute must contribute to the support of the dismissed Sister. As long as it is fulfilling this obligation, it need not even restore the income of the dowry as such. When the Holy See determines the status of the delinquent religious, the matter of the dowry will be finally settled.

According to canon 551, § 1, the fruits of the dowry which have already matured from investment [22] should not be restored to the dismissed woman religious. From the definition and purpose of the dowry it is evident that the religious institute has an absolute title of ownership to the income from the invested dowry up till the moment of dismissal. Such income is juridically distinct from the capital and accrues irrevocably to the religious institute.[23]

The obligation of restoring the dowry to the dismissed woman religious has equal application to solemn and simple vow institutes. It is an obligation not of equity or charity but an obligation of justice. And it should be noted that if superioresses of any institute, even exempt organizations, withhold this dowry from the dismissed person contrary to canon 551, § 1, they shall be punished by the local ordinary conformably to the gravity of the offense, even by deposition from office,[24] if that be deemed necessary.[25] The Holy

Congregations of Women Religious of Pontifical Approval, The Catholic University of America Canon Law Studies, n. 128 (Washington, D. C.: The Catholic University of America Press, 1941), p. 145; Goyeneche, *De Religiosis,* n. 126; Maroto, "Annotationes,"—*CpR,* V (1924), 321-322; Schaefer, *De Religiosis,* n. 596. Notice that this interpretation was expressed in the explanatory body of a question which was submitted to the Holy See in reference to supplementing the sum of the dowry in certain cases. The question commenced, "Ad normam cc. 551 et 643 Religiosa professa, e Religione egrediens aut *ex ea eadem dimissa,* si quidem dotem attulerit, eam, absque fructibus iam maturis, recipiendi ius habet. . . ."—S. C. de Rel., resp. 2 mart. 1924—*AAS,* XVI (1924), 165.

20 Canon 653.

21 Cf. Larraona, "Commentarium Codicis,"—*CpR,* XXI (1940), 147.

22 Canon 549.

23 Kealy, *op. cit.,* p. 119.

24 Canon 2412, n. 1.

25 Farrell, *op. cit.,* p. 145; Ayrinhac-Lydon, *Penal Legislation in the New Code of Canon Law* (New York: Benziger Bros., 1936), n. 388.

See is solicitous concerning the fulfillment of this law, requiring the restoration of the dowry to the dismissed, since the thirty-fourth question of the quinquennial report which must be submitted by institutes of pontifical approval, demands an explicit statement on the observance of this law.[26]

A difficulty presents itself in regard to the dismissal of a nun who professed solemn vows before the promulgation of the new Code. Pre-Code authors generally agreed that from the moment of solemn profession, the dowry was acquired irrevocably by the monastery, irrespective of whether the nun persevered in the institute or not.[27] The Holy See also recognized this right, as is evident in several cases brought before the Sacred Congregation of Bishops and Regulars.[28] Now since true acquisition took place according to the discipline of the old law, it may be asked if the monastery is bound to restore an acquired dowry to a nun who is dismissed after the promulgation of the Code.

In virtue of canon 4, the right of the monastery is protected against the obligation of restoring the dowry,[29] at the dismissal of such a nun. According to canon 4, acquired rights, acknowledged by the Holy See before the Code, remain in force unless they are explicitly revoked by the present law. The question must be settled on the principle of acquired rights. This statement stands even though history attests that the jurisprudence of the Sacred Congregation of Bishops and Regulars gradually showed an increasing

[26] "(In Institutis sororum). Num egressis quacumque de causa dos, quomodolibet constituta, integre tradita fuerit, una cum supellectili quam ad Institutum attulerant, in eo statu in quo tempore egressus reperiebatur."—S. C. de Rel., instruct., 25 mart. 1922, n. 34—*AAS*, XIV (1922), 280. There is an official translation of this questionnaire in *AAS*, XV (1923), 459-466, and in *IER*, XXII (1923), 653-660.

[27] Suarez, Tract. VIII, lib. III, c. XIV, n. 15; Ferraris, *Prompta Bibliotheca*, s. v. "Moniales," II, n. 51; Piatus Montensis, *Praelectiones Juris Regularis*, I, q. 93.

[28] *Baren. Seu Tranen*, 30 maii 1856—Bizzarri, pp. 645-648; *Viterbien*, 2 aug. 1580; *Neapolitana*, 20 iul 1583; *Paduana*, 20 mart. 1601; *Trapien*, 25 febr. 1603; *Concardien.*, 4 mart. 1603; *Massanen*, 29 apr. 1603; *Carmelitar. discal.*, 3 aug. 1635—Ferraris, *Prompta Bibliotheca*, s. v. "Moniales," II, n. 50. These cases refer to transfer from one monastery to another, or from one institute to another.

[29] Canon 551, § 1.

tendency in favor of the restoration of the dowry. At the beginning of the present century, authors pointed out that although the dowry was acquired by the monastery at solemn profession, yet equity demanded restoration of it in certain cases. Vermeersch testified that the Sacred Congregation was accustomed to prescribe the restoration of the dowry to nuns who were without means of support.[30] Certainly this principle found application in the dismissal of nuns after solemn profession, but few cases can be cited for the simple reason that the dismissal of such religious was a very rare occurrence. There is a record of a case in 1796, in which the Sacred Congregation of Bishops and Regulars dismissed a nun after solemn profession and then prescribed the restoration of the dowry.[31] It seems that the basis of such restoration should be merely an obligation in equity and an obligation of obedience to the Holy See, not an obligation in justice, since it was admitted that the monastery had acquired the dowry from the moment of solemn profession.

Therefore although certain authors have proposed the opinion that the restoration of the dowry required by canon 551, § 1, is also to be applied to women religious who were solemnly professed before the Code,[32] the opposite opinion seems to be the correct one.[33] The obligation of canon 551, § 1, is an obligation in justice, so it can hardly be applied to monasteries which have legitimately acquired the dowry before the promulgation of the Code.

It is true that the question is not a very practical one at this late date, but if such a nun were dismissed according to the statutes of the present law, an obligation of *equity* might demand the restoration of the dowry. Without doubt, it must be said that such dismissed nuns have a right to the charitable subsidy required by the

[30] *De Religiosis Institutis et Personis* (4. ed., 2 vols., Brugis, 1907-1909), Tom. I, pars IV, sect. I, c. II, n. 181.

[31] S. C. Ep. et Reg., *Fulginaten.*, mart. 1796—*Fontes,* n. 1889.

[32] Fuchs, "Rückgabe der Mitgift an die Ausscheidende Klosterfrau,"—*ThPrQs,* LXXXVIII (1935), 364-365; Goyeneche, "Consultationes,"—*CpR,* V (1924), 392; Coronata, *Institutiones,* n. 577.

[33] Vermeersch-Creusen, *Epitome,* I, n. 702; D'Ambrosio, De Dote Monialis ante Codicis Promulgationem Solemniter Professae et ad aliud Monasterium post Codicem Transeuntis,"—*Apollinaris,* I (1928), 297-300; Wernz-Vidal, *De Religiosis,* p. 226, note 21; Kealy, *Dowry of Women Religious,* pp. 133-134.

present law, whereby they may be able to return home in a safe and proper manner and may be able to provide for themselves for a certain period.[34] If the present legislation demands the payment of this charitable subsidy for those who have been received without the dowry, it *a fortiori* would apply to monasteries which have already acquired the dowry under pre-Code discipline. This obligation of charity would certainly be present even though the Sacred Congregation would state nothing about the dowry or the charitable subsidy in its decree of dismissal.

The above question does not refer to any women religious who have made profession after the promulgation of the Code. Under present legislation, it is clear that the dowry is acquired irrevocably only at the time of the death of the religious.[35] In like manner, the question has no reference to Sisters who professed simple vows before May 19, 1918, for in pre-Code law and practice, the dowry was restored to them at dismissal.[36]

B. *Obligations Supplementary to the Restoration of the Dowry*

It has been stated that the obligation to restore the dowry is an obligation in justice. The religious institute has a further obligation in charity to extend funds in certain circumstances, which funds are over and above the sum of the dowry. Thus the Code demands that if a woman religious has been received without a dowry,[37] and if she cannot provide for herself out of her own goods, the religious organization should give her out of charity that which is required for the safe and proper return to her home, and also that it should provide for her for a certain period with the means for a decent livelihood, in accordance with natural equity.[38] Moreover, the Sacred Congregation of Religious has decided that when the dowry is so small a sum that it is insufficient for the proper return

[34] Canon 643, § 2.

[35] Canon 548.

[36] S. C. C., *Civitatis Castellanae*, 3 mart. 1792—*Fontes*, n. 3875; *Normae* (1901), Art. 95; S. C. Ep. et Reg., decr. *Perpensis*, 3 maii 1902, art. 13—*Fontes*, n. 2039.

[37] Canon 547, §§ 3, 4.

[38] Canons 643, § 2; 652, §§ 2, 3.

of the woman religious to her home, or for her sustenance during a certain period, the religious organization is not freed from all obligation merely by returning the dowry. It must supply in charity what is necessary for the above purposes.[39] The constitutions of the religious institute will decide whether the province or house to which the religious is attached will be immediately responsible for the discharge of these obligations.[40]

Neither of these obligations, namely, to supply funds when no dowry is present or to supplement the dowry, is binding when the dismissed religious has goods of her own which she can use after dismissal.[41] Vermeersch-Creusen propose as the minimum equitable sum, according to the norms of canon 643, § 2, an amount between one hundred and fifty and two hundred dollars.[42] No such sum can be stated in the case of dismissal. If a dismissed woman religious lives in the vicinity of the convent which dismissed her, as happens frequently in the United States, and if such a dismissed person has the opportunity to acquire a position in the world almost immediately, there is no obligation of granting a sum even approaching the amount stated by Vermeersch-Creusen.

The destination of the dismissed woman religious and the possibility of future employment within a certain time, must be discussed by the dismissing superioress and the subject who is dismissed, for the Code speaks of mutual consent in reference to this obligation.[43] Where no satisfactory agreement can be reached it is the place of the local ordinary to decide the matter. The same is true if difficulties arise concerning the arrangement after dismissal. The local ordinary spoken of is the ordinary of the place of the religious house from which the woman religious was dismissed.[44] This is the law even if there is question of an exempt religious organization.[45]

[39] S. C. de Rel., resp., 2 mart. 1924—*AAS*, XVI (1924), 165-166.

[40] Berutti, *De Religiosis*, n. 155, II.

[41] Berutti, *loc. cit.*

[42] *Epitome*, I, n. 801.

[43] Canon 643, § 2.

[44] Palombo, *De Dimissione Religiosorum*, n. 188; Berutti, *De Religiosis*, n. 155, II.

[45] Berutti, *loc. cit.*; Chelodi, *Ius de Personis*, n. 281.

Canon 643, § 2, states that provision be made for the departing religious *for a certain period of time.* In any case this help which is given by the former community should never have the character of a pension for life.[46] The period of such provision is determined at the time of dismissal and the lump sum is then given to the dismissed religious. A further obligation in charity may arise if the dismissed woman religious fails to find employment or a means of support, but there is no obligation present if she neglects to accept suitable work when it is procurable or if she has squandered the amount given for the determined period. If the dismissed religious should be old and infirm and without resources, and if it is impossible for her to find relatives or friends with whom she may live in the world, she must agree to enter a suitable institute intended for persons of that condition.[47] These prescriptions of the obligations supplementary to the restoration of the dowry should always be observed in dismissal, even though the Sacred Congregation of Religious in the decree of dismissal should state nothing concerning these matters.[48] The Sacred Congregation demands a statement on the observance of these prescriptions when the Supreme Moderators of religious institutes of pontifical approval with simple vows make their quinquennial report.[49]

Above all it should be remembered that these obligations are only temporary and should not be prolonged. Lack of support from the religious institute is one of the punishments of dismissal and therefore if this temporary provision should become a regular means of support over a long period, one of the purposes of dismissal, namely, the amendment of the guilty party, might be defeated. There would be little incentive to conversion and to return to the religious life if the dismissed subject could remain

[46] Creusen-Garesché-Ellis, *Religious Men and Women in the Code,* n. 338.

[47] Creusen-Garesché-Ellis, *Religious Men and Women in the Code,* n. 338.

[48] Palombo, *De Dimissione Religiosorum,* n. 188.

[49] "Num iis quae, sine dote deceptae, ex propriis bonis sibimet providere non valebant, in casu eggressus ex Instituto, necessaria ex caritate suppeditata fuerint, quibus modo tuto ac convenienti domum redire et per aliquod tempus honeste vivere potuerint."—S. C. de Rel., instruc., 25 mart. 1922, n. 35—*AAS,* XIV (1922), 280.

freely in the world, enjoying the support of the religious institute which dismissed her.

C. *Charitable Maintenance of Clerics*

The charitable maintenance of dismissed clerics which is expressly prescribed by law refers only to those religious who have been dismissed for the less serious crimes. If such a religious obeys the commands of the Holy See and takes up his residence in the determined diocese, the religious institute shall in charity render him pecuniary air through the assigned ordinary.[50] The extent of this support is merely for those things which are necessary for the proper maintenance of life. Thus the religious institute is obliged to meet the expenses of the dismissed cleric in regard to clothing, board and lodging. It must pay the debts arising from hospital care or medical treatment, if he should become ill. It must bear the expenses of burial, if he should die in the assigned diocese. However, it has no responsibility for any debts which the religious contracts in making unnecessary or superfluous expenditures.

The quantity of the maintenance of the cleric by the religious institute is not determined by law. At the time of dismissal the religious is under an obligation of justice to reveal whether he has any means of livelihood, when he and the religious superior discuss the question. If they cannot come to a mutual agreement on the matter, no arbiter is determined by law, but a norm may be taken from a similar instance in the Code.[51] With regard to the charitable subsidy which is required for a dismissed Sister, who has been received without a dowry, the Code designates the local ordinary as the judge in any disputes that may arise.[52] This ordinary is the ordinary of the place of the house from which the woman religious is dismissed,[53] even when there is question of dismissal from an exempt organization.[54] It seems that the same prescription may

[50] Canon 671, n. 5.

[51] Canon 20.

[52] Canon 643, § 2.

[53] Palombo, *De Dimissione Religiosorum*, n. 188; Berutti, *De Religiosis*, n. 155, II.

[54] Berutti, *loc. cit.*; Chelodi, *Ius de Personis*, n. 128.

be applied to disputes which may arise in reference to the maintenance of a dismissed cleric.[55]

It might be suggested that preferably the assigned ordinary should settle the matter since the Holy See has placed him in a special way over the dismissed cleric. However, this opinion is opposed for the following reason. Since the assigned ordinary will have so important a part in the future direction of the cleric's amendment, it would seem more profitable to the cleric that another ordinary should settle the dispute. By such a measure there would be no danger of the cleric's entering upon the period of amendment with prejudice or misgivings toward the assigned ordinary. In most cases, it will so happen that the assigned ordinary and the local ordinary suggested will not be the same person. It is therefore stated that the ordinary of the place of the house from which the dismissal takes place should judge such disputes, even when there is question of religious organizations which are exempt. This opinion can be held more legitimately than the opinion favoring the assigned ordinary, since it can be supported by argument from a similar case in law.

The obligation of maintaining dismissed clerics is imposed on the religious institute always on one condition, namely, that the dismissed cleric has no other means of support. When a cleric is dismissed after the profession of simple vows, he may possess property in his own name. Royalties and civil pensions, bonuses and other payments may be addressed to all religious personally at regular intervals, whether they have professed solemn or simple vows.[56] In such cases, provided these means are sufficient for the proper maintenance of the dismissed cleric, there is no obligation on the religious institute to supply anything.[57]

[55] Goyeneche, *De Religiosis*, n. 129; Coronata, *Institutiones*, n. 660; Schaefer, *De Religiosis*, n. 597. Palombo states that these disputes should be referred to the Sacred Congregation of Religious. He also deduces his opinion from canon 643, § 2.—*op. cit.*, n. 203.

[56] In all of these cases, the dismissed religious may not have the right of dominion over these goods, but permission to use and administer them is given in an implicit and general permission at dismissal.

[57] Cocchi, *De Religiosis et Laicis*, n. 158; Goyeneche, *De Religiosis*, n. 129; Jansen, *Ordensrecht*, p. 306; Augustine, *A Commentary*, III, 413; Blat, *Ius de Religiosis*, n. 718; Schaefer, *De Religiosis*, n. 597, note 152.

If the dismissed cleric concerned has no means of self-support, this obligation of maintenance must be borne by the religious institute from the moment of dismissal. Thus all expenses of travel to the assigned place must be borne by the religious institute. It would seem that the law infers that the maintenance should be extended only through the assigned ordinary.[58] However, canon 671, n. 3, presupposes that the religious institute is under obligation as long as the cleric obeys the commands of the Holy See. Therefore the obligation is present even before he reaches the assigned diocese.[59]

The obligation ceases for a number of reasons. First it must be stated that if the religious leads a worthy life during his time of probative amendment, and if he cannot meet his necessary expenses, the obligation never ceases until he is received back into the institute, or until the Holy See dispenses him from his vows. The obligation will hardly ever extend for this entire time. Pejška has expressly stated that from the text of the canon, it may clearly be deduced that the charitable maintenance can never be prolonged for more than the period of a year.[60] Certainly, if the limitations placed on the dismissed clerics are so strict that they do not allow for a sufficient income, the obligation of the religious institute still remains. This seems to be the sense of the canon rather than the opinion which Pejška has expressed.[61] The obligation of the institute is suspended before the religious returns, (a) if he does not obey the commands of the Holy See to prove his amendment in a certain diocese; [62] (b) if the religious does not obey the ordinary's assignment to a house of penance or to the care and vigilance of a certain priest; [63] (c) if he does not lead a life worthy of a cleric and the ordinary deprives him of the charitable maintenance; [64] (d) if he, by the exercise of the sacred ministry, acquires the necessary means for his livelihood.[65] When the cleric has been absolved from sus-

[58] Canon 671, n. 5.

[59] Blat, *loc. cit.*

[60] *Ius Canonicum Religiosorum,* p. 197.

[61] Cf. Fanfani, *De Iure Religiosorum,* n. 519.

[62] Canon 671, n. 3.

[63] Canon 671, n. 4.

[64] Canon 671, n. 6.

[65] Canon 671, n. 6.

pension, and can legitimately exercise his Orders, the religious institute is not freed from the obligation by that very fact. Only if the cleric acquires sufficient means for livelihood from the exercise of his Orders will the obligation cease.

It is the assigned ordinary who has immediate control over the maintenance concerned.[66] The reason for this prescription of law is that maintenance should be extended only as long as there is hope of amendment and as long as the religious is seriously striving to prove his good dispositions. The assigned ordinary is the immediate judge of these matters. Therefore he should have the power to deprive the religious of the charitable maintenance immediately if he does not live up to his sacred calling.

It is evident that in the Code more consideration is shown for dismissed clerics who are sincere about their amendment than was shown to like clerics in the pre-Code discipline. Formerly it was the common opinion that the religious institute was obliged to maintain no religious who was justly dismissed.[67] The obligation of maintenance, as expressed in the present legislation, may seem rather burdensome for the religious community, after the repeated crimes and incorrigibility of the religious. However, if one considers that the delinquent member of the secular clergy must be sustained by his bishop while at least some hope of amendment appears,[67a] then it seems only proper that the same principle should be applied to the religious institute, when there is question of clerics in like condition.[68]

D. *The Obligation to Accept the Dismissed Religious*

In the explanation of the obligation to return to the religious institute, a twofold source of obligation was postulated. The same division is now applied to the obligation of the institute to accept the amended religious. This obligation can arise either from common law or from the bond of religious profession. Each of these sources of obligation will now be treated.

[66] Canon 671, n. 5.

[67] Cf. *supra*, p. 36.

[67a] Cf. canons 2303, § 2; 2304.

[68] Prümmer, *Manuale Iuris Canonici*, Q. 264.

1. *The Obligation from Canon Law.* In the discussion on the extent of the obligation of canon 672, § 1,[69] the following conclusion was attained. The canon refers only to dismissed clerical religious in Holy Orders. Furthermore, it does not apply to those who have been automatically dismissed,[70] and it is more probable that it does not refer to those clerical religious in Holy Orders who have been dismissed because of the crimes intimated in canon 670.[71]

Therefore the obligation of readmittance expressed in canon 672, § 1, applies only to clerics in major orders who have been dismissed for the less serious crimes. If such clerics have given signs of true amendment for a period of three years, the religious institute is obliged to receive them back immediately upon the lapse of that time, provided no serious reason stands in the way of readmittance.[72] The judgment of the ordinary assigned for the dismissed religious will be the main factor in the evidence of full amendment. Moreover, the religious institute may also make further investigations into the life of the dismissed cleric, if it wishes to do so.

The obligation of accepting the cleric arises only after a period of three full years computed from the date of dismissal.[73] This is said of those clerics who have shown obedience to the Holy See and to the assigned ordinary from the time of dismissal.[74] Before the lapse of the three year period, there is no obligation of receiving the cleric, no matter how perfect are the signs of amendment.[75] It may be asked if the dismissed religious may be accepted before the period of three years expires. In some cases the religious institute may readmit the cleric before the stated time,[76] but these would be cases of special merit in amendment. No special permission would be needed for this action, since in such cases it is neither against the injunctions of canon 672, § 1, nor against the purpose of dismissal.

[69] Cf. *supra,* pp. 98-108.

[70] P. C. I., 30 iul. 1934—*AAS,* XXVI (1934), 494.

[71] Cf. *supra,* pp. 103-108.

[72] Canon 672, § 1.

[73] Blat, *Ius de Religiosis,* n. 720.

[74] If they have been disobedient and have been deprived of the ecclesiastical garb, the Holy See will give special directions for their amendment.

[75] Coronata, *Institutiones,* n. 658.

[76] Goyeneche, *De Religiosis,* n. 130; Schaefer, *De Religiosis,* n. 598.

It is not contrary to canon 672, § 1, because that canon merely states when the obligation of readmitting the cleric arises. Hence if the institute wishes to accept the cleric before it is legally obliged to, it is failing in no way against the canon. Furthermore, it is not failing against the purpose of dismissal, provided it is satisfied that the life which the dismissed cleric has led since dismissal vouches for his complete and proved amendment.

Nevertheless, except in extraordinary cases, this action is not to be recommended. Even though the cleric himself testifies to genuine sorrow for his crimes and for the scandal he has caused in the religious community; even though he vouches that he has come to a new realization of the sacredness of his vocation; even though he promises that his future life will in no way cause disedification to his confreres and even though the life which he has led since his dismissal testifies to his sincerity, readmittance should be delayed. The religious institute should demand not only sincere amendment, but *complete* and *proved* amendment. The repeated crimes of the cleric and the futility of the superior's former warnings have placed the cleric under suspicion. It will be the better procedure in the greater majority of cases to let the full term of three years lapse before readmittance is allowed.

If in any case, the religious institute judges that there is a grave cause why the religious cleric should not return to the communal life, the matter should be referred to the Holy See. It is not the place of the religious superiors to inform these dismissed clerics, or even lay religious, that they will never be allowed to return no matter how complete their reformation. To dismiss a religious with such an impression may be a serious injustice. Certainly a cleric will be greatly hampered in the fulfillment of his religious obligations and in observing the rigid prescriptions of canon 671 if he has been thus informed by his superiors. It is solely the place of the Holy See to state that acceptance will not be allowed because of grave reasons against it. When the Holy See decides this point, it will also determine the future status of the cleric. Reasons which may be considered grave enough to refer to the Holy See will be treated in the following section. Suffice it to add here that a more serious reason is required for not wishing to readmit a cleric than is required in regard to a dismissed lay religious.[77]

2. *The Obligation Arising from the Bond of Religious Profession.* The following is stated concerning those clerics who are dismissed because of the crimes intimated in canon 670. The Pontifical Commission decided in 1934 that canon 672, § 1, is not to be extended to religious who are automatically dismissed.[78] From this decision, it can be stated with certainty that there is no obligation of readmitting clerics who have been automatically dismissed, even though they have given signs of complete amendment for a period of three years. Regarding the other clerics referred to in canon 670, it is more probable that canon 672, § 1, does not refer to them.[79] Therefore, neither has the institute any obligation of receiving them, even though they have given signs of amendment for three years.

However, it cannot be stated that the religious institute is entirely free from the obligation of ever accepting these dismissed clerics. The religious institute is still bound by the obligation of the bilateral contract made at the profession of these clerics. The obligations of that contract remain as long as the cleric is bound by the religious vows. Furthermore, it is not possible for dismissal to destroy the full obligation of the bilateral contract of religious profession, unless the Holy See or Apostolic indults give it that effect. Dismissal in itself is not meant to separate the religious completely from the institute. One of its purposes is to take the last drastic step in an effort to correct the delinquent as a religious. Therefore, if he corrects himself and proves his amendment, that purpose of dismissal is attained and the religious institute is obliged to readmit him. Sometimes this obligation may be almost impossible of fulfillment, *e. g.*, when the cleric has been degraded, but yet, it remains as long as the cleric is bound by the religious vows. Thus although nothing definite can be stated in reference to the time at which the religious institute is obliged to readmit such clerics, yet the following general principle remains. Due to the bilateral contract made in religious profession, the religious institute is obliged to accept them,

[77] Palombo, *De Dimissione Religiosorum,* n. 209.

[78] P. C. I., 30 iul. 1934—*AAS,* XXVI (1934), 494.

[79] Cf. *supra,* pp. 103-108.

provided they have proved their complete amendment and provided no grave reasons stand in the way of readmittance.

This is evidently contrary to the opinion of those authors who stated after the decision of 1934 that the religious institute is never obliged to readmit those who have been automatically dismissed.[80] However, it has been shown that this interpretation certainly goes beyond the statement of the Pontifical Commission, which merely stated that canon 672, § 1, does not apply to such religious.

In practice such clerics must approach the Holy See, if they intend to amend and to attempt return to the institute,[81] or if they seek a dispensation from the vows. If they pursue the latter course, all obligation to accept them ceases. If they attempt the former method, the Holy See will send directions to guide their amendment and probation. At the same time the Holy See may settle the question in regard to return to the institute, or it may reserve it till a later date. When the Holy See has settled nothing about their obligation to return and the obligation of the institute to accept them, the religious institute may receive them when it judges that there are signs of proved amendment. It is suggested that in all cases, the usual circumstances arising from the crimes committed by these clerics may be advanced to the Holy See as reasons against readmittance. This is stated because the crimes concerned are against the very foundation of religious life and it seems that scandal to the innocent and cause for wonderment would always be occasioned by the presence of such clerics among the confreres who are publicly aware of their past crimes.

In the majority of such cases, the cleric never returns to the religious institute. Thus it would be advisable for him to seek a dispensation from the religious vows, to take up his residence at a distance from the place where he is known and to lead a life worthy of a secular priest. This will always be on the condition that the Holy See will again affiliate him with the clerical state after having

[80] Maroto, "Annotationes,"—*CpR,* XV (1934), 356; Goyeneche, "Annotationes,"—*Apollinaris,* VIII (1935), 553-554; Berutti, *De Religiosis,* n. 177; Vermeersch, "Annotationes,"—*Periodica,* XXIII (1934), 147; cf. *supra,* pp. 109-110.

[81] Palombo, *De Dimissione Religiosorum,* n. 209; Beste, *Introductio in Codicem,* p. 453.

forbidden him to wear the ecclesiastical garb.[82] The seeking of a dispensation from the religious vows can be recommended as a suggestion or in advice, but it cannot be imposed, even on such clerics, since the Holy See alone can judge that the cleric is not obliged to fulfill his obligation to return, or the institute to receive him even though he is sincere in amendment and truly desires to lead a fervent religious life.

Concerning dismissed lay religious, although the obligation of accepting them, when they have proved their amendment is not stated in law, yet it remains as long as the dismissed religious is bound by the vows. Again, this obligation has its source in the bilateral contract made between the institute and the religious at the time of profession. Fanfani states that the religious institute is not obliged to receive any dismissed religious who is not in major orders.[83] He has incorrectly failed to consider the obligation arising from religious profession, which obligation certainly exists. Moreover, he cites this opinion as the opinion of Larraona,[84] but as has been pointed out before, this is not Larraona's opinion. Larraona treated merely the obligation arising from canon law,[85] and he expressly mentions that there *is* an obligation from religious profession.[86]

It has been pointed out that most authors advise the dismissed lay religious to seek a dispensation from the vows after dismissal.[87] This is without doubt the most advisable procedure. However, if the lay religious persists in a serious desire to return, if he believes that despite his former crimes, his vocation and his place is in the

[82] Canon 670.

[83] *De Iure Religiosorum,* n. 519.

[84] Wernz-Vidal also cite this opinion as the opinion of Larraona.—*De Religiosis,* n. 452, note 6.

[85] Canon 672, § 1.

[86] "Religiones, etiamsi vi can. 672, § 1, et ad normam ipsius, scilicet post triennium emendationis, non tenerentur ad religiosos huiusmodi votis ligatos recipiendos, tamen non solum possent eos recipere, sed aliqua ratione et, nisi graves obessent causae, deberent quoque, ex vinculo professionis, quod dimissione, ex neutra parte, plene rumpitur.—"Quaestio Canonica circa Canonem 672, § 1,"—*CpR,* III (1922), 320.

[87] Cf. *supra,* pp. 110-111.

religious community and not in the world, no religious superior, confessor or spiritual director can force him to seek a dispensation from his vows. Only the Holy See has the power to state that because of special reasons in particular cases, the institute is not obliged to receive the religious, even though he is amended and that consequently the religious is not obliged to return.

Since the Pontifical Commission has decided that canon 672, § 1, does not refer to those who have been automatically dismissed, it is evident that no religious institute is obliged to receive a lay religious who was automatically dismissed, even though he has given signs of complete amendment for a period of three years. After that time the obligation arises only when the institute is convinced that the religious has given signs of complete and proved amendment. It is suggested again in reference to lay religious that the institute may consider the usual circumstances following upon such crimes as grave reasons against readmittance, and can therefore refer the case to the Holy See for settlement. Since the same suggestion has been made concerning clerics who have committed crimes punished by the Code with infamy of law,[88] it could also be followed when the infamy of law has been incurred by a lay religious.

When dismissal of lay religious has taken place by the legitimate action of superiors and the religious wishes to fulfill his obligation to return to the institute, the following norms are given. Certainly there is no obligation to accept him before a period of three years is completed. This norm is taken from a comparison with a similar case given in law, namely, the obligation expressed in canon 672, § 1, regarding dismissed clerics. The clerics referred to in that canon are clerics dismissed for the less serious crimes. It is evident that they have been dismissed for crimes which are no more serious than the crimes of the lay religious who has been dismissed by the legitimate action of superiors. Now if the legislator does not impose the obligation of readmittance in regard to clerics until three years have lapsed, *a fortiori*, the institute cannot be obliged to accept the lay religious before that time. In reference to the clerics, constant vigilance and care is prescribed during the time of amendment; whereas no such precautions are laid down by law in the case of the

[88] Cf. *supra*, p. 156.

lay religious. Therefore, if despite the constant care and vigilance exercised in the case of the cleric, the legislator does not place an obligation in this matter before the expiration of three years, how can the obligation arise before that time in regard to lay religious, who are free to live in the world wherever they please? Furthermore, the legislator has a special reason for anxiety in urging the return of a dismissed cleric. It is true that all religious on professing perpetual vows, whether solemn or simple, lose their own proper diocese which they had as seculars.[89] By perpetual profession they are absolutely affiliated with their religious institute. For the religious as a cleric the bond of affiliation has a greater significance than it has for lay religious, since it takes the place of the incardination of clerics among the secular clergy. Hence the legislator has greater anxiety that the bond be retained in the case of religious clerics. And if, despite his anxiety, he does not oblige the institute to readmit the cleric before the lapse of three years, *a fortiori* the religious institute is not obliged to accept a dismissed lay religious before that time.

It is now asked if the religious institute is obliged to accept a lay religious after the term of three years. It is answered that no general statement can be made in reference to time. A fitting norm can be taken from canon 672, § 1, whereby proved amendment is legally accepted if the religious has given signs of complete amendment for three years. However, that is merely a norm in reference to lay religious. Beste states that even though the extent of canon 672, § 1, is disputed, *i. e.*, as to whether it comprehends both lay and clerical religious, yet its norms hold in regard to dismissed lay religious by an application of canon 20.[90] Thus he states that the institute is always obliged to receive an amended lay religious (with the exception of those automatically dismissed) after a period of three years. The previously advanced reasons show, however, that the amendment of the lay religious and the amendment of the cleric are not entirely similar. The norms of canon 672, § 1, cannot be applied in all cases to lay religious. The guiding principle of the question is that the religious institute becomes obliged to accept a

[89] Canons 115, 585.

[90] *Introductio in Codicem*, p. 454.

lay religious only when two conditions are fulfilled; namely, first, when the religious institute is convinced that the religious has given signs of complete and proved amendment, and secondly, when no grave reason exists contrary to acceptance. If these conditions are not realized after three or more years, no obligation exists for the religious institute. In summary it is stated that the religious institute certainly has no obligation to accept a dismissed lay religious before a period of three years. After that time the obligation is present only when the religious institute is convinced that there are signs of complete and proved amendment and that there is no grave reason contrary to readmittance.

It is added here that in all cases where readmittance is allowed by the superiors, no further permission is necessary [91] to admit the religious into the community.[92]

A word should be said about the grave reasons which may exist in all cases contrary to readmittance. Here, only reasons on the part of the religious institute are concerned.[93] Such reasons would be scandal to innocent souls, grave detriment to the good standing of the religious institute, or a realization that the character of the dismissed subject is too hostile to the common life. In some particular cases a reason may be present if due to the small number of members, the superiors will be forced to readmit the religious into the company of the identical community from which he was dismissed. Such action might prove dangerous either to the religious himself or to the community.[94] Augustine offers as a further grave reason the contraction of an incurable contagious disease,[95] and many authors advanced this reason before the Code.[96] However,

[91] Religious who were dismissed before the promulgation of the Code by intervention of the Holy See needed an Apostolic indult to be readmitted into the institute. This would seem to bind even after the promulgation of the Code for those particular dismissed religious. Cf. Vermeersch-Creusen, *Epitome,* I, n. 764; Schaefer, *De Religiosis,* n. 598.

[92] Fanfani, *De Iure Religiosorum,* n. 519, B.

[93] Cf. *supra,* p. 112, for reasons on the part of the dismissed religious.

[94] Cf. Palombo, *De Dimissione Religiosorum,* n. 207; Augustine, *A Commentary,* III, 415.

[95] *Loc. cit.*

[96] Donatus, *Rerum Regularium Praxis Resolutoria,* Tom. I, pars II, tract.

the opinion of Palombo is more preferable. He states that the grave reason can never be an infirmity, even though it was contracted during the time in which the dismissed subject was outside the religious community.[97]

Article II. The Obligations of the Assigned Ordinary

Canon 671 refers to a local ordinary who may be assigned by the Holy See for the purpose of directing the amendment of dismissed religious who are clerics. The norms of that canon refer to those clerics who have been dismissed for the less serious crimes. When there is question of clerics who have committed the more serious crimes, the matter must be treated in a different manner. If the Holy See commands one of this latter class of clerics to live in a certain diocese and to there prove his amendment, the ordinary of that diocese shall consider first of all the mandates which the Holy See will send to the delinquent cleric and also any directions which he might receive personally. Over and above these directions and mandates, the ordinary may take fitting norms from the prescripts of canon 671.

It is evident that all dismissed clerics who are placed by the Holy See under the jurisdiction and obedience of a local ordinary are subject to that ordinary in a manner similar to that of the secular clergy of the diocese. Thus the ordinary can inflict on them penalties and penal remedies, in order to punish their faults, to correct them, or to protect them from relapse into their former crimes. The religious is not bound to this ordinary by virtue of religious obedience and therefore no formal precept of religious obedience can be imposed by the assigned ordinary, acting under his own proper power.[98]

The Code states that when a cleric who has been dismissed for the less serious crimes is sent to a particular diocese by the Holy

VIII, q. 26; Rotarius, *Theologia Moralis Regularium,* Tom. I, lib. III, c. II, punct. VII, n. 4; Piatus Montensis, *Praelectiones Juris Regularis,* I, q. 246. Passerinus rejected this reason as a basis for refusing readmittance.—*De Hominum Statibus,* Q. CLXXXIX, art. VIII, n. 656.

[97] *De Dimissione Religiosorum,* n. 207.

[98] Cf. *supra,* pp. 78-81.

See, the causes that led to his dismissal shall be communicated to the said ordinary.[99] When the dismissed cleric subjects himself to the assigned ordinary, the latter is from then on personally responsible for the direction of the delinquent cleric. The religious institute should show itself most cooperative in revealing to the ordinary the causes for dismissal, the character and dispositions of the delinquent, the circumstances of his crimes and all else that may aid in his proper direction. It is only with such information that the ordinary can prudently place the religious and profitably direct his amendment.

Even though the Code states that the ordinary may place the religious under the care and vigilance of a holy and prudent priest, it is evident from the general tenor of the canon that the first obligation of vigilance and care rests upon the ordinary himself. It is he who will determine what particular care must be taken and what norms shall be used in the way of vigilance, when he assigns the cleric to a place in his diocese. He should make certain prescripts before placing the religious either in a house of penance or in the personal care of a priest. Such prescripts could be a prohibition to go to certain places, a prohibition to leave a certain territory, an obligation to ask permission of an assigned priest each time the delinquent leaves the house of penance, and an obligation to appear at certain times before him or some person delegated by him.[100] That the ordinary should make some prescripts of this kind is evident from the canon itself. Although it is his duty to watch over and care for each member of his flock, the vigilance and care here in question is something special; so much so that vigilance in this sense is considered as a remedy to be used only in exceptional and grave cases.[101] Naturally, any prescriptions which the ordinary makes in reference to this matter shall be communicated both to the delinquent and to those who are immediately charged with his care. The obedience of the delinquent in reference to such prescripts will show in great part whether he has finally amended or not.

The knowledge which the ordinary has of the delinquent shall

[99] Canon 671, n. 2.

[100] Cf. Vermeersch-Creusen, *Epitome,* III, n. 505.

[101] Canon 2311.

be the basis of the injunctions which he will impose on the dismissed cleric. From the same knowledge the ordinary shall judge whether in a particular case it will be more profitable to send the delinquent to a house of penance or to commit him to the care of a priest of his diocese.[102] The prudence of the ordinary will determine that often the latter course will be the more useful and effective one, even though he has a house of penance in his diocese.[103] It should be pointed out here that great prudence and consideration should be employed in these first steps toward the direction of the dismissed religious, for in regard to complete amendment, a great deal will depend upon the special prescriptions which the ordinary will make and upon the place of penance which he will assign.

It is the place of the assigned ordinary to judge that the religious can be considered as truly amended. This he must do before he shall recommend to the Holy See the petition for the absolution from suspension. The signs of amendment by which the ordinary may judge the case are not determined in law, but they can be readily discerned. If the cleric carefully avoids the occasion of his former crimes, if he does not refuse to do public penance to repair the scandal he has caused, if he has proved himself in obedience to the injunctions and restrictions imposed on him, if he has been regular in his religious observances and in devotional practices these signs can be accepted as evidence of true amendment.[104] If the ordinary has found these signs in the life of the dismissed cleric after a year's probation, he should judge the cleric worthy of absolution from the censure and recommend to the Holy See the petition of the delinquent.[105]

Two questions now arise concerning the ordinary's judgment on the worthiness of the cleric in reference to this matter. First, may the ordinary recommend to the Holy See the petition of the delinquent before the term of one full year has expired? Canon 671, n. 7, which concerns the recommendation, does not explicitly state the exact time required for probation. It merely refers back to the

[102] Cf. Palombo, *De Dimissione Religiosorum*, n. 203.

[103] Vermeersch-Creusen, *Epitome*, I, n. 822.

[104] Cf. Goyeneche, "Quando censeatur emendatus in ordine ad dimissionem religiosus delinquens,"—*CpR*, V (1924), 25.

[105] Canon 671, n. 7.

preceding number of the canon, which treats of clerics who have not led a worthy life while residing in the place of penance. In that number it is stated that the ordinary *after a year or even sooner,* may dismiss the cleric and inflict on him further penalties. It seems that the entire phrase, *after a year or even sooner,* can be embraced in the reference of canon 671, n. 7. Certainly such an interpretation is concordant with the end intended by the legislator in stating this number of the canon. That end is evidently and primarily the proved amendment of the guilty party. By the above interpretation, proved amendment will be more eagerly sought since the privilege of offering the Holy Sacrifice and of exercising his Orders at an earlier date is presented to the cleric should he lead a life so worthy that his amendment is apparent to all even before the full year has lapsed. Therefore it is the opinion of this writer that the ordinary may at times recommend the petition of the dismissed religious before the close of the year, unless the Holy See has stated otherwise when it assigned the religious to the diocese. Blat,[106] Palombo,[107] and Beste,[108] also sponsor this interpretation, although some authors oppose it.[109]

Ordinaries, however, are well aware that the Code has first suggested a period of a year for very good reasons. They know that such clerics have been dismissed by the action of religious superiors and therefore that they have been guilty of repeated offenses even after being warned. Therefore amendment must be proved rather than accepted without doubt. Certainly a long period of probation is justified to prove a change of dispositions in one who has merited dismissal from the religious communal life, despite the frequent efforts of religious superiors to correct him. Yet when there are extraordinary signs of amendment, or when the life which the religious leads, leaves no room for doubt about his change of dispositions, the ordinary can be justified in commending the petition before the end of the year. Without doubt it will be necessary in

106 *Ius de Religiosis,* n. 718.

107 *De Dimissione Religiosorum,* n. 205.

108 *Introductio in Codicem,* p. 454.

109 Chelodi, *Ius de Personis,* n. 294; Augustine, *A Commentary,* III, 413; Fanfani, *De Iure Religiosorum,* n. 517.

uch cases for him to cite in his recommendation special reasons why ie judges the religious truly amended at the particular time.

The second question about the ordinary's recommendation of he petition for absolution is now advanced. May the ordinary pro-ong the time in which the cleric remains under suspension by not ecommending the petition after a full year? It is evident that he can dismiss the religious altogether if he discovers that the delinquent is not leading a life worthy of a cleric. If this is the ordinary's udgment after a year, the cleric must be dismissed. He can legitimately dismiss him even before the close of the year if the case warrants it. However it seems that if the ordinary is still in doubt about the matter after a full year, he should refer the case to the Holy See. Such a doubt may arise when the cleric cannot be said to have passed his time of probation in a manner unworthy of the clerical state, but yet his character, piety and dispositions are not worthy enough to show that he has acted as praiseworthily as the case demands. Certainly if the efforts of the ordinary, plus dismissal from the religious communal life are not sufficient incentives to urge a thorough change of dispositions, after the lapse of a year further steps ought to be taken in the matter. It seems that the most effective action in such cases would be recourse to the Holy See for further instructions concerning the suspension and the delinquent cleric.

After the dismissed religious has been absolved from the suspension, he remains in the diocese which has been assigned to him. It is still the duty of the local ordinary to direct his life after this time. The Code states that he shall impose on the cleric certain precautions and limitations concerning the celebration of Holy Mass. Thus the ordinary can limit the celebration of Mass to certain feasts or to Sundays. He may restrict it to certain oratories or to a determined church, or he may demand that the celebration take place in the presence of trustworthy persons.[110] The restrictions may also be negative in character, e. g., that the priest shall not celebrate in certain churches, or that he shall not celebrate with any solemnity.[111]

110 Augustine, *A Commentary*, III, 413; Beste, *Introductio in Codicem*, p. 454; Coronata, *Institutiones*, n. 660.

111 Palombo, *De Dimissione Religiosorum*, n. 205.

It seems that it is not within the power of the ordinary to dispense with all limitations in this matter,[112] and it is certain that he cannot allow the religious the full exercise of his sacred ministry. He can however, at his own discretion, allow to the cleric some other exercise of the sacred ministry which is not prohibited by canon 642. He could therefore allow him to preach sermons or to act as chaplain in some home or hospital.[113]

After a period of three years, computed from the date of dismissal, the religious institute is obliged to accept the cleric according to the norms of canon 671, § 1. The testimony of the ordinary will be the main factor in the proofs which will be demanded concerning amendment.

Concerning the ordinary's power with regard to a disobedient cleric, the following is stated. If a dismissed religious takes up his residence in the assigned place of penance, the ordinary can inflict further penalties on him if he does not lead a life worthy of a cleric.[114] The penalties which the law states for such a case are most drastic. They entail not only dismissal from the place of penance, but also the cessation of the charitable maintenance and the privation of the right of wearing the ecclesiastical garb. These effects point to the fact that serious delinquency is in question. Thus if the cleric should at times infringe some of the injunctions of the ordinary without serious violation, these offenses would not be sufficient reasons for the infliction of the penalties. If the cleric should run away from the place of penance, if he should deliberately disregard the injunctions of the ordinary and commit the same crimes for which he was dismissed, or if his life in general is unworthy of his sacred calling, the penalties should be imposed. It hardly need be said that the ordinary should be slow to inflict these drastic measures and should attempt any means at his command to bring the delinquent to his senses before placing him in a state so debasing for one who has been ordained to Holy Orders. However, if the cleric shows himself truly unworthy of further mercy, the ordinary should inflict all the stated penalties cumulatively. It

[112] Blat, *Ius de Religiosis,* n. 718.

[113] Palombo, *De Dimissione Religiosorum,* n. 205.

[114] Canon 671, n. 6.

seems that the incurring of one of these penalties without the others would redound rather to the dishonor of the clerical state than to the good of the delinquent.[115]

After the ordinary has punished the unworthy cleric according to law, he should report his action both to the Holy See and to the religious institute. There is a further legal obligation of sending this report without delay.[116] In content the report should relate fully all things concerning the dismissed cleric, namely, all the penalties which have been applied, and all the pertinent facts concerning his life, his morals and his incorrigibility.[117]

Perhaps a doubt might arise about the extent of the word "ordinary" in canon 671. In numbers 6 and 7 of this canon the word is used without any immediate modification. The Code states that unless major superiors of clerical exempt organizations are expressly excluded they are included in the term "ordinary" in reference to their subjects.[118] By a literal interpretation then, it might be proposed that the major superiors of clerical exempt organizations are included in numbers 6 and 7 of this canon. Now it is the first principle of interpretation of law to consider individual terms in their context.[119] And if one studies numbers 6 and 7 of canon 671, it is evident from the context that the word can refer only to the assigned ordinary and not to any religious major superior. In the first number, namely in canon 671, n. 6, the law states that the ordinary should inflict the penalties and then it imposes a further obligation. It states that the same ordinary should report the matter to the Holy See and *to the religious institute.* The last phrase shows beyond doubt that no religious superior is concerned.[120] In number 7 of the canon it is very evident from the context that the assigned ordinary alone is referred to. It states that the ordinary should commend to the Holy See the cleric's petition for absolution from censure, if he

115 Palombo, *De Dimissione Religiosorum,* n. 205.

116 Canon 671, n. 6.

117 Cf. Palombo, *loc. cit.*

118 Canon 198, § 1.

119 Canon 18.

120 Keene includes canon 671, n. 6 under a list of canons which refer only to local ordinaries.—*Religious Ordinaries and Canon 198,* p. 12; cf. Blat, *Ius de Religiosis,* n. 718.

considers him worthy. Later in the same number, without repeating any subject, it is stated that the ordinary should permit the cleric to celebrate Mass *in his diocese (in sua diocesi)*. Because of this phrase, it is evident that religious ordinaries, as mere religious superiors, are excluded. Therefore it must be said that the major superior in exempt clerical organizations has no power to recommend to the Holy See the dismissed cleric's petition for absolution from the censure of suspension, even if he judges the cleric truly amended. Neither can such a superior inflict the punishments referred to in canon 671, n. 6, once the religious has taken up his residence in the assigned diocese. Both of these powers refer to the ordinary who has been assigned by the Holy See to direct the dismissed religious.

It is also the obligation of the assigned ordinary to inform the Holy See concerning these dismissed religious clerics in his quinquennial report. If he is drawing up his report while they are proving themselves in his diocese, he must include a full account about them in reference to canons 669-672.[121] Moreover if the dismissed cleric is later dispensed from his religious vows and incardination takes place, the ordinary shall include a statement of the matter in the quinquennial report.[122] No special obligations are placed on an ordinary in reference to dismissed lay religious.

[121] "Si adsint religiosi viri ordinibus sacris iam initiati, qui exclaustrati, saecularizati aut dimissi a religione fuerint, referat Ordinarius quid de ipsis dicendum iuxta cann. 639, 640, 669 seqq."—"De Relationibus Dioecesanis," n. 82—*AAS,* X (1918), 500.

[122] "An aliquem incardinaverit, qua de causa, et num iuxta legem can. 111 seqq."—"De Relationibus Dioecesanis," n. 29—*AAS,* X (1918), 493.

CHAPTER IX

DISMISSED RELIGIOUS DISPENSED FROM THE VOWS

Article I. In Reference to All Dismissed Religious

This chapter will treat of those dismissed religious who are dispensed from the religious vows. Such dispensation may be effected at the moment of dismissal in virtue of the constitutions of the religious institute, or it may be granted, either at dismissal or at a later date, by the Holy See. Although the general rule is that dismissed religious are still restricted by the obligations of the perpetual vows which they have professed, yet the Code admits of such exceptions.[1]

Certain religious constitutions have the express prescript that a dispensation from the vows takes place automatically at the moment of dismissal, even when perpetual vows are concerned. In such institutes the religious members make their perpetual profession with the tacit condition that if dismissal takes place, the religious vows will cease.[2] Some examples of this point may be given. In the Society of Jesus all vows, except the vows of those who have made solemn profession, cease automatically at dismissal.[3] The Constitutions of the Congregation of the Most Holy Redeemer[4] and of the Congregation of Missionaries of Mariannhill[5] state that dismissal from the institute effects an automatic dispensation from the vows. The same effect is found in the new statutes of the extern sisters of monasteries of nuns with solemn vows.[6] Finally the members of the Congregation of the Holy Cross are automatically dispensed

[1] Canon 669, § 1.

[2] Fanfani, *De Iure Religiosorum*, n. 517.

[3] Vermeersch-Creusen, *Epitome*, I, n. 822, note 1.

[4] Palombo, *De Dimissione Religiosorum*, n. 200.

[5] *Constitutiones Congregationis Missionariorum de Mariannhill*, n. 108.

[6] *Apollinaris*, IV (1931), 360.

from the vows of poverty and obedience at dismissal, but the perpetual vow of chastity remains.[7]

It should be added that in regard to those members of institutes with solemn vows, who professed simple perpetual vows before the Code, automatic dispensation also takes place at dismissal. This was the discipline of pre-Code law concerning such religious.[8] The vows professed by such religious were peculiar in this that they were perpetual on the part of the one vowing and temporary on the part of the religious institute. All religious who professed such vows and were dismissed after May 19, 1918, are judged both as regards dismissal and its effects by the law existing before the promulgation of the Code.[9] Also any religious institutes which had special indults or privileges concerning this matter of dispensation before the Code, still retain them and they are officially respected in the present common law.[10]

If after dismissal the religious remains bound by the vows, it is his right to petition at any time for a dispensation from them, provided he has sufficient reason. Such a petition should be sent through the hands of the religious superior, since it is evident from the usual indult of secularization that the Holy See will consult the religious organization on the reasons alleged for the dispensation.

The general effects of a dispensation from the vows are the effects of an indult of secularization. There is no substantial or practical difference between the two.[11] Thus there is no longer any bond between the dismissed and the religious institute. The dismissed person ceases entirely to be a religious. Consequently he is no longer bound to the obligations of the religious vows or of the constitutions of the institute. He regains full property rights, and

[7] "Dimissio religiosorum sequitur adamussim tramitem juris communis. Hoc tamen habetur speciale, quod scilicet professus perpetuus dimissus a Congregatione, eo ipso solvitur a votis paupertatis et obedientiae, manente vinculo solius castitatis, sine praejudicio tamen onerum S. Ordinum."—Sauvage, "Notae historicae et juridicae de Congregatione a Sancta Cruce."—*CpRM,* XX (1939), 334.

[8] Cf. *supra,* p. 27.

[9] P. C. I., 16 oct. 1919—*AAS,* XI (1919), 476.

[10] Canon 669, § 1; cf. Prümmer, *Manuale Iuris Canonici,* Q. 264, 1.

[11] Toso, *Commentaria Minora,* Lib. II, pars II, p. 154; Geser, *The Canon Law Governing Communities of Sisters,* n. 1104.

the cession of the administration of goods and any disposition concerning their use and usufruct which have been made,[12] cease automatically.[13] The ex-religious may freely dispose of all his property and may without further permission change the will which he drafted before his profession.[14] Finally, he has no obligation to return to the religious institute and the institute has no obligation to receive him.

The renunciation of the goods which the religious makes before solemn profession is still effective after a dispensation from the vows has been granted. The goods concerned have been legitimately acquired by an unconditional grant and therefore they cannot be lost by subsequent action of the donor. However, equity would demand that the beneficiary of the said goods would at least see to it that the ex-religious has sufficient means for a proper livelihood, provided the beneficiary still enjoys a sufficient amount of the goods to make that possible.

By dispensation from the vows, a lay religious occupies the same status as any lay person in the world; whereas a cleric in major orders is freed from all the obligations of the religious life, but is still bound by all the obligations arising from Holy Orders.[15] The Pontifical Commission declared in 1922 that the regulations of canon 640 regarding the effects of secularization apply to all who obtain the indult, either from the Apostolic See or from the local ordinary.[16]

If any dismissed ex-religious should desire to enter a seminary, he can not be admitted unless the bishop confers with the Sacred Congregation of Studies and Universities.[17] If admittance is to be allowed the bishop must first obtain information from the former superiors and from other trustworthy persons who are well acquainted with the ex-religious. The information given by the former

[12] Canon 569, § 1.

[13] Canon 580, § 3.

[14] Canon 569, § 3.

[15] Clerics in minor orders are reduced to the lay state by dismissal.—Canon 669, § 2.

[16] P. C. I., 12 nov. 1922—*AAS,* XIV (1922), 662.

[17] S. CC. de Religiosis atque de Seminariis et Studiorum Universitatibus, decr. *Consiliis initis,* 25 iul. 1941—*AAS,* XXXIII (1941), 371.

superiors shall concern the reasons for dismissal and shall include testimonials as to the morals, dispositions and talents of the former religious. Before admitting him, the bishop must be convinced that there is nothing in his character which would be unbecoming to the sacerdotal state.[18]

In conclusion to these general effects of secularization, one final difficulty may be proposed. When religious are dismissed from a clerical exempt organization and have been dispensed from the vows, it is evident that the jurisdiction of the superiors ceases in their regard. What must be said, then, of those who have incurred canonical penalties or censures reserved to the religious major superior? A practical example is the case of a lay brother who runs away from a clerical exempt institute and contracts a valid but illicit marriage. The contraction of such a marriage is punished with an automatic excommunication reserved to the ordinary.[19] The proper ordinary of the lay brother as a religious is his major superior. However, if the lay brother obtains a dispensation from the vows, either in the act of dismissal or at a later date, the major superior can no longer exercise jurisdiction over him as a religious. Thus the ex-religious cannot have recourse to the religious major superior for an absolution from the excommunication. In this case, the excommunication is not reserved to the major superior of the religious institute, but to the ordinary of the place where the former lay brother lives.[20] This is stated because it follows the general principle governing those who do not belong to a clerical exempt institute.

Article II. In Reference to Dismissed Clerics

At the profession of perpetual vows, whether solemn or simple, a religious automatically loses his own proper diocese which he had as a secular.[21] After such profession a religious, as a cleric, is incardinated in no diocese, but is absolutely affiliated [22] with the re-

[18] Canon 1363, § 3.

[19] Canon 2388, § 2.

[20] Cf. Riesner, *Apostates and Fugitives from Religious Institutes*, p. 81.

[21] Canon 585.

[22] Religious are not properly said to become "incardinated" into their religious institute. The Code uses the term "adscriptio" which may best be rendered

ligious institute.[23] This effect of perpetual profession takes place even though there is question of an institute of merely diocesan approval.[24] Furthermore, it refers to all perpetually professed religious, including even those who were ordained to Holy Orders before they were admitted into the institute. Now it is evident that once a dispensation from the religious vows is effected, all bonds between the religious and the institute are broken. This complete separation from the religious institute includes the severance of the bond of absolute affiliation. A serious difficulty may arise then, with regard to dismissed clerics who are dispensed from their vows, since the Code demands that every cleric must belong either to some diocese or to some religious organization and it extends no recognition to clerical *vagi*.[25]

If a dismissed cleric is dispensed from his religious vows before he has found a bishop who is willing to receive him, he becomes a clerical *vagus*. This is apparent when one considers that in such cases the cleric has no claim on the religious institute or on his former proper ordinary, and the said ordinary and the religious institute have no further obligations toward the cleric.

Before commencing a further discussion on this matter, a more fundamental question must be proposed. It is asked if the present legislation has done away with all possibility of the presence of clerical *vagi*. Evidently the Church has made great efforts to suppress clerical *vagi* wherever they were found.[26] However, notwithstanding the fundamental prescript of law, stating that every cleric must belong either to some diocese or to some religious organization,

by "affiliation." Cf. Maroto, *Institutiones Iuris Canonici* (2 vols., Vol. I, 3. ed., Romae: Apud Commentarium pro Religiosis, 1921), I, n. 492; Blat, *De Personis* (2. ed., Romae: Apud "Angelicum," 1921), n. 45; McBride, *Incardination and Excardination of Seculars*, The Catholic University of America Canon Law Studies, n. 145 (Washington, D. C.: The Catholic University of America Press, 1941), p. 298.

[23] Canon 115.

[24] Cervia, *De Professione Religiosa* (Bologna: Via Bellinzona, 1938), p. 158; Vermeersch-Creusen, *Epitome*, I, n. 798; Gerster, *Ius Religiosorum*, p. 119; Fanfani, *De Iure Religiosorum*, n. 273.

[25] Canon 111, § 1.

[26] Cf. McBride, *Incardination and Excardination of Seculars*, pp. 291-292.

and that no recognition is given to clerical *vagi*, yet it cannot be said that the Code did away with all possibility of their presence.[27] McBride has stated correctly that with regard to the secular clergy, the present legislation has made the presence of clerical *vagi* impossible, although he cites a few illegal ways (highly improbable in actuality) which would give rise to their presence.[28] Yet, it must be said that the Code was not as thorough in the matter with regard to religious clerics.

Immediately after the promulgation of the Code, it was the practice of the Holy See for a short while to grant absolutely the indult of secularization to religious clerics. Such action was not against the canons of the Code. In fact the Code presupposes it, by the norm of canon 641, § 1, which states that when a religious in major orders has lost his proper diocese,[29] and is dispensed from the vows, he cannot exercise his Orders outside the religious organization until he has found a bishop willing to receive him, or until the Holy See has made other provisions. This law takes it for granted that it is possible for a secularized religious to be without either incardination or absolute affiliation with a religious institute. If this is not admitted, then there is no purpose for that particular canon.

However, within a short time after the promulgation of the Code, certainly by 1928, the practice arose in the Roman Curia of not granting an indult of secularization absolutely. From that time on, the indult has been granted on the condition of the incardination of the cleric into a diocese. Vermeersch explains the new form of the indult in this manner. It does not immediately grant secularization, but in *forma commissoria* it gives to the ordinary who wishes to accept the religious for experiment the faculty of exclaustration of the religious. When the total time allowed for experiment has lapsed, or also sooner, if the cleric is formally received, the religious becomes secularized.[30] This practice obviates the difficulty in re-

[27] Kinane, "Incardination and Excardination,"—*IER*, XI (1918), 298-310.

[28] *Op. cit.*, pp. 293, 294.

[29] Canon 585.

[30] "Quaesita varia,"—*Periodica*, XVII (1928), 50*-51*. An example of the new form of the indult of secularization is found in *Periodica*, XVII (1928), 51*

gard to dismissed clerics who seek a dispensation from the vows after dismissal. They will receive the same conditional indult explained above and therefore there will be no moment in which they are not either affiliated with the religious institute or incardinated into a diocese.[31]

However, the difficulty still remains concerning those clerics who have been automatically dispensed from the vows at dismissal in virtue of the constitutions of the religious institute. There is no way of showing that such ex-religious, as clerics, are subject to anyone except to the Holy See. They are incardinated in no diocese and they are no longer affiliated with their religious institute. They are clerical *vagi* in the sense of canon 111, § 1. Therefore the difficulty which has been proposed is not a mere theoretical point, despite the change of practice in granting the indult of secularization since the promulgation of the Code. In practice, clerics who are automatically dispensed from the vows at dismissal can rarely find a bishop who is willing to receive them immediately after dismissal. It is also often impossible to retain the cleric in the convent until he has found such a bishop, for such a measure would defeat the first purpose of dismissal, namely, to protect the common good of the religious community. And even if such measures could be taken, they would not solve the difficulty, because during the time in which the cleric would remain in the convent after dismissal and up till the moment when the bishop would incardinate him, he would be without a proper ordinary and he would not be affiliated to the religious institute.

The principle of canon 641 that such clerics cannot exercise their sacred orders while outside the religious institute, until they find a bishop who is willing to receive them, also applies here. By the perpetual prohibition to wear the ecclesiastical garb, affecting those who have committed the more serious crimes,[32] and by the suspension of orders, affecting those who have committed the less serious

and in *CpR,* IX (1928), 302. Also an example of the new form of the indult of secularization so-called "pure et simpliciter" in *CpR,* XIII (1932), 90.

[31] Canon 111, § 1.

[32] Canon 670.

crimes,[33] the same effect is attained for a time. After the prohibition or the suspension is removed by the Holy See, the cleric is still bound by the prohibition of canon 641, unless the Holy See states otherwise. If he cannot find a bishop who is willing to receive him, the Holy See may grant him permission with limitations to celebrate the Sacrifice of the Mass and to exercise the sacred ministry, provided he is truly amended. It has granted this permission often in the past.[34]

Ojetti has stated that the condition of such clerics is not a juridic condition, and that clerical *vagi* do not exist juridically, but at most exist in fact.[35] It is the opinion of the present writer that the possibility of such a condition is recognized by the Code and can therefore be called a juridic condition. It is true that it is against the mind of the legislator as expressed in canon 111, § 1, yet the legislator has introduced canon 641, §1, in recognition of the possibility of clerical *vagi*. Hence it must be said that such cases exist and exist juridically.

In summary it should be stated that in reference to religious clerics, the enactment of canon 111, § 1, does not destroy all possibility of the presence of a clerical *vagus*, under the present legislation. In cases which may arise, the prohibition to exercise Orders, as stated in canon 641, § 1, is always effective until the religious finds a bishop willing to receive him, or until the Holy See provides for him.

For all those who have been dispensed from the religious vows in or after dismissal, the Code states that if they have found a bishop willing to receive them, they shall remain under his jurisdiction and special vigilance. If they cannot find such a bishop, they shall refer the matter to the Holy See.[36] If the cleric finds such a bishop, he may be received either immediately and abso-

[33] Canon 671, n. 1.

[34] De Meester, *Compendium*, n. 1064; Raus, *Institutiones Canonicae*, n. 208; Biederlack-Führich, *De Religiosis* (Oeniponte: Rauch, 1919), n. 178; Vermeersch-Creusen, *Epitome*, I, n. 823; Prümmer, *Manuale Iuris Canonici*, Q. 254; Coronata, *Institutiones*, n. 660.

[35] *Commentarium in Codicem Iuris Canonici* (4 vols., Romae: Apud Aedes Universitatis Gregorianae, 1927-1931), III, 32.

[36] Canon 672, § 2.

lutely or, as will usually happen, for an experiment of three years.[37] If the former method is resorted to, the cleric is immediately incardinated in the diocese. If the latter course is taken and if the bishop wishes to prolong the time of experiment, he may do so, but not for a longer period than another three years. It is understood that the bishop intends to prolong the time of experiment unless he expressly incardinates the dismissed cleric at the expiration of the first three years. No express statement of prorogation is necessary to continue the time of experiment.[38] Once the period of six years of experiment has lapsed, incardination takes place automatically, provided the cleric has not been dismissed in the meantime.[39]

The religious cleric who has been dismissed for the less serious crimes remains suspended after dismissal until he is absolved by the Holy See.[40] If immediately after dismissal the cleric finds a bishop willing to receive him, he may go to his diocese unless the Holy See states otherwise. After he has been absolved from the suspension, then the bishop may incardinate him absolutely, or he may begin the period of experiment. All during this time, up till the final incardination, the cleric dispensed from religious vows is subject to the Holy See since he is not affiliated with any religious institute and is not incardinated in any diocese. Thus if the bishop dismisses him during the time of experiment, and the cleric cannot find another bishop willing to receive him, he must have recourse to the Holy See.[41] Pending such recourse he cannot exercise his sacred orders,[42] unless the Holy See has granted him that permission without reference to incardination or experiment in a particular diocese.

It is evident, then, that if the bishop allows the dispensed cleric in his diocese immediately after dismissal, the time in which he is under suspension does not count in the reckoning of the years of experiment. The relative position of canon 672, § 2, shows that it

[37] Canon 641, § 2.
[38] P. C. I., 27 iul. 1942—*AAS,* XXXIV (1942), 241.
[39] Canon 641, § 2.
[40] Canon 671, n. 1.
[41] Canon 672, § 2.
[42] Canon 641, § 1.

is treating of an amended cleric and therefore amendment is presupposed before reception can take place according to canon 642, § 2.

Once the cleric who has been absolved from suspension is received by a bishop, he immediately has the full use of his ecclesiastical powers of Orders, without any further permission, despite the former restrictions placed on the exercise of his ministry since dismissal.[43] It is evident that the ex-religious exercises the sacred functions as the secular clergy, after he has received the dispensation from the vows. Therefore he then becomes as the secular clergy in the celebration of Mass,[44] in the recitation of the Divine Office,[45] and in the use and dispensation of the Sacraments.[46]

Although the dismissed ex-religious is received by a bishop, he is not eligible for every office or benefice in the Church. He is forbidden without a new and special indult of the Holy See to hold the following offices and benefices; (a) any benefice in major and minor basilicas and in cathedral churches; (b) any professorship or office in major or minor seminaries, in colleges in which clerics are educated and in universities and institutions which enjoy the papal privilege of conferring academic degrees; (c) any office or position in the curia of bishops, or in religious houses of either men or women, even in the case of congregations of diocesan approval.[47]

The subjects of these prohibitions are only those ex-religious who were ordained to Holy Orders at the time in which they were dispensed from the religious vows.[48] This is apparent from the text

[43] Berutti, *De Religiosis,* n. 179.

[44] For example this point would refer to a priest dismissed from the Order of Preachers.

[45] This would affect all those who have a breviary different from that which is used by the secular clergy.

[46] Canon 640, § 1.

[47] Canon 642, § 1.

[48] Raus, *Institutiones Canonicae,* p. 238, note 1; Biederlack-Führich, *De Religiosis,* n. 157; Vermeersch-Creusen, *Epitome,* I, n. 824; Oesterle, *Praelectiones Iuris Canonici,* I, pp. 364, 377; Fanfani, *De Iure Religiosorum,* n. 488; Toso, *Commentaria Minora,* Lib. II, pars II, p. 237; Blat, *Ius de Religiosis,* n. 721; Leitner, *Handbuch des katholischen Kirchenrechts* (2. ed., 2 vols., Regensburg: Kosel und Pustet, 1921-1927), I, 555; Goyeneche, "Consultationes,"—*CpR,* V (1924), 28; (Anonymous), "Can Ex-Religious Become Pastors?"—*ER,* LXXXIX (1933), 32.

of the canon 642, § 1, for although it speaks in the beginning of "*any professed*" who returns to the world, it immediately states that although they may exercise their Orders according to canon 641, they are forbidden these offices and benefices. The phrase concerning the exercise of Orders shows that only those who have already been ordained to Holy Orders are comprehended in the canon.[49] Moreover, the reason for the enactment is undoubtedly a legal precaution against the abandonment of the religious vocation in the proximate hope of securing positions of honor and advantage outside the religious institute.[50] This proximate hope is not found in those who have not yet received Holy Orders. Furthermore, these prohibitions were first enacted in the decree *Quum minoris*, of 1909,[51] and it was expressly declared in that enactment that only priests and those in major orders were referred to. Finally the strict interpretation of the canon is in accord with the prescript of common law which states that laws which involve a penalty or restrict the free exercise of one's rights or establish an exception from the law must be interpreted strictly.[52] For these reasons it is evident that the above prohibitions do not refer to those who have received a dispensation from the religious vows before they have been ordained to Holy Orders. If such persons aspire to Orders and are later ordained as members of the secular clergy, these prohibitions do not affect their clerical life.[53]

The Holy See declared in 1920 that these prohibitions also affect those religious who had obtained from the Holy See permission to stay outside the religious organization before the promulgation of the Code.[54] However, must the same be said of those who took simple perpetual vows in orders which professed solemn vows before the Code? If such religious were dismissed and were allowed to remain outside the religious institute before the promulgation of the

[49] Fanfani, *loc. cit.*; Goyeneche, *loc. cit.*

[50] Vermeersch-Creusen, *Epitome,* I, nn. 799, 824.

[51] S. C. de Rel., decr. *Quum minoris,* 15 iun. 1909—*AAS,* I (1909), 523.

[52] Canon 19.

[53] Vermeersch-Creusen, *Epitome,* I, n. 824; Fanfani, *De Iure Religiosorum,* n. 488.

[54] P. C. I., 24 nov. 1920—*AAS,* XII (1920), 575; cf. Maroto, "Annotationes"—*CpR,* II (1921), 38-39.

Code, they are not comprehended in the above prohibitions.[55] The vows which such religious professed were peculiar in so far as they were temporary on the part of the religious institute and perpetual on the part of the person making the profession. Now it is evident from canon 642, § 1, that in institutes which have perpetual vows, only those who are perpetually professed are comprehended. Hence those who have professed temporary vows in such institutes can freely leave the institute at the end of the time of temporary vows without being further restricted. Since this is so, the canon should not comprehend those who in pre-Code law made profession which was not thoroughly perpetual. Moreover, in the decree *Quum minoris* which first enacted these prohibitions the religious concerned here were not comprehended. The decree referred only to those with solemn vows in religious orders and to those with simple perpetual vows in other religious institutes. Finally there is question here of interpreting a law of the Code in the light of pre-Code legislation,[56] so that it must be held that such religious are not comprehended under the prohibitions of canon 642, § 1.

Those clerics who have been dismissed as well as dispensed from their religious vows, are certainly under these prohibitions by an express enactment of common law,[57] even though the prohibitions themselves are listed under a title of the Code which treats of voluntary egress from the religious institute. It may now be asked if the prohibitions of canon 642, § 1, comprehend those who have been dismissed and are not dispensed from the religious vows. It is evident that such religious have an obligation to return to their religious institute. The time which they spend outside the religious community is a time of amendment directed toward their final return. Therefore they have not a permanency outside the community which would warrant the reception of the prohibited offices and benefices. Canon 642, § 1, does not apply to dismissed clerics who are still bound by the religious vows.[58] However, although they are not

[55] Cf. Goyeneche, "Consultationes,"—*CpR,* V (1924), 26-27.

[56] Canon 6, n. 2.

[57] Canon 672, § 2.

[58] Cf. (Anonymous), "Can Ex-Religious Become Pastors?"—*ER,* LXXXIX (1933), 432; Geser, *The Canon Law Governing Communities of Sisters,* n. 620.

expressly included under canon 642, none of the mentioned benefices and offices should be conferred on them. After they have been allowed with limitations the celebration of the Holy Sacrifice, permission for all further exercise of the sacred ministry is left to the prudent judgment of the ordinary assigned to the dismissed cleric by the Holy See. No assigned ordinary would confer such positions of responsibility upon the dismissed religious. In their prudence the ordinaries will discern that if the legislator does not favor the reception of such benefices and offices by ex-religious who are in good standing, certainly they should not be conferred on religious who are still proving their amendment after being dismissed from the religious community.

It is only after the dismissed clerics have been dispensed from the vows that they are comprehended in these prohibitions. Particular offices forbidden to such clerics would be the offices of Vicar General, *Officialis,* Chancellor, *Promotor Justitiae,* Canon Penitentiary in a cathedral church, Defender of the Bond, Synodal Judge, Synodal Examiner, Parochial Consultor, Auditor, Notary, and the offices of rector, chaplain, confessor,[59] regular preacher,[60] spiritual director and visitor of a religious house. Also the offices of rector, magister spiritus or spiritual director, professor and bursar (oeconomus) in seminaries, both diocesan or interdiocesan or regional, are also forbidden to them.[61] Moreover, such ex-religious cannot be diocesan consultors.[62] Such ex-religious are not excluded from obtaining all parishes, but they cannot be pastors in the cathedral churches or in the major and minor basilicas.[63]

If a bishop wishes to confer one of these offices or benefices on

[59] Of course the prohibition to be such a confessor does not affect the prescriptions of canons 519 and 522. Cf. Schaaf, "Ex-Religious as Confessors of Religious,"—*ER,* XCI (1934), 420-421.

[60] Canon 1327. This prohibition does not forbid an occasional sermon in the religious house, if the needed permission to preach is had.

[61] Cf. "Formula Servanda in Relatione de Statu Seminarii," nn. 8, 10, 11, 14,—*AAS,* XVII (1925), 549.

[62] P. C. I., 29 ian. 1931—*AAS,* XXIII (1931), 110; cf. Cappello, "Annotationes,"—*Periodica,* XX (1931), 154.

[63] Cf. (Anonymous), "Can Ex-Religious Become Pastors?"—*ER,* LXXXIX (1933), 431-432.

the ex-religious, he must first obtain a special indult from the Holy See. The indult should be sought from the Sacred Congregation of Religious. This may seem strange, since the cleric is no longer a religious, but the reason is that the former institute or the Sacred Congregation itself may have grave reasons why the petition should be denied.[64] It may be added, too, that it is within the power of the Sacred Congregation to lift all the prohibitions in one indult.[65]

If it should happen that a prohibited office or benefice is conferred without an apostolic indult on the cleric mentioned in canon 672, § 2, the provision would be valid, but could be declared void by the sentence of a legitimate superior.[66] If the words of the canon are studied, the presence of a mere prohibition is found and therefore there is no question of absolute invalidity. These offices or benefices can therefore be obtained validly but not licitly without an apostolic indult.[67]

[64] Toso, *Commentaria Minora,* Lib. II, pars II, p. 238.

[65] Toso, *loc. cit.*

[66] Canon 153, § 3.

[67] Vermeersch-Creusen, *Epitome,* I, n. 799; Gerster, *Ius Religiosorum,* p. 142; Oesterle, *Praelectiones Iuris Canonici,* I, p. 364; Toso, *Commentaria Minora,* Lib. II, pars II, p. 237.

CHAPTER X

RETURN TO THE RELIGIOUS INSTITUTE

ARTICLE I. RETURN TO THE INSTITUTE WHICH DISMISSED THE RELIGIOUS

WHEN a dismissed religious who was not dispensed from the vows has sufficiently amended and is readmitted by his institute, he is not bound to make a new novitiate or profession. This is evident from the fact that the dismissed person remained a religious while he was absent from the community. He was by no means expelled from the religious state. It is the opinion of all authors that such religious need not make another novitiate or profession.[1]

Since the amendation of the dismissed religious is proved before he is readmitted, there is no further need for a long term of probative penance. A retreat for the purpose of resuming religious fervor and a renewal of the vows at its close may well be imposed, but such measures are left to the superior's discretion. Once a cleric has been readmitted into the institute, he immediately has the full use of his powers of Orders without any further permission. The former limitations and restrictions on the exercise of his sacred ministry then cease automatically.[2]

The question arises concerning the place which the dismissed religious should take among the other professed members after his return. The constitutions should first be consulted in this matter. Thus the General Constitutions of the Friars Minor state that a Friar who returns after dismissal takes precedence from the day of his new reception.[3] When the constitutions state nothing about this

[1] Cocchi, *De Religiosis et Laicis*, n. 159; Geser, *The Canon Law Governing Communities of Sisters*, n. 1215; Fanfani, *De Iure Religiosorum*, n. 519; Palombo, *De Dimissione Religiosorum*, n. 207; Coronata, *Institutiones*, n. 658; Creusen-Garesché-Ellis, *Religious Men and Women in the Code*, n. 1215; Schaefer, *De Religiosis*, n. 598.

[2] Berutti, *De Religiosis*, n. 179.

[3] "If it happens that a Friar legitimately expelled, and according to the

point, the authors are not in agreement on how the question should be settled. Many pre-Code authors were of the opinion that the seniority of such a religious should be dated not from the day of his return, but from the time of his profession.[4] Berutti also adheres to this opinion after the promulgation of the Code.[5]

However, it does not seem fitting that such a religious should after return precede those religious who, since their profession have striven to lead a worthy and fervent life, remaining under the immediate direction of their superiors in obedience, and exercising constantly religious charity within the community. Furthermore, if a dismissed religious who has returned were placed below those who have always striven for perfection by a worthy religious life since the day of their profession, it would be a salutary reminder of the gravity of disobedience and incorrigibility in the religious life, and would act as a deterrent for other religious who might be tempted to rebel against the obligations of their vows and rules. For these reasons the present author holds the opposite view, namely, that such a religious should take precedence, not from the day of his profession, but from the day of his return. This opinion was also proposed by several pre-Code authors.[6] After the promulgation of the code, Fanfani,[7] and Palombo[8] state it as a common custom among the religious institutes. This opinion has gradually gained the favor of many authors who now represent a well estab-

standard of law, being fully amended, is again readmitted to the Order, he shall reside for a year in a solitary convent where regular discipline is more perfectly observed. His precedence takes effect only from the day of his new reception."—*The Rule and General Constitutions of the Friars Minor,* n. 390; The Franciscan Friars of the Atonement also have an identical rule.—*Constitutions of the Franciscan Friars of the Atonement,* n. 364.

[4] Barbosa, *Collectanea Doctorum in Jus Pontificium Universum,* Lib. III, tit. XXXI, c. XXIV, n. 8; Passerinus, *De Hominum Statibus,* Q. CLXXXIX, art. VIII, n. 660; Schmalzgrueber, Lib. III, tit. XXXI, n. 257.

[5] *De Religiosis,* n. 177.

[6] Leurenius, Lib. III, tit. XXXI, q. DCCCLXI, n. 2; Donatus, *Rerum Regularium Praxis Resolutoria,* Tom. I, pars II, tract. VIII, q. XXVII, n. 3; Rotarius, *Theologia Moralis Regularium,* Tom. I, lib. III, c. II, punct. VII, n. 6.

[7] *De Iure Religiosorum,* n. 519.

[8] *De Dimissione Religiosorum,* n. 207.

lished majority.[9] However, as Larraona has pointed out, this privation of the former precedence can hardly be said to be automatic on return, but it can be justly applied *ab homine* and such is the usual practice of religious superiors.[10] Following such a privation of former precedence all the rights that depend upon it in the community would be computed not from the day of profession but from the day of return.

If, after a dispensation from the vows, an ex-religious returns to his former institute a dispensation from the Holy See is necessary,[11] otherwise he would be received invalidly into the novitiate. If the dispensation were granted, the ex-religious would be obliged to make a new novitiate and profession and precedence in the community would always be reckoned from the date of the new profession.[12]

Article II. Transfer to Another Institute

No dismissed religious, who has not been dispensed from the vows, can without permission of the Holy See enter a religious institute other than the one which dismissed him. Since he is still bound by the vows and still a member of the institute in which he made his profession, such action involves real transfer from one institute to another. And without authorization from the Apostolic See, no religious can transfer either to another institute or from one independent monastery to another.[13] If such a religious were admitted into a second institute without an Apostolic indult, his admission into the novitiate would be invalid.[14] To accomplish this transfer, testimonial letters of the former major superior would be necessary.[15] Besides these, testimonials should also be demanded

[9] Cocchi, *De Religiosis et Laicis*, n. 159; Vermeersch-Creusen, *Epitome*, I, n. 823; Gerster, *Ius Religiosorum*, p. 162; Geser, *The Canon Law Governing Communities of Sisters*, n. 1216; Schaefer, *De Religiosis*, n. 598; Creusen-Garesché-Ellis, *Religious Men and Women in the Code*, n. 364; Beste, *Introductio in Codicem*, p. 453.

[10] "Commentarium Codicis,"—*CpR*, IV (1923), 332.

[11] Canon 542, n. 1.

[12] Canon 640, § 2.

[13] Canon 632.

[14] Canon 542, n. 1.

[15] Canon 544, § 5.

from the ordinary of the place where the dismissed person has stayed for more than one morally continuous year after dismissal.

If the religious were legitimately received into a second institute, it is required that he make a new novitiate. In the meantime the vows which he has professed remain intact, but the particular obligations of the former institute are suspended and he is bound to obey the superiors of the new organization, including the master of novices, in virtue of his vow of obedience.[16] If he does not make profession in the second organization, the obligation remains of returning to the institute which dismissed him.[17] The privilege granted to the Society of Jesus whereby the Superior General could grant to dismissed members permission to enter certain orders,[18] does not do away with the necessity of the Apostolic indult now demanded by law.[19]

If a dismissed religious receives a dispensation from his vows and then wishes to enter a second religious institute, he must petition for a dispensation of the Holy See from the invalidating impediment of canon 542, n. 1. As for required testimonials, nothing is explicitly stated in law. Certainly, as Larraona points out, canon 544, § 5, does not treat of such an ex-religious. It is merely concerned with cases of transfer of a perpetually professed religious who has received apostolic authorization.[20] Arguing from analogy, it seems that besides the information of the superior of the religious institute which dismissed him, which is asked for *ex officio* by the Holy See before it grants the dispensation, the superior of the second institute ought to demand only testimonials for the time after secularization, *i. e.*, testimonials from the ordinaries of the places where the person lived after secularization for more than one morally continuous year and testimonials from the rector or superior of a seminary or college in which the ex-religious lived after the dispensation from the vows.[21]

[16] Canon 633, § 1.

[17] Canons 633, § 2; 634.

[18] Gregorius XIII, const. *Cum alias*, 22 sept. 1582—*Bull. Rom. Taur.*, VIII, 399.

[19] Goyeneche, "De Transitu ad alium Religionem,"—*CpR*, I (1920), 229-230.

[20] "Commentarium Codicis,"—*CpRM*, XIX (1938), 258.

[21] Larraona, *loc. cit.*

CONCLUSIONS

1. The usual terms found in the definition of dismissal after the profession of perpetual vows are confusing. Dismissal is here defined as an egress from the communal life of a religious organization imposed by legitimate ecclesiastical authority upon a delinquent religious.

2. Even though no expressed permission is given by religious superiors, the religious on dismissal receives an implicit and general permission to use and to administer goods for necessities. This applies to all goods in his possession whether he, or the religious institute, is the proper owner.

3. The dismissed religious has no obligation by reason of his vow to obey the ordinary of the place where he stays. He must obey that ordinary merely as a lay person or as a secular cleric of the diocese.

4. The dismissed religious must observe the obligations of the additional vows which are professed in certain religious organizations.

5. The dismissed religious must observe the obligations of the rules and constitutions of his institute, in so far as they do not conflict with the life which he leads outside the community. He is entirely freed from only those observances which necessitate the presence of a community.

6. The prescripts of canon 671, § 1, do not refer to dismissed lay religious or to those clerics who have been automatically dismissed. It is also more probable that they do not refer to those religious in holy orders who have been dismissed for crimes which are punished with infamy of law, with deposition or with degradation.

7. The obligation of the dismissed religious to return to the institute, and the obligation of the institute to accept the amended religious, remain as long as the dismissed is bound by the religious vows. The Holy See alone can decide that either of these obligations need not be fulfilled.

8. In all cases of dismissed religious the superiors should demand not mere amendment but complete and proved amendment, before the religious is allowed to return.

9. In justice the institute is not obliged to support a dismissed religious. There is an obligation in charity enforced by the common law to maintain clerics who are proving their amendment and to provide dismissed women religious with what is necessary for the safe and proper return to their home and for decent livelihood during a certain period. These obligations are not binding when the dismissed religious has means of self-support.

10. After a dismissed religious has returned to the institute, his precedence in the community should be reckoned not from the date of his religious profession, but from the date of his return.

BIBLIOGRAPHY

Sources

Acta Apostolicae Sedis, Commentarium Officiale, Romae, 1909—

Acta Sanctae Sedis, 41 vols., Romae, 1865-1908.

Bullarii Romani Continuatio Summorum Pontificum, 19 vols., Prati, 1756-1883.

Bullarum Diplomatum et Privilegiorum Sanctorum Romanorum Pontificum Taurinensis Editio, 24 tomes in 25 vols., Augustae Taurinorum, 1857-1872.

Canonical Legislation Concerning Religious, Authorized English Translation, Rome: Vatican Printing Office, 1918; also ed., 1919.

Codex Iuris Canonici Pii X Pontificis Maximi iussu digestus Benedicti Papae XV auctoritate promulgatus, Romae: Typis Polyglottis Vaticanis, 1917, Reimpressio, 1929.

Codicis Iuris Canonici Fontes cura Emi. Petri Card. Gasparri editi, 9 vols., Romae [postea Civitate Vaticana]: Typis Polyglottis Vaticanis, 1923-1939 (Vols. VII-IX ed. cura et studio Emi. Iustiniani Card. Serédi).

Collectanea in Usum Secretariae Sacrae Congregationis Episcoporum et Regularium, ed. noviss. Bizzarri, Romae, 1885.

Constitutiones Congregationis Missionariorum de Marianhill, 1936.

Constitutiones Ordinis Fratrum Minorum Sancti Francisci Conventualium, Romae, 1932.

Constitutions of the Brothers of Christian Doctrine, Jersey, 1936.

Constitutions of the Franciscan Friars of the Atonement, Garrison, N. Y., 1932.

Constitutions of the Institute of the Brothers of the Sacred Heart, Metuchen, N. J., 1928.

Constitutions of the Institute of the Marist Brothers of the Schools or the Little Brothers of Mary, Grugliasco, 1935.

Corpus Iuris Canonici, ed. Lipsiensis secunda, post Aemilii Richteri curas . . . instruxit Aemilius Friedberg, 2 vols., Lipsiae, 1879-1881.

Corpus Juris Civilis, ed. Gothofredi, Lugduni, 1781.

Corpus Iuris Civilis, Institutiones, quas recognovit P. Krueger, *Digesta,* quae recognovit T. Mommsen et retractavit P. Kreuger, *Codex Iustinianus,* quem recognovit et retractavit P. Kreuger, *Novellae,* quas recognovit R. Schoell et absolvit G. Kroll, 3 vols., Berolini, 1928-1929.

Institutum Societatis Iesu, 3 vols., Florentiae, 1892-1893.

Mansi, Joannes, *Sacrorum Conciliorum Nova et Amplissima Collectio,* 53 vols. in 59, Florentiae, Parisiis, Arnhem et Leipzig, 1901-1927.

Monumenta Germaniae Historica, Legum Sectio II, Capitularia Regum Francorum, 2 tomes in 5 vols., ed. A. Boretius et V. Krause, Hannoverae, 1883-1897.

Normae Secundum Quas S. Cong. Episcoporum et Regularium Procedere Solet in Approbandis Novis Institutis Votorum Simplicium, Romae, 1901.

Pallottini, Salvator, *Collectio Omnium Conclusionum et Resolutionum Quae in Causis Propositis apud Sacram Congregationem Cardinalium S. Concilii Tridentini Interpretum Prodierunt* . . . , 18 vols., Romae, 1868-1893.

Regulae ac Praescriptiones a variis Capitulis generalibus praesertim a decimo exartae accedit Statutum pro Missionibus (Congregatio Sacerdotum a Sacro Corde Jesu), Romae: apud Curiam Generalitiam, 1934.

Rule and General Constitutions of the Friars Minor, The, Paterson, N. J., 1936.

Sacrosancti et Oecumenici Concilii Tridentini Canones et Decreta, Parisiis et Vesontione, 1832.

Sancti Benedicti Regula Monasteriorum, 3. ed., D. Cuthbertus Butler, Friburgi Brisgoviae: Herder, 1935.

Thesaurus Resolutionum Sacrae Congregationis Concilii, 167 vols., Romae, 1718-1908.

Reference Works

Aertnys, Josephus, *Theologia Moralis juxta Doctrinam S. Alphonsi Mariae de Ligorio, Doctoris Ecclesiae,* 3. ed., 2 vols., Tornaci, 1893.

Aertnys, Josephus-Damen, Cornelius, *Theologia Moralis Secundum Doctrinam S. Alfonsi De Ligorio Doct. Ecclesiae,* 13. ed., 2 vols., Taurini: Marietti, 1939.

Alphonsus de Liguori, St., *Theologia Moralis,* ed. Gaudé, 4 vols., Romae, 1905-1912.

Appeltern, Victor, *Compendium Praelectiones Juris Regularis,* 2. ed., Parisiis, 1913.

Avanzini, Petrus, *De Constitutione Apostolicae Sedis,* 2. ed., Romae, 1874.

Ayrinhac, H. A.-Lydon, P. J., *Penal Legislation in the New Code of Canon Law,* New York: Benziger Bros., 1936.

Azor, Joannes, *Institutum Moralium in Quibus Universae Questiones,* 3 vols., Brixiae, 1617.

Bachofen (Augustine), *Compendium Juris Regularium,* New York, 1903.

[Bachofen], Charles Augustine, *A Commentary on the New Code of Canon Law,* 8 vols., Vol. III, 4. ed., 1929; Vol. VI, 2. ed., 1923, St. Louis: Herder.

Barbosa, Augustinus, *Collectanea Doctorum in Jus Pontificium Universum,* 6 tomes in 3 vols., Lugduni, 1716.

Bastien, Pierre, *Directoire Canonique a l'Usage des Congrégations à Voeux Simples,* 3. ed., Bruges: Beyaert, 1923.

Battandier, Albert, *Guide canonique pour les constitutions des instituts a voeux simples,* 5. ed., Paris, 1911. Also, 6. ed., Paris, 1923.

Benedictus XIV, *De Synodo Dioecesana,* ed. noviss., Prati, 1844.

Berutti, Christophorus, *Institutiones Iuris Canonici,* 6 vols., Vol. III, *De Religiosis,* Taurini, Romae: Marietti, 1936.

Beste, Udalricus, *Introductio in Codicem,* Collegeville, Minn.: St. John's Abbey Press, 1938.

Biederlack, Josephus-Führich, Maximillianus, *De Religiosis,* Oeniponte: Rauch, 1919.

Blat, Albertus, *Commentarium Textus Codicis Iuris Canonici,* 5 vols. in 6, lib. II, pars II-III, *Ius de Religiosis,* 3. ed., 1938, Romae: Apud "Angelicum."

Bonacina, Martinus, *Opera Omnia,* 3 tomes, Lugduni, 1639.

———, *Theologia Moralis,* 3 tomes, Venetiis, 1687.

Bouix, Dominicus, *Tractatus de Iure Regularium,* 2. ed., 2 tomes, Bruxellis, 1867.

Bouuaert, F., *Selecta Capita Codicis Iuris Canonici Analytica Proposita et Brevi Commentario Adaucta,* Gandae, 1919.

Cappello, Felix, *Summa Iuris Canonici in Usum Scholarum Concinnata,* 2 vols., Romae: Apud Aedes Universitatis Gregorianae, 1928.

———, *Tractatus Canonico-Moralis de Censuris Iuxta Codicem Canonici,* 3. ed., Romae: Marietti, 1933.

Catholic Encyclopedia, The, 15 vols., index and 2 sups., New York, 1907-1922.

Cervia, Augenius, *De Professione Religiosa,* Bologna: Via Bellinzona, 1938.

Chelodi, Ioannes, *Ius de Personis iuxta Codicem Iuris Canonis,* 2. ed., a Sac. Ernesto Bertagnolli recognita et aucta, Tridenti: Libr. edit. Tridentum, 1927.

———, *Ius Poenale et Ordo Procedendi in Iudiciis Criminalibus iuxta Codicem Iuris Canonici,* Tridenti: Libr. Edit. Tridentum, 1925.

Cicognani, Hamletus J., *Commentarium ad Librum I Codicis,* Romae: ex Schola Typographica "Pio X," 1925.

Cipollini, Albertus, *De Censuris Latae Sententiae iuxta Codicem Iuris Canonici,* Taurini: Marietti, 1925.

Cocchi, Guidus, *Commentarium in Codicem Iuris Canonici,* 5 vols. in 8, Vol. IV, *De Religiosis et Laicis,* 2. ed., Taurinorum Augustae: Marietti, 1926.

Connell, Franciscus, *De Sacramentis Ecclesiae,* Brugis: Beyaert, 1933.

Coronata, Matthaeus Conte a, *Institutiones Iuris Canonici,* 5 vols., Vols. I and II, 2. ed., 1939, Taurini: Marietti, 1933-1939.

Craisson, D., *Manuale Totius Juris Canonici,* 6. ed., 4 vols., Pictavii, 1880.

Creusen, Joseph-Garesché, Edward-Ellis, Adam, *Religious Men and Women in the Code,* 3. English ed., Milwaukee: Bruce, 1940.

D'Anibale, Iosephus, *In Constitutionem Apostolicae Sedis qua Censurae Latae Sententiae Limitantur Commentarii,* Prati, 1894.

De Ameno, *Opera Omnia,* 3 tomes, Romae, 1753-1754.

De Meester, A., *Juris Canonici et Juris Canonico-Civilis Compendium,* nova ed., 3 vols. in 4, Brugis: Desclée, De Brouwer & Si, 1921-1928.

Donatus, Hyacentus, *Rerum Regularium Praxis Resolutoria,* 2 tomes, Neapoli, 1652.

Elbel, Benjamin, *Theologia Moralis per Modum Conferentiarum,* 2. ed., 3 vols., Paderbornae, 1894.

Engel, Ludovicus, *Collegium Universi Juris Canonici,* Venetiis, 1760.

Fagnanus, Prosperus, *Commentaria in Quinque Libros Decretalium,* 5 vols., Romae, 1661.

Fanfani, Ludovicus, *De Iure Religiosorum,* 2. ed., Taurini, Romae: Marietti, 1925.

Farrell, Benjamin, *The Rights and Duties of the Local Ordinary Regarding Congregations of Women Religious of Pontifical Approval,* The Catholic University of America Canon Law Studies, n. 128, Washington, D. C.: The Catholic University of America Press, 1941.

Ferraris, Lucius, *Prompta Bibliotheca Canonica, Juridica, Moralis, Theologica, necnon Ascetica, Polemica, Rubristica, Historica,* 8 vols., Parisiis, 1860-1863.

Findlay, Stephen, *Canonical Norms Governing the Deposition and Degradation of Clerics,* The Catholic University of America Canon Law Studies, n. 130, Washington, D. C.: The Catholic University of America Press, 1941.

Gasparri, Petrus Card., *Tractatus Canonicus de Matrimonio,* ed. nova, 2 vols., Civitate Vaticana: Typis Polyglottis Vaticanis, 1932.

Gerster a Zeil, Thomas Villanova, *Ius Religiosorum in Compendium Redactum,* Taurini: Marietti, 1935.

Geser, Fintan, *The Canon Law Governing Communities of Sisters,* St. Louis: Herder, 1938.

Gonzalez-Tallez, *Commentaria Perpetua in Singulos Textus Quinque Librorum Decretalium,* 5 tomes in 4 vols., Venetiis, 1699.

Goyeneche, Servus, *Iuris Canonici Summa Principia, De Religiosis,* Romae: Tip. Pol. "Cuore di Maria," 1938.

Hannan, Jerome, *The Canon Law of Wills,* The Catholic University of America Canon Law Studies, n. 86, Washington, D. C.: The Catholic University of America, 1934.

Huguenin, Ludovicus, *Expositio Methodica Juris Canonici ad Usum Scholarum Clericalium,* 4. ed., Parisiis, 1887.

Iorio, Thomas A., *Theologia Moralis Iuxta Methodum Compendii Ioannis P. Gury et Raphaelis Tummulo,* 6. ed., 3 vols., Neapoli: D'Auria, 1938-1939.

Jansen, J., *Ordensrecht,* 3. ed., Paderborn: Schöningh, 1931.

Jardí, Antonio de la C., *El Derecho de las Religiosas según las Praescripciones Vigentes del Codigo Canonico y Civil,* 2. ed., Vich: Serafica, 1927.

Kealy, Thomas, *The Dowry of Women Religious,* The Catholic University of America Canon Law Studies, n. 134, Washington, D. C.: The Catholic University of America Press, 1941.

Keene, Michael, *Religious Ordinaries and Canon 198,* The Catholic University of America Canon Law Studies, n. 135, Washington, D. C.: The Catholic University of America Press, 1942.

Lanslots, D. I., *Handbook of Canon Law for Congregations of Women Under Simple Vows,* 6. ed., New York, 1911.

Laurentius, Ioannes, *Institutiones Iuris Ecclesiastici Quas in Usum Scholarum Scripsit,* 3. ed., Friburgi Brisgoviae, 1914.

Leitner, Martin, *Handbuch des katholischen Kirchenrechts,* 2. ed., 2 vols., Regensburg: Kosel und Pustet, 1921-1927.

Lessius, Leonardus, *De Iustitia et Iure,* 3. ed., Mediolani, 1613.

Leurenius, Petrus, *Forum Ecclesiasticum, in quo Jus Canonicum Universum Explanatur,* 5 vols. in 3, Venetiis, 1729.

Marc, Clement-Gestermann, Fr. X., *Institutiones Morales Alphonsianae,* 19. ed. (4. ed. post Codicem), 2 vols., Lugduni: Emmanuel Vitte, 1934.

Maroto, Philippus, *Institutiones Iuris Canonici,* 2 vols., Romae, 1919-1921. Vol. I, 3. ed., Romae: Apud Commentarium pro Religiosis, 1921.

McBride, James, *Incardination and Excardination of Seculars,* The Catholic University of America Canon Law Studies, n. 145, Washington, D. C.: The Catholic University of America Press, 1941.

Merkelbach, Benedictus Henricus, *Summa Theologiae Moralis ad Mentem D. Thomae et ad Normam Iuris Novi,* 3. ed., 3 vols., Parisiis, Desclée de Brouwer, 1938-1939.

Michiels, P. Gomarrus, *Normae Generales Juris Canonici,* 2 vols., Lublin in Polonia: Universitas Catholica, 1929.

———, *Principia Generalia de Personis in Ecclesia,* Lublin in Polonia: Universitas Catholica, 1932.

Migne, Jacques P., *Patrologiae Cursus Completus, Series Graeca,* 161 vols., Parisiis, 1856-1866.

———, *Patrologiae Cursus Completus, Series Latina,* 221 vols., Parisiis, 1844-1864.

Mocchegiani, Petrus, *Jurisprudentia Ecclesiastica ad Usum et Commoditatem Utriusque Cleri,* 3 vols., Ad Claras Aquas, 1904-1905.

Molina, Ludovicus, *De Iustitia et Iure Tractatus,* 2 tomes, Venetiis, 1611.

Montensis, Piatus, *Praelectiones Juris Regularis,* 3. ed., 2 vols., Tornaci, 1906.

Navarrus (Martinus de Azpilcueta), *Opera Omnia,* 6 vols., Venetiis, 1618-1621.

Oesterle, Gerardus, *Praelectiones Iuris Canonici,* Vol. I, Romae: In Collegio S. Anselmi, 1931.

Official Catholic Directory, The, New York: Kenedy & Sons, 1943.

Ojetti, B., *Commentarium in Codicem Iuris Canonici,* 4 vols., Romae: Apud Aedes Universitatis Gregorianae, 1927-1931.

Orth, Raymond, *The Approbation of Religious Institutes,* The Catholic University of America Canon Law Studies, n. 71, Washington, D. C.: The Catholic University of America, 1931.

Palombo, Josephus, *De Dimissione Religiosorum, Taurini,* Romae: Marietti, 1931.

Papi, H., *Religious Profession,* New York, 1918.

Passerinus, Petrus, *De Hominum Statibus et Officiis Inspectiones Morales,* 3 vols., Lucae, 1732.

Pejška, Josephus, *Ius Canonicum Religiosorum,* 3. ed., Friburgi Brisgoviae: Herder, 1927.

Piontek, Cyrillus, *De Indulto Exclaustrationis Necnon Saecularizationis,* The Catholic University of America Canon Law Studies, n. 29, Washington, D. C.: The Catholic University of America, 1925.

Prümmer, Dominicus, *Manuale Iuris Canonici,* 5. ed., Friburgi Brisgoviae: Herder, 1927.

Raus, Joannes B., *De Sacra Obedientiae Virtute et Voto,* Lugduni: Apud Emmanuelem Vitte, 1923.

———, *Institutiones Canonicae,* 2. ed., Lugduni: Typis Emmanuelis Vitte, 1931.

Reiffenstuel, A., *Jus Canonicum Universum,* 5 vols., Antverpiae, 1743.

Riesner, Albert, *Apostates and Fugitives from Religious Institutes,* The Catholic University of America Canon Law Studies, n. 168, Washington, D. C.: The Catholic University of America Press, 1942.

Rotarius, Thomas, *Theologia Moralis Regularium,* 3 tomes in 2 vols., Venetiis, 1735.

Sabetti-Barrett, *Compendium Theologiae Moralis,* 8. ed. post Codicem, Neo-Eboraci: Frederick Pustet Co., 1939.

Sanchez, Thomas, *Opus Morale in Praecepta Decalogi,* 2 vols., Parmae, 1723.

Schaefer, Timotheus, *De Religiosis,* 3. ed., Romae: Typis Polyglottis Vaticanis, 1940.

Schmalzgrueber, F., *Ius Ecclesiasticum Universum,* 5 vols. in 12, Romae, 1843-1845.

Schroeder, H. J., *Disciplinary Decrees of the General Councils,* St. Louis: Herder, 1937.

Sebastianelli, Gulielmus, *Praelectiones Iuris Canonici, De Personis,* Romae, 1896.

Smith, Mariner, *The Penal Law for Religious,* The Catholic University of America Canon Law Studies, n. 98, Washington, D. C.: The Catholic University of America, 1935.

Sole, Iacobus, *De Delictis et Poenis Praelectiones in Lib. V Codicis Iuris Canonici,* Romae, 1920.

Soto, D., *De Iustitia et Iure,* Venetiis, 1568.

Suarez, Franciscus, *Opera Omnia,* 26 vols., Parisiis, 1856-1861, Vols. XIII-XVI, *De Virtute et Statu Religiosorum.*

Tanquerey, A., *Synopsis Theologiae Moralis et Pastoralis,* 3 vols., Vol. I, *De Poenitentia, Matrimonio et Ordine,* 10. ed., Tornaci: Desclée, 1925.

Thomas Aquinas, St., *Opera Omnia,* 24 tomes in 15, Parmae, 1852-1869.

Toso, Albertus, *Ad Codicem Iuris Canonici Commentaria Minora,* 5 vols., lib. II, pars II, Romae: Jus Pontificium, 1927.

Turner, Sidney, *The Vow of Poverty,* The Catholic University of America Canon Law Studies, n. 54, Washington, D. C.: The Catholic University of America, 1929.

Van Espen, Zegerus Bernardus, *Jus Ecclesiasticum Universum,* ed. noviss., 10 tomes in 5 vols., Venetiis, 1769.

Van Hove, A., *Commentarium Lovaniense in Codicem Iuris Canonici,* Vol. I, tom. I, *Prolegomena,* Mechliniae, Romae: Dessain, 1928.

Vesquez, Gabriel, *Commentarii in Summam S. Thomae,* 2 tomes in 6 vols., Lugduni, 1631.

Vecchiotti, Septimius M., *Institutiones Canonicae ex Operibus Joannis Card. Soglia,* 16. ed., 3 vols., Augustini Taurinorum, 1875.

Vermeersch, Arthurus, *De Religiosis Institutis et Personis,* 4. ed., 2 vols., Brugis, 1907-1909.

Vermeersch, Arthurus, *Theologiae Moralis Principia, Responsa, Concilia,* ed. altera, 3 vols., Brugis: Charles Beyaert, 1926-1928.

Vermeersch, Arthurus-Creusen, Josephus, *Epitome Iuris Canonici,* 3 vols., Vol. I, 6. ed., 1937; Vol. II, 5. ed., 1934; Vol. III, 5. ed., 1936, Mechliniae-Romae: H. Dessain.

Vromant, G., *De Bonis Ecclesiae Temporalibus ad Usum praesertim Missionariorum et Religiosorum,* Louvain: Desbarax, 1927.

Wernz, Franciscus, *Ius Decretalium ad usum Praelectionum in Scholis Textus Iuris Canonici, sive Iuris Decretalium,* 2. ed., 6 vols., Romae et Prati, 1905-1914.

Wernz, Franciscus-Vidal, Petrus, *Ius Canonicum ad Codicis Normam Exactum,* 7 tomes in 8 vols., Romae: Apud Aedes Universitatis Gregorianae, Tom III, *De Religiosis,* 1933; Tom. VI, *De Processibus,* 1927.

Wouters, Ludovicus, *Manuale Theologiae Moralis,* 2 vols., Brugis (Belgii): Carolus Beyaert, 1932.

Woywod, Stanislaus, *A Practical Commentary on the Code of Canon Law,* 3. ed., 2 vols., New York: Wagner, 1929.

PERIODICALS

Analecta Iuris Pontificii, Romae, 1855-1868; Parisiis, 1869-1890.

Apollinaris, Romae, 1928—

Commentarium pro Religiosis (later, [1935] *Commentarium pro Religiosis et Missionariis*), Romae, 1920—

Ecclesiastical Review, The (originally *The American Ecclesiastical Review*), Philadelphia, 1889—

Irish Ecclesiastical Record, The, Dublin, 1864—

Jus Pontificium, Romae, 1921—

Periodica de Re Canonica et Morali utili praesertim Religiosis et Missionariis, Bruges, 1905—

Theologisch-praktische Quartalschrift, Linz, 1832—

ARTICLES

(Anonymous), "Can Ex-Religious Become Pastors?"—*ER,* LXXXIX (1933), 431-432.

Bastien, P., "De Evolutione Historico-Iuridica Processus Dimissionis,"—*Jus Pontificium,* XI (1931), 20-29.

Cappello, Felix, "Annotationes,"—*Periodica,* XX (1931), 151-154.

Commentator, "De Suspensione lata in religiosos eiectos extra Religionem degentes,"—*ASS,* XIX (1886), appendix XLVI, 389-403.

D'Ambrosio, Franciscus, "De Dote Monialis ante Codicis Promulgationem Solemniter Professae et ad aliud Monasterium post Codicem Transeuntis,"—*Apollinaris,* I (1928), 297-300.

Fuchs, Vinzenz, "Rückgabe der Mitgift an die ausscheidende Klosterfrau,"—*ThPrQs,* LXXXVIII (1935), 359-368.

Gearin, M. A., "The Confessor and Vow of Religious Poverty,"—*ER,* LXI (1919), 136-153.

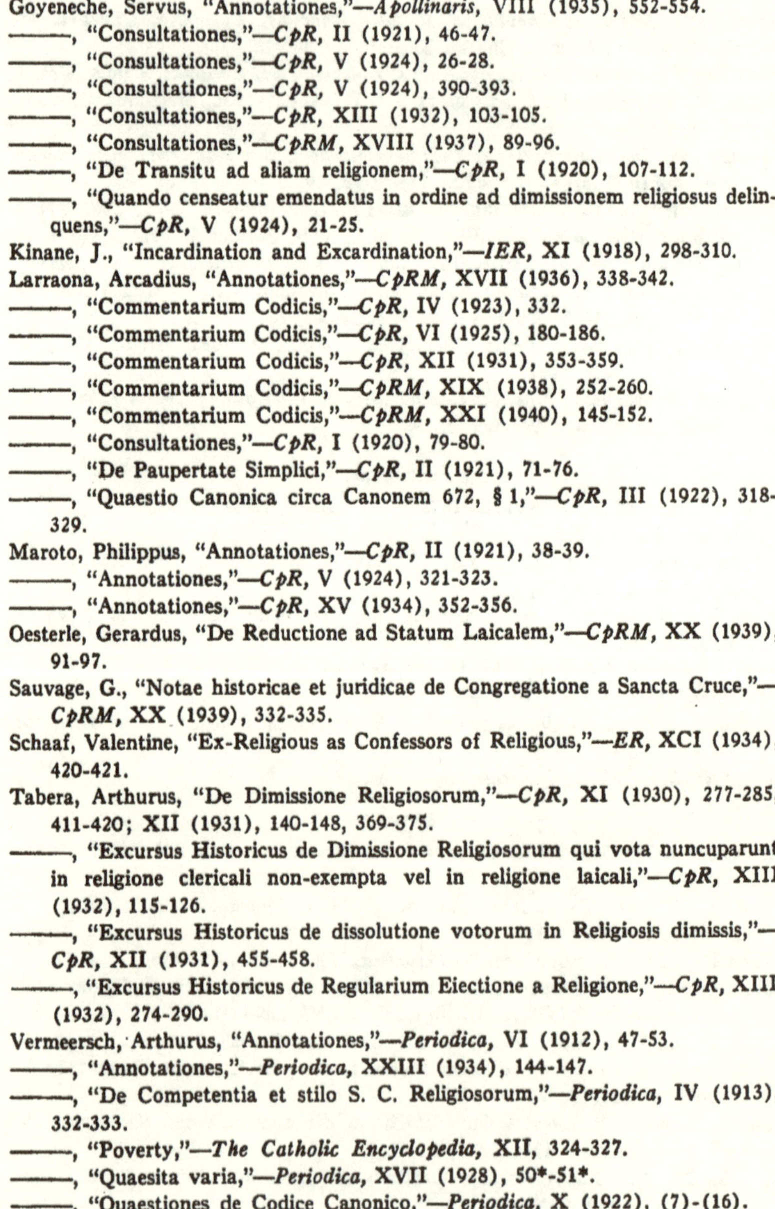

Goyeneche, Servus, "Annotationes,"—*Apollinaris*, VIII (1935), 552-554.

———, "Consultationes,"—*CpR*, II (1921), 46-47.

———, "Consultationes,"—*CpR*, V (1924), 26-28.

———, "Consultationes,"—*CpR*, V (1924), 390-393.

———, "Consultationes,"—*CpR*, XIII (1932), 103-105.

———, "Consultationes,"—*CpRM*, XVIII (1937), 89-96.

———, "De Transitu ad aliam religionem,"—*CpR*, I (1920), 107-112.

———, "Quando censeatur emendatus in ordine ad dimissionem religiosus delinquens,"—*CpR*, V (1924), 21-25.

Kinane, J., "Incardination and Excardination,"—*IER*, XI (1918), 298-310.

Larraona, Arcadius, "Annotationes,"—*CpRM*, XVII (1936), 338-342.

———, "Commentarium Codicis,"—*CpR*, IV (1923), 332.

———, "Commentarium Codicis,"—*CpR*, VI (1925), 180-186.

———, "Commentarium Codicis,"—*CpR*, XII (1931), 353-359.

———, "Commentarium Codicis,"—*CpRM*, XIX (1938), 252-260.

———, "Commentarium Codicis,"—*CpRM*, XXI (1940), 145-152.

———, "Consultationes,"—*CpR*, I (1920), 79-80.

———, "De Paupertate Simplici,"—*CpR*, II (1921), 71-76.

———, "Quaestio Canonica circa Canonem 672, § 1,"—*CpR*, III (1922), 318-329.

Maroto, Philippus, "Annotationes,"—*CpR*, II (1921), 38-39.

———, "Annotationes,"—*CpR*, V (1924), 321-323.

———, "Annotationes,"—*CpR*, XV (1934), 352-356.

Oesterle, Gerardus, "De Reductione ad Statum Laicalem,"—*CpRM*, XX (1939), 91-97.

Sauvage, G., "Notae historicae et juridicae de Congregatione a Sancta Cruce,"—*CpRM*, XX (1939), 332-335.

Schaaf, Valentine, "Ex-Religious as Confessors of Religious,"—*ER*, XCI (1934), 420-421.

Tabera, Arthurus, "De Dimissione Religiosorum,"—*CpR*, XI (1930), 277-285, 411-420; XII (1931), 140-148, 369-375.

———, "Excursus Historicus de Dimissione Religiosorum qui vota nuncuparunt in religione clericali non-exempta vel in religione laicali,"—*CpR*, XIII (1932), 115-126.

———, "Excursus Historicus de dissolutione votorum in Religiosis dimissis,"—*CpR*, XII (1931), 455-458.

———, "Excursus Historicus de Regularium Eiectione a Religione,"—*CpR*, XIII (1932), 274-290.

Vermeersch, Arthurus, "Annotationes,"—*Periodica*, VI (1912), 47-53.

———, "Annotationes,"—*Periodica*, XXIII (1934), 144-147.

———, "De Competentia et stilo S. C. Religiosorum,"—*Periodica*, IV (1913), 332-333.

———, "Poverty,"—*The Catholic Encyclopedia*, XII, 324-327.

———, "Quaesita varia,"—*Periodica*, XVII (1928), 50*-51*.

———, "Quaestiones de Codice Canonico,"—*Periodica*, X (1922), (7)-(16).

ABBREVIATIONS

AAS—Acta Apostolicae Sedis.
ASS—Acta Sanctae Sedis.
ER—Ecclesiastical Review.
CpR—Commentarium pro Religiosis (1920-1934).
CpRM—Commentarium pro Religiosis et Missionariis (1935—).
Fontes—Codicis Iuris Canonici Fontes.
Ibid—(Ibidem) The preceding reference.
IER—The Irish Ecclesiastical Record.
Loc. cit.—Loco citato.
MPL—(Migne, *Patrologia Latina*), Migne, Jacques Paul, *Patrologiae Cursus Completus, Series Latina.*
Op. cit.—Opere citato.
Periodica—Periodica de Re Canonica et Morali utili Praesertim Religiosis et Missionariis.
S. C. C.—Sacra Congregatio Concilii.
S. C. de Rel.—Sacra Congregatio de Religiosis.
S. C. Ep. et Reg.—Sacra Congregatio Episcoporum et Regularium.
ThPrQs—Theologisch-praktische Quartalschrift.

ALPHABETICAL INDEX

BIOGRAPHICAL NOTE

CHARLES GERARD O'LEARY was born on August 22, 1913, in Boston, Massachusetts. After completing his elementary education in the parochial school of Our Lady of Perpetual Help, Roxbury, Massachusetts, he entered St. Mary's College, the Juvenate of the Redemptorist Fathers at North East, Pennsylvania, in September, 1927. On August 1, 1933, he received the habit of the Congregation of the Most Holy Redeemer at Ilchester, Maryland, and made his religious profession on August 2nd of the following year. His seminary course was made at the Redemptorist House of Studies, Mount St. Alphonsus, Esopus, New York, where he was ordained to the priesthood on June 18, 1939, by the Most Reverend Stephen J. Donahue, D.D., Bishop Auxiliary of New York. In September of 1940 he entered the Catholic University of America to pursue a graduate course of studies in the School of Canon Law. He received his Baccalaureate in Canon Law in June, 1941, and his Licentiate in Canon Law in May, 1942.

CANON LAW STUDIES *

1. Freriks, Rev. Celestine A., C.PP.S., J.C.D., Religious Congregations in Their External Relations, 121 pp., 1916.
2. Galliher, Rev. Daniel M., O.P., J.C.D., Canonical Elections, 117 pp., 1917.
3. Borkowski, Rev. Aurelius L., O.F.M., J.C.D., De Confraternitatibus Ecclesiasticis, 136 pp., 1918.
4. Castillo, Rev. Cayo, J.C.D., Disertacion Historico-Canonica sobre la Potestad del Cabildo en Sede Vacante o Impedida del Vicario Capitular, 99 pp., 1919 (1918).
5. Kubelbeck, Rev. William J., S.T.B., J.C.D., The Sacred Penitentiaria and Its Relation to Faculties of Ordinaries and Priests, 129 pp., 1918.
6. Petrovits, Rev. Joseph, J.C., S.T.D., J.C.D., The New Church Law on Matrimony, X-461 pp., 1919.
7. Hickey, Rev. John J., S.T.B., J.C.D., Irregularities and Simple Impediments in the New Code of Canon Law, 100 pp., 1920.
8. Klekotka, Rev. Peter J., S.T.B., J.C.D., Diocesan Consultors, 179 pp., 1920.
9. Wanenmacher, Rev. Francis, J.C.D., The Evidence in Ecclesiastical Procedure Affecting the Marriage Bond, 1920 (Printed 1935).
10. Golden, Rev. Henry Francis, J.C.D., Parochial Benefices in the New Code, IV-119 pp., 1921 (Printed 1925).
11. Koudelka, Rev. Charles J., J.C.D., Pastors, Their Rights and Duties According to the New Code of Canon Law, 211 pp., 1921.
12. Melo, Rev. Antonius, O.F.M., J.C.D., De Exemptione Regularium, X-188 pp., 1921.
13 Schaaf, Rev. Valentine Theodore, O.F.M., S.T.B., J.C.D., The Cloister, X-180 pp., 1921.
14. Burke, Rev. Thomas Joseph, S.T.D., J.C.D., Competence in Ecclesiastical Tribunals, IV-117 pp., 1922.
15. Leech, Rev. George Leo, J.C.D., A Comparative Study of the Constitution "Apostolicae Sedis" and the "Codex Juris Canonici," 179 pp., 1922.
16. Motry, Rev. Hubert Louis, S.T.D., J.C.D., Diocesan Faculties According to the Code of Canon Law, II-167 pp., 1922.
17. Murphy, Rev. George Lawrence, J.C.D., Delinquencies and Penalties in the Administration and the Reception of the Sacraments, IV-121 pp., 1923.
18. O'Reilly, Rev. John Anthony, S.T.B., J.C.D., Ecclesiastical Sepulture in the New Code of Canon Law, II-129 pp., 1923.

* Below n. 100 only the following numbers are still available: Nn. 3, 4, 9, 25, 34, 57 and 75. Beginning with n. 100 only the following are unavailable: Nn. 100, 101, 102, 104, 105, 107, 108, 109, 111 and 113.

19. MICHALICKA, REV. WENCESLAS CYRILL, O.S.B., J.C.D., Judicial Procedure in Dismissal of Clerical Exempt Religious, 107 pp., 1923.
20. DARGIN, REV. EDWARD VINCENT, S.T.B., J.C.D., Reserved Cases According to the Code of Canon Law, IV-103 pp., 1924.
21. GODFREY, REV. JOHN A., S.T.B., J.C.D., The Right of Patronage According to the Code of Canon Law, 153 pp., 1924.
22. HAGEDORN, REV. FRANCIS EDWARD, J.C.D., General Legislation on Indulgences, II-154 pp., 1924.
23. KING, REV. JAMES IGNATIUS, J.C.D., The Administration of the Sacraments to Dying Non-Catholics, V-141 pp., 1924.
24. WINSLOW, REV. FRANCIS JOSEPH, O.F.M., J.C.D., Vicars and Prefects Apostolic, IV-149 pp., 1924.
25. CORREA, REV. JOSE SERVELION, S.T.L., J.C.D., La Potestad Legislativa de la Iglesia Catolica, IV-127 pp., 1925.
26. DUGAN, REV. HENRY FRANCIS, A.M., J.C.D., The Judiciary Department of the Diocesan Curia, 87 pp., 1925.
27. KELLER, REV. CHARLES FREDERICK, S.T.B., J.C.D., Mass Stipends, 167 pp., 1925.
28. PASCHANG, REV. JOHN LINUS, J.C.D., The Sacramentals According to the Code of Canon Law, 129 pp., 1925.
29. PIONTEK, REV. CYRILLUS, O.F.M., S.T.B., J.C.D., De Indulto Exclaustrationis necnon Saecularizationis, XIII-289 pp., 1925.
30. KEARNEY, REV. RICHARD JOSEPH, S.T.B., J.C.D., Sponsors at Baptism According to the Code of Canon Law, IV-127 pp., 1925.
31. BARTLETT, REV. CHESTER JOSEPH, A.M., LL.B., J.C.D., The Tenure of Parochial Property in the United States of America, V-108 pp., 1926.
32. KILKER, REV. ADRIAN JEROME, J.C.D., Extreme Unction, V-425 pp., 1926.
33. McCORMICK, REV. ROBERT EMMETT, J.C.D., Confessors of Religious, VIII-266 pp., 1926.
34. MILLER, REV. NEWTON THOMAS, J.C.D., Founded Masses According to the Code of Canon Law, VII-93 pp., 1926.
35. ROELKER, REV. EDWARD G., S.T.D., J.C.D., Principles of Privilege According to the Code of Canon Law, XI-166 pp., 1926.
36. BAKALARCZYK, REV. RICHARDUS, M.I.C., J.U.D., De Novitiatu, VIII-208 pp., 1927.
37. PIZZUTI, REV. LAWRENCE, O.F.M., J.U.L., De Parochis Religiosis, 1927. (Not Printed.)
38. BLILEY, REV. NICHOLAS MARTIN; O.S.B., J.C.D., Altars According to the Code of Canon Law, XIX-132 pp., 1927.
39. BROWN, MR. BRENDAN FRANCIS, A.B., LL.M., J.U.D., The Canonical Juristic Personality with Special Reference to its Status in the United States of America, V-212 pp., 1927.
40. CAVANAUGH, REV. WILLIAM THOMAS, C.P., J.U.D., The Reservation of the Blessed Sacrament, VIII-101 pp., 1927.

41. DOHENY, REV. WILLIAM J., C.S.C., A.B., J.U.D., Church Property: Modes of Acquisition, X-118 pp., 1927.
42. FELDHAUS, REV. ALOYSIUS H., C.PP.S., J.C.D., Oratories, IX-141 pp., 1927.
43. KELLY, REV. JAMES PATRICK, A.B., J.C.D., The Jurisdiction of the Simple Confessor, X-208 pp., 1927.
44. NEUBERGER, REV. NICHOLAS J., J.C.D., Canon 6 or the Relation of the Codex Juris Canonici to the Preceding Legislation, V-95 pp., 1927.
45. O'KEEFE, REV. GERALD MICHAEL, J.C.D., Matrimonial Dispensations, Powers of Bishops, Priests, and Confessors, VIII-232 pp., 1927.
46. QUIGLEY, REV. JOSEPH A. M., A.B., J.C.D., Condemned Societies, 139 pp., 1927.
47. ZAPLOTNIK, REV. JOHANNES LEO, J.C.D., De Vicariis Foraneis, X-142 pp., 1927.
48. DUSKIE, REV. JOHN ALOYSIUS, A.B., J.C.D., The Canonical Status of the Orientals in the United States, VIII-196 pp., 1928.
49. HYLAND, REV. FRANCIS EDWARD, J.C.D., Excommunication, Its Nature, Historical Development and Effects, VIII-181 pp., 1928.
50. REINMANN, REV. GERALD JOSEPH, O.M.C., J.C.D., The Third Order Secular of Saint Francis, 201 pp., 1928.
51. SCHENK, REV. FRANCIS J., J.C.D., The Matrimonial Impediments of Mixed Religion and Disparity of Cult, XVI-318 pp., 1929.
52. COADY, REV. JOHN JOSEPH, S.T.D., J.U.D., A.M., The Appointment of Pastors, VIII-150 pp., 1929.
53. KAY, REV. THOMAS HENRY, J.C.D., Competence in Matrimonial Procedure, VIII-164 pp., 1929.
54. TURNER, REV. SIDNEY JOSEPH, C.P., J.U.D., The Vow of Poverty, XLIX-217 pp., 1929.
55. KEARNEY, REV. RAYMOND A., A.B., S.T.D., J.C.D., The Principles of Delegation, VII-149 pp., 1929.
56. CONRAN, REV. EDWARD JAMES, A.B., J.C.D., The Interdict,, V-163 pp., 1930.
57. O'NEILL, REV. WILLIAM H., J.C.D., Papal Rescripts of Favor, VII-218 pp., 1930.
58. BASTNAGEL, REV. CLEMENT VINCENT, J.U.D., The Appointment of Parochial Adjutants and Assistants, XV-257 pp., 1930.
59. FERRY, REV. WILLIAM A., A.B., J.C.D., Stole Fees, V-136 pp., 1930.
60. COSTELLO, REV. JOHN MICHAEL, A.B., J.C.D., Domicile and Quasi-Domicile, VII-201 pp., 1930.
61. KREMER, REV. MICHAEL NICHOLAS, A.B., S.T.B., J.C.D., Church Support in the United States, VI-136 pp., 1930.
62. ANGULO, REV. LUIS, C.M., J.C.D., Legislation de la Iglesia sobre la intencion en la application de la Santa Misa, VII-104 pp., 1931.
63. FREY, REV. WOLFGANG NORBERT, O.S.B., A.B., J.C.D., The Act of Religious Profession, VIII-174 pp., 1931.

64. Roberts, Rev. James Brendan, A.B., J.C.D., The Banns of Marriage, XIV-140 pp., 1931.
65. Ryder, Rev. Raymond Aloysius, A.B., J.C.D., Simony, IX-151 pp., 1931.
66. Campagna, Rev. Angelo, Ph.D., J.U.D., Il Vicario Generale del Vescovo, VII-205 pp., 1931.
67. Cox, Rev. Joseph Godfrey, A.B., J.C.D., The Administration of Seminaries, VI-124 pp., 1931.
68. Gregory, Rev. Donald J., J.U.D., The Pauline Privilege, XV-165 pp., 1931.
69. Donohue, Rev. John F., J.C.D., The Impediment of Crime, VII-110 pp., 1931.
70. Dooley, Rev. Eugene A., O.M.I., J.C.D., Church Law on Sacred Relics, IX-143 pp., 1931.
71. Orth, Rev. Clement Raymond, O.M.C., J.C.D., The Approbation of Religious Institutes, 171 pp., 1931.
72. Pernicone, Rev. Joseph M., A.B., J.C.D., The Ecclesiastical Prohibition of Books, XII-267 pp., 1932.
73. Clinton, Rev. Connell, A.B., J.C.D., The Paschal Precept, IX-108 pp., 1932.
74. Donnelly, Rev. Francis B., A.M., S.T.L., J.C.D., The Diocesan Synod, VIII-125 pp., 1932.
75. Torrente, Rev. Camilo, C.M.F., J.C.D., Las Procesiones Sagradas, V-145 pp., 1932.
76. Murphy, Rev. Edwin J., C.PP.S., J.C.D., Suspension Ex Informata Conscientia, XI-122 pp., 1932.
77. MacKenzie, Rev. Eric F., A.M., S.T.L., J.C.D., The Delict of Heresy in its Commission, Penalization, Absolution, VII-124 pp., 1932.
78. Lyons, Rev. Avitus E., S.T.B., J.C.D., The Collegiate Tribunal of First Instance, XI-147 pp., 1932.
79. Connolly, Rev. Thomas A., J.C.D., Appeals, XI-195 pp., 1932.
80. Sangmeister, Rev. Joseph V., A.B., J.C.D., Force and Fear as Precluding Matrimonial Consent, V-211 pp., 1932.
81. Jaeger, Rev. Leo A., A.B., J.C.D., The Administration of Vacant and Quasi-Vacant Episcopal Sees in the United States, IX-229 pp., 1932.
82. Rimlinger, Rev. Herbert T., J.C.D., Error Invalidating Matrimonial Consent, VII-79 pp., 1932.
83. Barrett, Rev. John D. M., S.S., J.C.D., A Comparative Study of the Third Plenary Council of Baltimore and the Code, IX-221 pp., 1932.
84. Carberry, Rev. John J., Ph.D., S.T.D., J.C.D., The Juridical Form of Marriage, X-177 pp., 1934.
85. Dolan, Rev. John L., A.B., J.C.D., The Defensor Vinculi, XII-157 pp., 1934.
86. Hannan, Rev. Jerome D., A.M., S.T.D., LL.B., J.C.D., The Canon Law of Wills, IX-517 pp., 1934.

87. Lemieux, Rev. Delise A., A.M., J.C.D., The Sentence in Ecclesiastical Procedure, IX-131 pp., 1934.
88. O'Rourke, Rev. James J., A.B., J.C.D., Parish Registers, VII-109 pp., 1934.
89. Timlin, Rev. Bartholomew, O.F.M., A.M., J.C.D., Conditional Matrimonial Consent, X-381 pp., 1934.
90. Wahl, Rev. Francis X., A.B., J.C.D., The Matrimonial Impediments of Consanguinity and Affinity, VI-125 pp., 1934.
91. White, Rev. Robert J., A.B., LL.B., S.T.B., J.C.D., Canonical Ante-Nuptial Promises and the Civil Law, VI-152 pp., 1934.
92. Herrera, Rev. Antonio Parra, O.C.D., J.C.D., Legislacion Ecclesiastica sobra el Ayuno y la Abstinencia, XI-191 pp., 1935.
93. Kennedy, Rev. Edwin J., J.C.D., The Special Matrimonial Process in Cases of Evident Nullity, X-165 pp., 1935.
94. Manning, Rev. John J., A.B., J.C.D., Presumption of Law in Matrimonial Procedure, XI-111 pp., 1935.
95. Moeder, Rev. John M., J.C.D., The Proper Bishop for Ordination and Dimissorial Letters, VII-135 pp., 1935.
96. O'Mara, Rev. William A., A.B., J.C.D., Canonical Causes for Matrimonial Dispensations, IX-155 pp., 1935.
97. Reilly, Rev. Peter, J.C.D., Residence of Pastors, IX-81 pp., 1935.
98. Smith, Rev. Mariner T., O.P., S.T.Lr., J.C.D., The Penal Law for Religious, VIII-169 pp., 1935.
99. Whalen, Rev. Donald W., A.M., J.C.D., The Value of Testimonial Evidence in Matrimonial Procedure, XIII-297 pp., 1935.
100. Cleary, Rev. Joseph F., J.C.D., Canonical Limitations on the Alienation of Church Property, VIII-141 pp., 1936.
101. Glynn, Rev. John C., J.C.D., The Promoter of Justice, XX-337 pp., 1936.
102. Brennan, Rev. James H., S.S., M.A., S.T.B., J.C.D., The Simple Convalidation of Marriage, VI-135 pp., 1937.
103. Brunini, Rev. Joseph Bernard, J.C.D., The Clerical Obligations of Canons 139 and 142, X-121 pp., 137.
104. Connor, Rev. Maurice, A.B., J.C.D., The Administrative Removal of Pastors, VIII-159 pp., 1937.
105. Guilfoyle, Rev. Merlin Joseph, J.C.D., Custom, XI-144 pp., 1937.
106. Hughes, Rev. James Austin, A.B., A.M., J.C.D., Witnesses in Criminal Trials of Clerics, IX-140 pp., 1937.
107. Jansen, Rev. Raymond J., A.B., S.T.L., J.C.D., Canonical Provisions for Catechetical Instruction, VII-153 pp., 1937.
108. Kealy, Rev. John James, A.B., J.C.D., The Introductory Libellus in Church Court Procedure, XI-121 pp., 1937.
109. McManus, Rev. James Edward, C.SS.R., J.C.D., The Administration of Temporal Goods in Religious Institutes, XVI-196 pp., 1937.

110. MORIARTY, REV. EUGENE JAMES, J.C.D., Oaths in Ecclesiastical Courts, X-115 pp., 1937.

111. RAINIER, REV. ELIGIUS GEORGE, C.SS.R., J.C.D., Suspension of Clerics, XVII-249 pp., 1937.

112. REILLY, REV. THOMAS F., C.SS.R., J.C.D., Visitation of Religious, VI-195 pp., 1938.

113. MORIARTY, REV. FRANCIS E., C.SS.R., J.C.D., The Extraordinary Absolution from Censures, XV-334 pp., 1938.

114. CONNOLLY, REV. NICHOLAS P., J.C.D., The Canonical Erection of Parishes, X-132 pp., 1938.

115. DONOVAN, REV. JAMES JOSEPH, J.C.D., The Pastor's Obligation in Prenuptial Investigation, XII-322 pp., 1938.

116. HARRIGAN, REV. ROBERT J., M.A., S.T.B., J.C.D., The Radical Sanation of Invalid Marriages, VIII-208 pp., 1938.

117. BOFFA, REV. CONRAD HUMBERT, J.C.D., Canonical Provisions for Catholic Schools, VII-211 pp., 1939.

118. PARSONS, REV. ANSCAR JOHN, O.M.Cap., J.C.D., Canonical Elections, XII-236 pp., 1939.

119. REILLY, REV. EDWARD MICHAEL, A.B., J.C.D., The General Norms of Dispensation, XII-156 pp., 1939.

120. RYAN, REV. GERALD ALOYSIUS, A.B., J.C.D., Principles of Episcopal Jurisdiction, XII-172 pp., 1939.

121. BURTON, REV. FRANCIS JAMES, C.S.C., A.B., J.C.D., A Commentary on Canon 1125, X-222 pp., 1940.

122. MIASKIEWICZ, REV. FRANCIS SIGISMUND, J.C.D., Supplied Jurisdiction According to Canon 209, XII-340 pp., 1940.

123. RICE, REV. PATRICK WILLIAM, A.B., J.C.D., Proof of Death in Prenuptial Investigation, VIII-156 pp., 1940.

124. ANGLIN, REV. THOMAS FRANCIS, M.S., J.C.D., The Eucharistic Fast, VIII-183 pp., 1941.

125. COLEMAN, REV. JOHN JEROME, J.C.D., The Minister of Confirmation, VI-153 pp., 1941.

126. DOWNS, REV. JOSEPH EMMANUEL, A.B., J.C.D., The Concept of Clerical Immunity, XI-163 pp., 1941.

127. ESSWEIN, REV. ANTHONY ALBERT, J.C.D., Extrajudicial Penal Powers of Ecclesiastical Superiors, X-144 pp., 1941.

128. FARRELL, REV. BENJAMIN FRANCIS, M.A., S.T.L., J.C.D., The Rights and Duties of the Local Ordinary Regarding Congregations of Women Religious of Pontifical Approval, V-195 pp., 1941.

129. FEENEY, REV. THOMAS JOHN, A.B., S.T.L., J.C.D., Restitutio in Integrum, VI-169 pp., 1941.

130. FINDLAY, REV. STEPHEN WILLIAM, O.S.B., A.B., J.C.D., Canonical Norms Governing the Deposition and Degradation of Clerics, XVII-279 pp., 1941.

131. GOODWINE, REV. JOHN, A.B., S.T.L., J.C.D., The Right of the Church to Acquire Property, VIII-119 pp., 1941.
132. HESTON, REV. EDWARD LOUIS, C.S.C., Ph.D., S.T.D., J.C.D., The Alienation of Church Property in the United States, XII-222 pp., 1941.
133. HOGAN, REV. JAMES JOHN, A.B., S.T.L., J.C.D., Judicial Advocates and Procurators, XIII-200 pp., 1941.
134. KEALY, REV. THOMAS M., A.B., Litt.B., J.C.D., Dowry of Women Religious, IX-152 pp., 1941.
135. KEENE, REV. MICHAEL JAMES, O.S.B., J.C.D., Religious Ordinaries and Canon 198, V-164 pp., 1942.
136. KERIN, REV. CHARLES A., S.S., M.A., S.T.B., J.C.D., The Privation of Christian Burial, XVI-279 pp., 1941.
137. LOUIS, REV. WILLIAM FRANCIS, M.A., J.C.D., Diocesan Archives, X-101 pp., 1941.
138. MCDEVITT, REV. GILBERT JOSEPH, A.B., J.C.D., Legitimacy and Legitimation, X-247 pp., 1941.
139. MCDONOUGH, REV. THOMAS JOSEPH, A.B., J.C.D., Apostolic Administrators, X-217 pp., 1941.
140. MEIER, REV. CARL ANTHONY, A.B., J.C.D., Penal Administrative Procedure Against Negligent Pastors, XI-240 pp., 1941.
141. SCHMIDT, REV. JOHN ROGG, A.B., J.C.D., The Principles of Authentic Interpretation in Canon 17 of the Code of Canon Law, XII-331 pp., 1941.
142. SLAFKOSKY, REV. ANDREW LEONARD, A.B., J.C.D., The Canonical Episcopal Visitation of the Diocese, X-197 pp., 1941.
143. SWOBODA, REV. INNOCENT ROBERT, O.F.M., J.C.D., Ignorance in Relation to the Imputability of Delicts, IX-271 pp., 1941.
144. DUBÉ, REV. ARTHUR JOSEPH, A.B., J.C.D., The General Principles for the Reckoning of Time in Canon Law, VIII-299 pp., 1941.
145. MCBRIDE, REV. JAMES T., A.B., J.C.D., Incardination and Excardination of Seculars, XX-585 pp., 1941.
146. KRÓL, REV. JOHN T., J.C.D., The Defendant in Ecclesiastical Trials, XII-207 pp., 1942.
147. COMYNS, REV. JOSEPH J., C.SS.R., A.B., J.C.D., Papal and Episcopal Administration of Church Property, XIV-155 pp., 1942.
148. BARRY, REV. GARRETT FRANCIS, O.M.I., J.C.D., Violation of the Cloister, XII-260 pp., 1942.
149. BOLDUC, REV. GATIEN, C.S.V., A.B., S.T.L., J.C.D., Les Études dans les Religions Cléricales, VIII-155 pp., 1942.
150. BOYLE, REV. DAVID JOHN, M.A., J.C.D., The Juridic Effects of Moral Certitude on Pre-Nuptial Guarantees, XII-188 pp., 1942.
151. CANAVAN, REV. WALTER JOSEPH, M.A., LITT.D., J.C.D., The Profession of Faith, XII-143 pp., 1942.
152. DESROCHERS, REV. BRUNO, A.B., PH.L., S.T.B., J.C.D., Le Premier Concile Plénier de Québec et le Code de Droit Canonique, XIV-186 pp., 1942.

153. Dillon, Rev. Robert Edward, A.B., J.C.D., Common Law Marriage, X-148 pp., 1942.
154. Dodwell, Rev. Edward John, Ph.D., S.T.B., J.C.D., The Time and Place for the Celebration of Marriage, X-156 pp., 1942.
155. Donnellan, Rev. Thomas Andrew, A.B., J.C.D., The Obligation of the Missa pro Populo, VII-131 pp., 1942.
156. Eltz, Rev. Louis Anthony, A.B., J.C.L., Cooperation in Crime.
157. Gass, Rev. Sylvester Francis, M.A., J.C.D., Ecclesiastical Pensions, XI-206 pp., 1942.
158. Guiniven, Rev. John Joseph, C.SS.R., J.C.D., The Precept of Hearing Mass, XIV-188 pp., 1942.
159. Gulczynski, Rev. John Theophilus, J.C.D., The Desecration and Violation of Churches, X-126 pp., 1942.
160. Hammill, Rev. John Leo, M.A., J.C.D., The Obligations of the Traveler According to Canon 14, VIII-204 pp., 1942.
161. Haydt, Rev. John Joseph, A.B., J.C.D., Reserved Benefices, XI-148 pp., 1942.
162. Huser, Rev. Roger John, O.F.M., A.B., J.C.D., The Crime of Abortion in Canon Law, XII-187 pp., 1942.
163. Kearney, Rev. Francis Patrick, A.B., S.T.L., J.C.L., The Principles of Canon 1127.
164. Linahen, Rev. Leo James, S.T.L., J.C.D., De Absolutione Complicis In Peccato Turpi, 114 pp., 1942.
165. McCloskey, Rev. Joseph Aloysius, A.B., J.C.D., The Subject of Ecclesiastical Law According to Canon 12, XVII-246 pp., 1942.
166. O'Neill, Rev. Francis Joseph, C.SS.R., J.C.D., The Dismissal of Religious in Temporary Vows, XIII-220 pp., 1942.
167. Prince, Rev. John Edward, A.B., S.T.B., J.C.D., The Diocesan Chancellor, X-136 pp., 1942.
168. Riesner, Rev. Albert Joseph, C.SS.R., J.C.D., Apostates and Fugitives from Religious Institutes, IX-168 pp., 1942.
169. Stenger, Rev. Joseph Bernard, J.C.D., The Mortgaging of Church Property, 186 pp., 1942.
170. Waldron, Rev. Joseph Francis, A.B., J.C.D., The Minister of Baptism, XII-197 pp., 1942.
171. Willett, Rev. Robert Albert, J.C.D., The Probative Value of Documents in Ecclesiastical Trials, X-124 pp., 1942.
172. Woeber, Rev. Edward Martin, M.A., J.C.D., The Interpellations, XII-161 pp., 1942.
173. Benko, Rev. Matthew Aloysius, O.S.B.. M.A., J.C.L., The Abbot *Nullius*.
174. Christ, Rev. Joseph James, M.A., S.T.L., J.C.L., Dispensation from Vindicative Penalties.
175. Clancy, Rev. Patricn M. J., O.P., A.B., S.T.Lr., J.C.D., The Local Religious Superior, X-229 pp., 1943.

176. CLARKE, REV. THOMAS JAMES, J.C.D., Parish Societies, XII-147 pp., 1943.
177. CONNOLLY, REV. JOHN PATRICK, S.T.L., J.C.L., Synodal Examiners and Parish Priest Consultors.
178. DRUMM, REV. WILLIAM MARTIN, A.B., J.C.L., Hospital Chaplains.
179. FLANAGAN, REV. BERNARD JOSEPH, A.B., S.T.L., J.C.L., The Canonical Erection of Religious Houses, X-147 pp., 1943.
180. KELLEHER, REV. STEPHEN JOSEPH, A.B., S.T.B., J.C.L., Discussions with Non-Catholics: Canonical Legislation, X-93 pp., 1943.
181. LEWIS, REV. GORDIAN, C.P., J.C.L., Chapters in Religious Institutes, XII-169 pp., 1943.
182. MARX, REV. ADOLPH, J.C.L., The Declaration of Nullity of Marriages Contracted Outside the Church, X-151 pp., 1943.
183. MATULENAS, REV. RAYMOND ANTHONY, O.S.B., A.B., J.C.L., Communication, a Source of Privileges.
184. O'LEARY, REV. CHARLES GERARD, C.SS.R., J.C.L., Religious Dismissed After Perpetual Profession.
185. POWER, REV. CORNELIUS MICHAEL, J.C.L., The Blessing of Cemeteries.
186. SHUHLER, REV. RALPH VINCENT, O.S.A., J.C.L., Privileges of Religious to Absolve and Dispense, XII-195 pp., 1943.
187. ZIOLKOWSKI, REV. THADDEUS STANISLAUS, A.B., J.C.L., The Consecration and Blessing of Churches, XII-151 pp., 1943.
188. HENEGHAN, REV. JOHN JOSEPH, S.T.D., J.C.L., The Marriages of Unworthy Catholics.

www.ingramcontent.com/pod-product-compliance
Lightning Source LLC
LaVergne TN
LVHW050242080826
844660LV00012B/586

* 9 7 8 0 8 1 3 2 2 3 7 3 5 *